THE *Art of* WORK

An Anthology of *Workplace Literature*

Christine LaRocco
Applied Communication
Trainer and Consultant
Former High School
English Instructor
Arlington, Virginia

Jim Coughlin
English Instructor
Capital City High School
Boise, Idaho

SOUTH-WESTERN EDUCATIONAL PUBLISHING

ACKNOWLEDGMENTS

"A Delicate Balance" by José Armas. Permission to reprint granted by José Armas.

"Balthazar's Marvelous Afternoon" from NO ONE WRITES TO THE
    COLONEL . . . by Gabriel Garcia Marquez. Copyright ©1968 in the English
    translation by HarperCollins, Publishers, Inc. Reprinted by permission of
    HarperCollins Publishers, Inc.

"Bargain" from THE BIG IT AND OTHER STORIES by A. B. Guthrie, Jr. Copyright
    ©1960 by A. B. Guthrie, Jr. Reprinted by permission of Houghton Mifflin
    Company. All rights reserved.

Continued on page 278

Continued on page 278

Editor-in-Chief: Peter McBride
Developmental Editor: Susan Freeman
Marketing Manager: Carolyn Love
Production Manager: Carol Sturzenberger
Senior Production Editor: Jane E. Congdon
Production Editor: Edna D. Stroble
Staff Designer: Nicola Hardy
Internal & Cover Design: Lamson Design
Illustrator: Dave Miller
Copyright © 1996
by SOUTH-WESTERN EDUCATIONAL PUBLISHING
Cincinnati, Ohio

ISBN: 0-538-63651-3

Library of Congress Number 94-074920

1 2 3 4 5 6 7 8 9 0 KI 99 98 97 96 95

Printed in the United States of America

I(T)P
International Thomson Publishing

South-Western Educational Publishing is a division of
International Thomson Publishing Inc. The ITP trademark is used under license.

The Art of Work: An Anthology of Workplace Literature is a collection of poetry, short stories, essays, and drama focusing on workers and their lives. Through the study of literature with workplace themes, students can focus on their lives as workers and participants in a society where most of our days are spent working. The fictional and nonfictional characters in this anthology seek meaning in their lives which transcends the time clock and the paycheck.

REAL-LIFE CONNECTIONS

Students seeking their first entry-level jobs will relate to Russell Baker and Louisa May Alcott's frustrations with first jobs. They will identify with young characters in stories by A. B. Guthrie, Jr., and Sinclair Lewis, who struggle with personal relationships on the job. Through the stories of these workers and others, readers will have opportunities to gain insight on universal themes of life's struggles and triumphs.

Readers will discover that workers from decades long forgotten experienced similar problems and emotions. The common themes encourage students to share their own experiences through a variety of workplace-related writing, reading, speaking, and listening activities.

Perhaps this is why, when we called poet Phil Hey for permission to include his poem "Old Men Working Concrete" in this anthology, he told us he always felt his old men belonged in a book of writings about workers. You'll find these old men in a section of poetry on "Pride in a Job."

FOR THE STUDENT

The anthology is organized by genre and also offers suggestions for grouping selections by theme. Poetry is divided by predominant themes. The selections represent a balance in the gender of authors and the rich cultures they represent. With each literature piece and group of poems, we've included:

- An Anticipating activity with suggested journal entries or discussion topics to interest readers in the central themes.
- A short profile on the author focusing on the writer's vision and philosophy as well as other major works and accomplishments.

FOR THE INSTRUCTOR

In the teacher's edition, we've included:

- An Overview of each piece.
- An Anticipating activity with suggested journal entries or discussion topics to interest readers in the central themes.
- Reading suggestions, including problem vocabulary words and a suggested approach to the text.
- Reflecting activities to review key elements of each selection.
- Applying activities offering opportunities to make personal and real-life applications.
- Suggestions for additional reading or viewing.
- Correlations to AIT's *Applied Communication* and the new South-Western/ AIT program *Communication 2000.*

We designed discussion questions to move students beyond knowledge and comprehension to analysis and evaluation. The application section suggests writing assignments in both academic and technical areas. Students are asked to reach out into communities for resources and to present findings as graphic and oral presentations. Projects require group collaboration, and all assignments are performance based and assessed.

SPECIAL THANKS

We are grateful to our diligent reviewers for their input, suggestions, and expert editing.

> Dorothy Hoover, Huntingdon Area High School, Huntingdon, PA
> Margie Jones, Greene County Central High School, Snow Hill, NC
> Judy Strand, Lincoln High School, Lincoln, NE

We thank, also, our teaching colleagues with whom we have collaborated through the years in developing the ideas for many of the lesson suggestions in the book.

We extend our greatest appreciation to our spouses, Jane and Larry, for their strong support and encouragement during this year-long project.

Christine LaRocco
James Coughlin

Contents

SHORT STORIES

In Service · **Louisa May Alcott** · 3
A Delicate Balance · **José Armas** · 17
Spring · **Italo Calvino** · 23
A Doctor's Visit · **Anton Chekhov** · 30
Bargain · **A. B. Guthrie, Jr.** · 44
The Hack Driver · **Sinclair Lewis** · 57
Balthazar's Marvelous Afternoon · **Gabriel Garcia Marquez** · 66
Forty-Five a Month · **R. K. Narayan** · 76
The Man to Send Rain Clouds · **Leslie Silko** · 83
Just Lather, That's All · **Hernando Tellez** · 89
The Catbird Seat · **James Thurber** · 95
The Richer, the Poorer · **Dorothy West** · 106

NONFICTION

Personal Memoirs

Cotton-Picking Time · **Maya Angelou** · 115
My Lack of Gumption · **Russell Baker** · 119
From Man to Boy · **John R. Coleman** · 128
True Stories and Other Dreams · **Judy Collins** · 131
Darkness at Noon · **Harold Krents** · 138
Shooting an Elephant · **George Orwell** · 142
The Indian Basket · **Mickey Roberts** · 151
The Boy and the Bank Officer · **Philip Ross** · 154
Of Dry Goods and Black Bow Tie · **Yoshiko Uchida** · 158

Process/Job Description

Perfection is an Insult to the Gods · **Tracy Kidder** · 165
To Bid the World Farewell · **Jessica Mitford** · 171
Sarcophagus · **Richard Selzer** · 178
Nancy Miles: The Political Conscience of the Class · **Studs Terkel** · 188
Nick Salerno · **Studs Terkel** · 192

Essay

Pablo Picasso: Living in His Own Shadow . Ellen Goodman 197
Insert Flap 'A' and Throw Away . S.J. Perelman 201
Shorthand Grad is Shortchanged . Mike Royko 206

POETRY

Theme: Coping

Woman Work . Maya Angelou 213
Factory Jungle . Jim Daniels 215
The Song of the Factory Worker . Ruth Collins 216
Pee Wee . Jim Daniels 218
Old Man Pike . David Budbill 219

Theme: Downtrodden

An Old Charcoal Seller . Po Chü-Yi 221
Share-Croppers . Langston Hughes 222
Weaving at the Window . Wang Chien 223
"Butch" Weldy . Edgar Lee Master 224
Song of the Weaving Woman . Yüan Chen 225

Theme: Endings

Enough . James Scully 228
Cooney Potter . Edgar Lee Masters 231
Their Bodies . David Wagoner 232

Theme: Family

Me and My Work . Maya Angelou 234
That Day . David Kherdian 235
The Rope . Patricia Dobler 236
Mag . Carl Sandburg 237

Theme: Pride

Old Men Working Concrete . Phil Hey 240
Old Florist . Theodore Roethke 242
Factory Work . Deborah Roe 243
The Closing of the Rodeo . William Jay Smith 245

Theme: Society

To Be of Use · **Marge Piercy** · 248

The Country of Everyday:
   Literary Criticism · **Tom Wayman** · · · · · · · · · · · · · · · · · · · 250

Theme: Survivors

Saturday's Child · **Countee Cullen** · · · · · · · · · · · · · · · · · · · 254

Dynamiter · **Carl Sandburg** · 256

5000 Apply for 100 Jobs · **Jim Daniels** · · · · · · · · · · · · · · · · · 257

DRAMA

The Oyster and the Pearl · **William Saroyan** · · · · · · · · · · · · · · · · 261

SHO
RTS
TOR
IES

1

In Service

BY LOUISA MAY ALCOTT

ANTICIPATING: Describe an embarrassing situation you've experienced at work, on a team, in school, at home, or in your neighborhood. Describe how you felt inside and how other people made you feel.

After several disappointments, Christie decided that her education was too old-fashioned for the city, and gave up the idea of teaching. Sewing she resolved not to try till every thing else failed; and, after a few more attempts to get writing to do, she said to herself, in a fit of humility and good sense: "I'll begin at the beginning, and work my way up. I'll put my pride in my pocket, and go out to service. Housework I like, and can do well, thanks to Aunt Betsey. I never thought it degradation to do it for her, so why should I mind doing it for others if they pay for it? It isn't what I want, but it's better than idleness, so I'll try it!" 🖋 Full of this wise resolution, she took to haunting that purgatory of the poor, an intelligence office. Mrs. Flint gave her a recommendation and she hopefully took her place among the ranks of buxom German, incapable Irish, and "smart" American women; for in those days foreign help had not driven farmers' daughters out of the field, and made domestic comfort a lost art. 🖋 At first Christie enjoyed the novelty of the thing, and watched with interest the anxious housewives who flocked in demanding that *raravis*, an angel at nine shillings a week; and not finding it, bewailed the degeneracy of the times. Being too honest to profess herself absolutely perfect in every known branch of house-work, it was some time before she suited herself. Meanwhile, she was

questioned and lectured, half engaged and kept waiting, dismissed for a whim, and so worried that she began to regard herself as the incarnation of all human vanities and shortcomings.

"A desirable place in a small, genteel family," was at last offered her and she posted away to secure it, having reached a state of desperation and resolved to go as a first-class cook rather than sit with her hands before her any longer.

A well-appointed house, good wages, and light duties seemed things to be grateful for, and Christie decided that going out to service was not the hardest fate in life, as she stood at the door of a handsome house in a sunny square waiting to be inspected.

rs. Stuart, having just returned from Italy, affected the artistic, and the new applicant found her with a Roman scarf about her head, a rosary like a string of small cannon balls at her side, and azure draperies which became her as well as they did the sea-green furniture of her marine boudoir, where unwary walkers tripped over coral and shells, grew sea-sick looking at pictures of tempestuous billows engulfing every sort of craft, from a man-of-war to a hencoop with a ghostly young lady clinging to it with one hand, and had their appetites effectually taken away by a choice collection of water-bugs and snakes in a glass globe that looked like a jar of mixed pickles in a state of agitation.

Madame was intent on a water-color copy of Turner's "Rain, Wind, and Hail," that pleasing work which was sold upsidedown and no one found it out. Motioning Christie to a seat she finished some delicate sloppy process before speaking. In that little pause Christie examined her, and the impression then received was afterward confirmed.

Mrs. Stuart possessed some beauty and chose to think herself a queen of society. She assumed majestic manners in public and could not entirely divest herself of them in private, which often produced comic effects. Zenobia troubled about fish-sauce, or Aspasia indignant to the price of eggs will give some idea of this lady when she condescended to the cares of housekeeping.

Presently she looked up and inspected the girl as if a new servant were no more than a new bonnet, a necessary article to be ordered home for examination. Christie presented her recommendation, made her modest little speech, and awaited her doom.

Mrs. Stuart read, listened, and then demanded with queenly brevity:

"Your name?"

"Christie Devon."

"Too long. I should prefer to call you Jane as I am accustomed to the name."

"As you please, ma'am."

"Your age?"

"Twenty-one."

"You are an American?"

"Yes, ma'am."

Mrs. Stuart gazed into space a moment, then delivered the following address with impressive solemnity.

"I wish a capable, intelligent, honest, neat, well-conducted person who knows her place and keeps it. The work is light, as there are just two in the family. I am very particular and so is Mr. Stuart. I pay two dollars and a half, allow one afternoon out, one service on Sunday, and no followers. My table-girl must understand her duties thoroughly, be extremely neat, and always wear white aprons."

"I think I can suit you ma'am, when I have learned the ways of the house," meekly replied Christie.

Mrs. Stuart looked graciously satisfied and returned the paper with a gesture that Victoria might have used in restoring a granted petition, though her next words rather marred the effect of the regal act. "My cook is black."

"I have no objection to color, ma'am."

An expression of relief dawned upon Mrs. Stuart's countenance, for, the black cook had been an insurmountable obstacle to all the Irish ladies who had applied. Thoughtfully tapping her Roman nose with the handle of her brush Madame took another survey of the new applicant, and seeing that she looked neat, intelligent, and respectful, gave a sigh of thankfulness and engaged her on the spot.

Much elated Christie rushed home, selected a bag of necessary articles, bundled the rest of her possessions into an empty closet (lent her rent-free owing to a profusion of cockroaches), paid up her board, and at two o'clock introduced herself to Hepsey Johnson, her fellow servant.

Hepsey was a tall, gaunt woman, bearing the tragedy of her race written in her face, with its melancholy eyes, subdued expression, and the pathetic patience of a wronged dumb animal. She received Christie with an air of resignation, and speedily bewildered her with an account of the duties she would be expected to perform.

 long and careful drill enabled Christie to set the table with but few mistakes, and to retain a tolerably clear recollection of the order of performances. She had just assumed her badge of servitude, as she called the white apron, when the bell rang violently and Hepsey, who was hurrying away to "dish up," said:

"It's de marster. You has to answer de bell, honey, and he likes it done bery spry."

Christie ran and admitted an impetuous, stout gentleman, who appeared to be incensed against the elements, for he burst in as if blown, shook himself like a Newfoundland dog, and said all in one breath:

"You're the new girl, are you? Well, take my umbrella and pull off my rubbers."

"Sir?"

Mr. Stuart was struggling with his gloves, and, quite unconscious of the astonishment of his new maid, impatiently repeated his request.

"Take this wet thing away, and pull off my over-shoes. Don't you see it's raining like the very deuce!"

Christie folded her lips together in a peculiar manner as she knelt down and removed a pair of muddy over-shoes, took the dripping umbrella, and was walking away with her agreeable burden when Mr. Stuart gave her another shock by calling over the banister:

"I'm going out again; so clean those rubbers, and see that the boots I sent down this morning are in order."

"Yes, sir," answered Christie meekly, and immediately afterward startled Hepsey by casting overshoes and umbrella upon the kitchen floor, and indignantly demanding:

"Am I expected to be a boot-jack to that man?"

"I 'spects you is, honey."

"Am I also expected to clean his boots?"

"Yes, chile. Katy did, and de work ain't hard when you gits used to it."

"It isn't the work; it's the degradation; and I won't submit to it."

Christie looked fiercely determined; but Hepsey shook her head, saying quietly as she went on garnishing a dish:

"Dere's more 'gradin works dan dat, chile, and dem dat's bin 'bliged to do um finds dis sort bery easy. You's paid for it, honey; and if you does it willin, it won't hurt you more dan washin' de marster's dishes, or sweepin' his rooms."

"There ought to be a boy to do this sort of thing. Do you think it's right to ask it of me?" cried Christie, feeling that being servant was not as pleasant a task as she had thought it.

"Dunno, chile. I'se shore I'd never ask it of any woman if I was a man, 'less I was sick or ole. But folks don't seem to 'member dat we've got feelin's, and de best way is not to mind dese ere little trubbles. You jes leave de boots to me; blackin' can't do dese ole hands no hurt, and dis ain't no deggydation to me now; I's a free woman."

"Why, Hepsey, were you ever a slave?" asked the girl, forgetting her own small injury at this suggestion of the greatest of all wrongs.

"All my life, till I run away five year ago. My ole folks and eight brudders and sisters, is down dere in de pit now, waitin' for the Lord to set 'em free. And He's gwine to do it soon, *soon!*" As she uttered the last words, a sudden light chased the tragic shadow from Hepsey's face, and the solemn fervor of her voice thrilled Christie's heart. All her anger died out in a great pity, and she put her hand on the woman's shoulder, saying earnestly:

"I hope so; and I wish I could help to bring that happy day at once!"

For the first time Hepsey smiled, as she said gratefully, "De Lord bless you for dat wish, chile." Then, dropping suddenly into her old, quiet way, she added, turning to her work:

"Now you tote up de dinner, and I'll be handy by to 'fresh your mind 'bout how de dishes goes, for missis is bery 'ticular, and don't like no 'stakes in tendin'.'"

Thanks to her own neat-handed ways and Hepsey's prompting through the slide, Christie got on very well; managed her silver dexterously, only upset one glass, clashed one dish-cover, and forgot to sugar the pie before putting it on the table; an omission which was majestically pointed out, and graciously pardoned as a first offence.

y seven o'clock the ceremonial was fairly over, and Christie dropped into a chair quite tired out with frequent pacings to and fro. In the kitchen she found the table spread for one, and Hepsey busy with the boots.

"Aren't you coming to your dinner, Mrs. Johnson?" she asked, not pleased at the arrangement.

"When you's done, honey; dere's no hurry 'bout me. Katy liked dat way best, and I'se used ter waitin'."

"But *I* don't like that way, and I won't have it. I suppose Katy thought her white skin gave her a right to be disrespectful to a woman old enough to be her mother just because she was black. I don't, and while I'm here, there must be no difference made. If we can work together, we can eat together; and because you have been a slave is all the more reason I should be good to you now."

If Hepsey had been surprised by the new girl's protest against being made a boot-jack of, she was still more surprised at this sudden kindness, for she had set Christie down in her own mind as "one ob dem toppin smart ones dat don't stay long nowheres." She changed her opinion now, and sat watching the girl with a new expression on her face, as Christie took boot and brush from her, and fell to work energetically, saying as she scrubbed:

"I'm ashamed of complaining about such a little thing as this, and don't mean to feel degraded by it, though I should be letting you do it for me. I never lived out before: that's the reason I made a fuss. There's a polish, for you, and I'm in a good humor again; so Mr. Stuart may call for his boots whenever he likes, and we'll go to dinner like fashionable people, as we are."

There was something so irresistible in the girl's hearty manner, that Hepsey submitted at once with a visible satisfaction, which gave a relish to

Christie's dinner, though it was eaten at a kitchen table, with a bare-armed cook sitting opposite, and three rows of burnished dish-covers reflecting the dreadful spectacle.

After this, Christie got on excellently, for she did her best, and found both pleasure and profit in her new employment. It gave her real satisfaction to keep the handsome rooms in order, to polish plate, and spread bountiful meals. There was an atmosphere of ease and comfort about her which contrasted agreeably with the shabbiness of Mrs. Flint's boarding-house and the bare simplicity of the old home. Like most young people, Christie loved luxury, and was sensible enough to see and value the comforts of her situation, and to wonder why more girls placed as she was did not choose a life like this rather than the confinements of a sewing room, or the fatigue and publicity of a shop.

She did not learn to love her mistress, because Mrs. Stuart evidently considered herself as one belonging to a superior race of beings, and had no desire to establish any of the friendly relations that may become so helpful and pleasant to both mistress and maid. She made a royal progress through her dominions every morning, issued orders, found fault liberally, bestowed praise sparingly, and took no more personal interest in her servants than if they were clocks, to be wound up once a day, and sent away the moment they got out of repair.

Mr. Stuart was absent from morning till night, and all Christie ever knew about him was that he was a kind hearted, hot tempered, and very conceited man; fond of his wife, proud of the society they managed to draw about them, and bent on making his way in the world at any cost.

If masters and mistresses knew how skillfully they are studied, criticised and imitated by their servants, they would take more heed to their ways, and set better examples, perhaps. Mrs. Stuart never dreamed that her quiet, respectful Jane kept a sharp eye on all her movements, smiled covertly at her affectations, envied her accomplishments, and practised certain little elegancies that struck her fancy.

Mr. Stuart would have become apoplectic with indignation if he had known that this too intelligent table-girl often contrasted her master with his guests, and dared to think him wanting in good breeding when he boasted of his money, flattered a great man, or laid plans to lure some lion into his house. When he lost his temper, she always wanted to laugh, he bounced and bumbled about so like an angry blue bottle fly, and when he got himself up elaborately for a party, this disrespectful hussy confided to Hepsey her opinion that "master was a fat dandy, with nothing to be vain of but his clothes,"— a sacrilegious remark which would have caused her to be summarily ejected from the house if it had reached the august ears of master or mistress.

"My father was a gentleman, and I shall never forget it, though I do go out to service. I've got no rich friends to help me up, but, sooner or later, I mean to find a place among cultivated people; and while I'm working and waiting, I can be fitting myself to fill that place like a gentlewoman, as I am."

With this ambition in her mind, Christie took notes of all that went on in the polite world, of which she got frequent glimpses while "living out." Mrs. Stuart received one evening of each week, and on these occasions Christie, with an extra frill on her white apron, served the company, and enjoyed herself more than they did, if the truth had been known.

hile helping the ladies with their wraps, she observed what they wore, how they carried themselves, and what a vast amount of prinking they did, not to mention the flood of gossip they talked while shaking out their flounces and settling their topknots.

Later in the evening, when she passed the cups and glasses, this demure-looking damsel heard much fine discourse, saw many famous beings, and improved her mind with surreptitious studies of the rich and great when on parade. But her best time was after supper, when through the crack of the door of the little room where she was supposed to be clearing away the relics of the feast, she looked and listened at her ease, laughed at the wits, stared at the lions, heard the music, was impressed by the wisdom, and much edified by the gentility of the whole affair.

After a time, however, Christie got rather tired of it, for there was an elegant sameness about these evenings that became intensely wearisome to the uninitiated, but she fancied that as each had his part to play he managed to do it with spirit. Night after night the wag told his stories, the poet read his poems, the singers warbled, the pretty women simpered and dressed, the heavy scientific was duly discussed by the elect precious, and Mrs. Stuart, in amazing costumes, sailed to and fro in her most swan-like manner; while my lord stirred up the lions he had captured, till they roared their best, great and small.

"Good heavens! why don't they do or say something new and interesting, and not keep twaddling on about art, and music, and poetry, and cosmos? The papers are full of appeals for help for the poor, reforms of all sorts, and splendid work that others are doing; but these people seem to think it isn't genteel enough to be spoken of here. I suppose it is all very elegant to go on like a set of trained canaries, but it's very dull fun to watch them, and Hepsey's stories are a deal more interesting to me."

Having come to this conclusion, after studying dilettanteism through the crack of the door for some months, Christie left the "trained canaries" to twitter and hop about their gilded cage, and devoted herself to Hepsey, who gave her glimpses into another sort of life so bitterly real that she never could forget it.

Friendship had prospered in the lower regions, for Hepsey had a motherly heart, and Christie soon won her confidence by bestowing her own. Her story was like many another, yet, being the first Christie had ever heard, and told with the unconscious eloquence of one who had suffered and escaped, it made a deep impression on her, bringing home to her a sense of obligation so forcibly that she began at once to pay a little part of the great debt which the white race owes the black.

Christie loved books, and the attic next her own was full of them. To this store she found her way by a sort of instinct as sure as that which leads a fly to a honey-pot, and, finding many novels, she read her fill. This amusement lightened many heavy hours, peopled the silent house with troops of friends, and, for a time, was the joy of her life.

Hepsey used to watch her as she sat buried in her book when the day's work was done, and once a heavy sigh roused Christie from the most exciting crisis of "The Abbot."

"What's the matter? Are you very tired, Aunty?" she asked, using the name that came most readily to her lips.

"No, honey. I was only wishin' I could read fast like you does. I's berry slow 'bout readin' and I want to learn a heap," answered Hepsey, with such a wistful look in her soft eyes that Christie shut her book, saying briskly:

"Then I'll teach you. Bring out your primer and let's begin at once."

"Dear chile, it's orful hard work to put learnin' in my ole head, and I wouldn't 'cept such a ting from you only I needs dis sort of help so bad, and I can trust you to gib it to me as I wants it."

hen in a whisper that went straight to Christie's heart, Hepsey told her plan and showed what help she craved.

For five years she had worked hard, and saved her earnings for the purpose of her life. When a considerable sum had been hoarded up, she confided it to one whom she believed to be a friend, and sent him to buy her old mother. But he proved false, and she never saw either mother or money. It was a hard blow, but she took heart and went to work again, resolving this time to trust no one with the dangerous part of the affair, but when she had scraped together enough money to pay her way she meant to go South and steal her mother at the risk of her life.

"I don't want much money, but I must know little 'bout readin' and countin' up, else I'll get lost and cheated. You'll help me do dis, honey, and I'll bless you all my days, and so will my old mammy, if I ever gets her safe away."

With tears of sympathy shining on her cheeks, and both hands stretched out to the poor soul who implored this small boon of her, Christie promised all the help that in her lay, and kept her word religiously.

From that time, Hepsey's cause was hers; she laid by a part of her wages for "ole mammy," she comforted Hepsey with happy prophecies of success, and taught with an energy and skill she had never known before. Novels lost their charms now, for Hepsey could give her a comedy and tragedy surpassing any thing she found in them, because truth stamped her tales with a power and pathos the most gifted fancy could but poorly imitate.

The select receptions upstairs seemed duller than ever to her now, and her happiest evenings were spent in the tidy kitchen, watching Hepsey laboriously shaping A's and B's, or counting up on her worn fingers the wages they had earned by months of weary work, that she might purchase one treasure,—a feeble, old woman, worn out with seventy years of slavery far away there in Virginia.

For a year Christie was a faithful servant to her mistress, who appreciated her virtues, but did not encourage them; a true friend to poor Hepsey, who loved her dearly, and found in her sympathy and affection a solace for many griefs and wrongs. But Providence had other lessons for Christie, and when this one was well learned she was sent away to learn another phase of woman's life and labor.

While their domestics amused themselves with privy conspiracy and rebellion at home, Mr. and Mrs. Stuart spent their evenings in chasing that bright bubble called social success, and usually came home rather cross because they could not catch it.

On one of these occasions they received a warm welcome, for, as they approached the house, smoke was seen issuing from an attic window, and flames flickering behind the half-drawn curtain. Bursting out of the carriage with his usual impetuosity, Mr. Stuart let himself in and tore upstairs shouting "Fire!" like an engine company.

In the attic Christie was discovered lying dressed upon her bed, asleep or suffocated by the smoke that filled the room. A book had slipped from her hand, and in falling had upset the candle on a chair beside her; the long wick leaned against a cotton gown hanging on the wall, and a greater part of Christie's wardrobe was burning brilliantly.

"I forbade her to keep the gas lighted so late, and see what the deceitful creature has done with her private candle!" cried Mrs. Stuart with a shrillness that roused the girl from her heavy sleep more effectually than the anathemas Mr. Stuart was fulminating against the fire.

Sitting up she looked dizzily about her. The smoke was clearing fast, a window having been opened, and the tableau was a striking one. Mr. Stuart with an excited countenance was dancing frantically on a heap of half-consumed clothes pulled from the wall. He had not only drenched them with water from bowl and pitcher, but had also cast those articles upon the pile like extinguishers, and was skipping among the fragments with an agility which contrasted with his stout figure in full evening costume, and his besmirched face, made the sight irresistibly ludicrous.

Mrs. Stuart, though in her most regal array, seemed to have left her dignity downstairs with her opera cloak, for with skirts gathered closely about her, tiara all askew, and face full of fear and anger, she stood upon a chair and scolded like any shrew.

The comic overpowered the tragic, and being a little hysterical with the sudden alarm, Christie broke into a peal of laughter that sealed her fate.

"Look at her! look at her!" cried Mrs. Stuart gesticulating on her perch as if about to fly. "She has been at the wine, or lost her wits. She must go, Horatio, she must go! I cannot have my nerves shattered by such dreadful scenes. She is too fond of books, and it has turned her brain. Hepsey can watch her to-night, and at dawn she shall leave the house for ever."

ot till after breakfast, my dear. Let us have that in comfort I beg, for upon my soul we shall need it," panted Mr. Stuart, sinking into a chair exhausted with the vigorous measures which had quenched the conflagration.

Christie checked her untimely mirth, explained the probable cause of the mischief, and penitently promised to be more careful for the future.

Mr. Stuart would have pardoned her on the spot, but Madame was inexorable, for she had so completely forgotten her dignity that she felt it would be impossible ever to recover it in the eyes of this disrespectful menial. Therefore she dismissed her with a lecture that made both mistress and maid glad to part.

She did not appear at breakfast, and after that meal Mr. Stuart paid Christie her wages with a solemnity which proved he had taken a curtain lecture to heart. There was a twinkle in his eye, however, as he kindly added a recommendation, and after the door closed behind him Christie was sure that he exploded into a laugh at the recollection of his last night's performance.

This lightened her sense of disgrace very much, so, leaving a part of her money to repair damages, she packed up her dilapidated wardrobe, and, making Hepsey promise to report progress from time to time, Christie went back to Mrs. Flint's to compose her mind and be ready *a la* Micawber "for something to turn up."

✤ ✤ ✤

Author's Profile

LOUISA MAY ALCOTT

The sentimental New England family tales of Louisa May Alcott have earned her acclaim as one of America's best-loved juvenile writers. Born in 1832 and raised in New England with her three sisters, the "little women" of her classic novel *Little Women* (1869), Alcott did not venture far from her family to find characters for her stories.

Her father, philosopher and educator Amos Bronson Alcott, dreamed of improving the education methods of those times, but times were hard. He had trouble finding positions, and the family drifted in and out of poverty. The family's financial setbacks actually helped form Alcott's personality. Often she was the only breadwinner in the family, shouldering the responsibility in her teens. She worked as seamstress, domestic helper, teacher, nurse, and traveling companion, but her greatest love was writing.

Alcott tried all forms of literature: short stories, poetry, realistic Civil War stories (based on those she heard from the soldiers she nursed in Georgetown during the war), and novels. She even tried her hand at bloody thrillers published under the pseudonym, A. M. Barnard.

In *Little Women*, Alcott romanticized and sentimentalized her early family life, even the poverty which was so harsh at times. Her style was simple and straightforward, for she believed, "Never use a long word when a short one will do as well." Her characterization is realistic and honest.

Her first book was an anthology of stories called *Flower Fables*, published in 1855. Her first novel *Moods*, a story of stormy violence and death, was published in 1865. In 1868, she became editor of a popular children's monthly, *Merry's Museum*, and during that year, a Boston publisher asked her to write a story especially for girls. She called it *Little Women* and wrote it in two volumes. Among the offshoots to this story were *Old Fashioned Girl* (1870), *Eight Cousins* (1875), *Under the Lilacs* (1878), and *Jo's Boys* (1886). None of these novels ever soared to the heights of *Little Women*.

Work: A Story of Experience (1869), one of her adult novels, reveals her concern that young women in the mid-1800s were powerless, exploited by a society which required them to support themselves but offered them no training or self-improvement. Alcott was active in the Women's Suffrage Movement, taking pride in working for political reform. She said she felt more pride in this work "than in all the books I ever wrote." She was the first woman in Concord, Massachusetts, to register to vote in 1879.

Alcott did not enjoy the fame her books brought. During the book tours and at home in Concord, she complained that, "I asked for bread, and got a stone — in the shape of a pedestal." She never married, but always claimed she had taken the "pen for a bridegroom." With that pen, she produced close to 300 different literary pieces.

In her later years, Alcott's family was continually a burden for her, especially her widowed sister and aging father. She was often ill, but not with any particular malady, so some critics believe her illness was psychosomatic in nature. The difficulties of carrying out the roles of responsible family member and moral crusader ended ironically on the day one of these responsibilities was lifted. She died on March 6, 1888, the day of her father's funeral, in Roxbury, Massachusetts.

A Delicate Balance

BY JOSÉ ARMAS

ANTICIPATING: Describe a situation in which you have helped someone. Maybe you have a neighbor who is elderly and needs a snowy walk shoveled or assistance with a household chore. Perhaps you have worked with an organization whose members served as volunteers in the community. Write about the projects you've been involved in as a volunteer, or specific incidents when you have helped someone who needed help. Analyze how you felt at the time. Describe your feelings. Share your journals with a small group.

Romero Estrada had his home near the Golden Heights Centro where he spent a lot of time. He would get up almost every morning and clean and shave, and then after breakfast he would get his broom and go up and down the block sweeping the sidewalks for everyone. He would sweep in front of the Tortillería América, the Tres Milpas Bar, Barelas' Barbershop, the used furniture store owned by Goldstein, the corner grocery store, the Model Cities office, and the print shop. In the afternoons, he would come back and sit in the barbershop and just watch the people go by. Sometimes, when there was no business, Barelas would let him sit in the barber chair, and Romero would love it. He would do this just about every day except Sundays and Mondays, when Barelas' was closed. Over time, people got to expect Romero to do his little task of sweeping the sidewalks. When he was feeling real good, he would sweep in front of the houses on the block also. Romero took great care to sweep cleanly, between the cracks and even between the sides of the buildings. Everything went into the gutter. The work took him the whole morning if he did it the way he wanted.

Romero was considered a little crazy by most people, but they pretty much tolerated him. Nobody minded much when he got too drunk at the Tres Milpas Bar and went around telling everyone he loved them. "I love youuu," he would tell everyone.

"*Ta bueno*, Romero, '*ta bueno. Ya vete*," they would tell him. Sometimes when he got too drunk and obnoxious, Tino, the bartender, would make him go home.

omero received some kind of financial support, but it wasn't much. He was not given any credit by anyone because he would always forget to pay his bills. He didn't do it on purpose; he just never remembered. The businessmen preferred just to do things for him and give him things when they wanted. Barelas would trim his hair when things were slow; Tortillería América would give him *menudo* with fresh tortillas; the grocery store would give him overripe fruit and broken boxes of food that no one would buy.

When Barelas' oldest son, Seferino, graduated from high school, he went to work in his shop. Seferino took notice of Romero and came to feel sorry for him. One day, Romero was in the shop and Seferino decided to act.

"*Mira, Romero. Yo te doy 50 centavos cada vez que me barras la acera.* Fifty cents for every day you do the sidewalk for us. *¿Qué te parece?*"

Romero thought about it carefully. "*Hecho.* Done," he exclaimed. He started for home right away, to get his broom.

"What did you do that for, *m'ijo*," asked Barelas.

"It don't seem right, Dad. The man works, and no one pays him for his work. Everyone should get paid for what they do."

"He don't need no pay. He has everything he needs."

"It's not the same, Dad. How would you like to do what he does and be treated the same way?"

"I'm not Romero. You don't know about these things, *m'ijo*. Romero would be unhappy if his routine was upset. Right now, everyone likes him and takes care of him. He sweeps the sidewalks because he wants something to do. Not because he wants some money."

"I'll pay him out of my money; don't worry about it."

"The money is not the point. The point is that money will not help Romero. Don't you understand that?"

"Look, Dad. Just put yourself in his place. Would you do it? Would you cut hair for nothing?"

Barelas knew his son was putting something over on him, but he didn't know how to answer. It made sense the way Seferino explained it, but it didn't seem right. On the other hand, Seferino had gone and finished high school. He must know something. Barelas didn't know many kids who had finished high school, much less gone to college. And his son was going to college in the fall. Barelas himself had never even gone to school. Maybe his son had something there; yet on the other hand. . . . Barelas had known Romero a long time. . . . Despite his uncertainty on the matter, Barelas decided to drop the issue and not say anything about it.

Just then, Romero came back and started to sweep in front of Barelas' shop again, pushing what little dirt was left into the curb. He swept up the gutter, put the trash in a box and threw it in a garbage can.

Seferino watched with pride as Romero went about his job, and when Romero was finished, Seferino went outside and told him he had done a good job and gave him his fifty cents.

Manolo was coming into the shop to get his hair cut as Seferino was giving Romero his wages. He noticed Romero with his broom.

"What's going on?" he asked. Barelas shrugged his shoulders. "What's with Romero? Is he sick or something?"

"No he's not sick," explained Seferino, who now was inside. He told Manolo the story.

"We're going to make Romero a businessman. Do you realize how much money he would make if people just paid him fifty cents a day, if everyone paid him just fifty cents? He does do a job, you know."

"Well, it makes sense," said Manolo.

"Maybe I'll ask people to do that," said Seferino. "That way the guy could make a decent wage. Do you want to help, Manolo? You can go with me to ask people to pay him."

"Well," said Manolo, "I'm not too good at asking people for money."

This did not stop Seferino. He contacted all the businesses in the neighborhood, but no one else wanted to contribute. Still, that didn't discourage Seferino either. He went on giving Romero fifty cents a day.

A couple of weeks later, Seferino heard that Romero had gotten credit at the grocery store. "See, Dad, what did I tell you? Things are getting better for him already. And look, it's only been a couple of weeks."

But, for the next week, Romero did not show up to sweep any sidewalks. He was around, but he didn't do any work for anybody. He walked around Golden Heights Centro in his best gray work pants and his slouch hat, trying his best to look important and walking right past the barbershop.

 he following week, he came and asked to talk with Seferino in private. They went into the back, where Barelas could not hear, and Romero informed Seferino that he wanted a raise.

"What! What do you mean a raise? You haven't worked for a week. You've only been doing this a couple of weeks, and now you want a raise?" Seferino was clearly angry, but Romero was calm and persistent. He pointed out that he had been sweeping the sidewalks for a long time—even before Seferino finished school.

"I deserve a raise," he insisted.

Seferino stared at Romero coldly. It was clearly a standoff in a labor-management confrontation.

Seferino said, "Look, maybe we should forget the whole thing. I was just trying to help you out, and now look at what you do."

Romero held his ground. "I helped you out, too. No one told me to do it, and I did it anyway. I helped you many years."

"Well, let's forget about the whole thing then," said Seferino.

"I quit then," said Romero.

"Quit!" exclaimed Seferino, laughing at the absurdity of the whole thing.

"Quit! I quit!" said Romero as he stormed out the front of the shop, passing Barelas, who was cutting Pedrito's hair.

Seferino walked into the shop, shaking his head and laughing.

"Can you imagine that old guy?" he said. Barelas, for his part, did not seem too amused. He felt he could have predicted something like this would happen.

The next day, Romero was back sweeping the sidewalks again, but when he came to the barbershop, he walked completely around it and then continued sweeping the rest of the sidewalks. After about a week of doing this every day, he began sweeping the sidewalk all the way up to Barelas' and then pushing the trash to the sidewalk in front of the barbershop.

He had also stopped coming to the shop altogether. When he and Barelas met in the street, they would still greet each other. And Barelas would never bring up the fact that Romero kept pushing the trash in front of the shop. Things went on like that for a long time, until fall came and Seferino went off to college and stopped helping his father in the shop.

It was then that Romero began sweeping *all* the sidewalk again. He was happier then, and he even whistled and sang at his job.

♧ ♧ ♧

Author's Profile
JOSÉ ARMAS

Until he was twenty, José Armas worked on farms in the San Joaquin Valley of California where he was raised. Since the 1960s he has been involved in social and political issues affecting Hispanic people.

Early in his career, Armas played a major role in landmark court cases which provided for the creation of bilingual education programs in schools across the country.

Becoming an authority in diversity training, Armas developed a cross-cultural communications program which was implemented in grade schools throughout the Southwest. He has written educational textbooks which rewrite history from a Native American and Hispanic perspective, and he founded Pajarito Publications, a large Chicano publishing house. Through an MIT Fellowship, Armas developed a bilingual television series in mathematics.

Many of Armas' short stories are anthologized in American literature texts. He designed *Hispanic Magazine*, based in Washington, D.C. Currently he is a syndicated columnist whose columns appear in 15 newspapers in seven states. Recently he developed a national newsletter, *Hispanic Agenda: Leadership Strategies for the 90's.*

Armas lives in Albuquerque, New Mexico, where he writes, lectures widely, appears on radio talk shows, and is working on a collection of short stories.

Spring

BY ITALO CALVINO

ANTICIPATING: **Discuss or write about a time when you went into business for yourself: lemonade stand, lawn mowing, leaf raking, baby-sitting, etc. Record what you did, how it went, and what you learned from the experience. If you cannot think of a personal experience, substitute a "get rich quick" episode someone you know became involved in.**

 very day the postman left some envelopes in the tenants' boxes; only in Marcovaldo's there was never anything, because nobody ever wrote him, and if it hadn't been for an occasional dun from the light or the gas company, his box would have been absolutely useless. "Papa! There's mail!" Michelino shouted. "Come off it!" he answered. "The same old ads!" From all the letter-boxes a blue-and-yellow folded sheet was protruding. It said that to achieve really good suds, Blancasol was the best of products; anyone who presented this blue-and-yellow paper would be given a free sample.

Since these sheets were narrow and long, some of them jutted from the slot of the boxes; others lay on the ground, crumpled, or only a bit mussed, because many tenants, opening the box, would promptly throw away all the advertising matter that crammed it. Filippetto, Pietruccio, and Michelino, collecting some from the floor, slipping some from the slots, and actually fishing others out with a bit of wire, began to make a collection of Blancasol coupons.

"I have the most!"

"No! Count them! I have the most! You want to bet?"

Blancasol had conducted the advertising campaign through the whole neighborhood, house to house. And house to house, the young brothers started covering the area, trying to corner the coupons. Some concierges drove them away, shouting: "You little crooks! What are you trying to steal? I'm going to call the police." Others were pleased to see the kids clean up some of the waste paper deposited there every day.

In the evening, Marcovaldo's two poor rooms were all blue and yellow with Blancasol ads; the children counted and recounted them and piled them into packs like bank tellers with banknotes.

"Papà, we have so many; couldn't we start a laundry?" Filippetto asked.

n those days, the detergent world was in great upheaval. Blancasol's advertising campaign had alarmed all the rival companies. To launch their products, they distributed through all the mailboxes of the city similar coupons, which entitled the recipient to larger and larger free samples.

Marcovaldo's children, in the days that followed, were kept very busy. Every morning the letter-boxes blossomed like peach-trees in spring: slips of paper with green drawings or pink, blue, orange, promised snow-white wash for those who used Washrite or Lavolux or Beautisuds or Handikleen. For the boys, the collecting of coupons and free-sample cards ramified into more and more new classifications. At the same time, their collection territory expanded, extending to the buildings on other streets.

Naturally, these maneuvers could not go unnoticed. The neighborhood kids soon realized what Michelino and his brothers went hunting for all day, and immediately those papers, to which none of them had paid any attention before, became a sought-after booty. There was a period of rivalry among the various bands of kids, when the collection in one zone rather than another gave rise to disputes and brawling. Then, after a series of exchanges and negotiations, they reached an agreement: an organized system of hunting was more profitable than helter-skelter grabbing. And the collection of coupons became so methodical that the moment the man from Washrite or Rinsequik went by on his round of doorways, his route was observed and shadowed, step by step, and as fast as the material was distributed, it was confiscated by the kids.

Commanding operations, naturally, were still Filippetto, Pietruccio, and Michelino, because the idea had been theirs in the first place. They even succeeded in convincing the other boys that the coupons were common property and should be preserved all together. "Like in a bank!" Pietruccio explained.

"Do we own a laundry or a bank?" Michelino asked.

"Whatever it is, we're millionaires!"

The boys were so excited they couldn't sleep any more, and they made plans for the future.

"We only have to redeem all these samples and we'll have a huge amount of detergent."

"Where are we going to keep it?"

"We'll rent a warehouse!"

"Why not a freighter?"

Advertising, like fruits and flowers, has its seasons. After a few weeks, the detergent season ended; in the letter-boxes you found only ads for corn-removers.

"Shall we start collecting these, too?" someone suggested. But the prevailing view was that they should devote themselves at once to the redemption of their accumulated wealth of detergents. It was merely a matter of going to the prescribed shops and making them give a sample for every coupon. But this new phase of their plan, apparently quite simple, proved to be much longer and more complicated than the first.

Operations had to be conducted in skirmishing order: one kid at a time in one shop at a time. They could present three or even four coupons at once, provided they were of different brands; and if the clerks wanted to give only one sample of one brand, they had to say: "My Mamma wants to try them all to see which one's best."

Things became difficult when, in many shops, they would give the free sample only to those who bought something; never had Mammas seen their children so eager to run errands to the grocery.

In other words, the transformation of coupons into goods was dragging out and required supplementary expenses because errands with Mamma's money were few and the shops to be covered were many. To procure funds the only course was to initiate phase three of the plan, namely the sale of the detergent already redeemed.

They decided to sell it door to door, ringing bells: "Signora! Are you interested? Perfect wash!" and they would hold out the box of Rinsequik or the packet of Blancasol.

"Yes, yes, thanks. Give it here," some of them said, and the moment they had the sample, they would slam the door in the boy's face.

ey? Where's the money?" And they would hammer their fists on the door.

"Money? Isn't it free? Go home, you naughty kids!"

In that same period, in fact, men hired by the various brands were going from home to home, leaving free samples: this was a new advertising offensive undertaken by the whole detergent industry, since the coupon campaign had not proved fruitful.

Marcovaldo's house looked like the basement of a grocery store, full as it was of products by Beautisuds, Handikleen, Lavolux; but from all this quantity of merchandise not a cent could be squeezed; it was stuff that's given away, like the water of drinking-fountains.

Naturally, among the company representatives the rumor soon spread that some kids were making the same rounds, door to door, selling the very product their representatives were begging housewives to accept free. In the world of trade waves of pessimism are frequent; they began to report that they, who were giving the stuff away, were told by housewives that they didn't have any use for detergents, while the same women actually bought the products from those who demanded money. The planning offices of the various firms got together, market research specialists were consulted: the conclusion they reached was that such unfair competition could be carried out only by receivers of stolen goods. The police, after bringing formal charges against criminals unknown, began to patrol the neighborhood, hunting for thieves and the hiding-place of their loot.

In a moment the detergents became as dangerous as dynamite. Marcovaldo was afraid. "I won't have even an ounce of this powder in my house!" But they didn't know where to put it; nobody wanted it at home. It was decided that the children would go and throw all of it into the river.

It was before dawn; on the bridge a little cart arrived, drawn by Pietruccio and pushed by his brothers, laden with boxes of Washrite and Lavolux, then another similar cart drawn by Uguccione, the son of the concierge across the street, and then others, many others. In the center of the bridge they stopped, they allowed a cyclist to pass. After he had cast a curious glance behind him, they cried: "Go!" Michelino began hurling boxes into the river.

"Stupid! Can't you see they float?" Filippetto cried. "You have to empty the powder into the river, not dump the box!"

And from the boxes, opened one by one, a soft white cloud drifted down, rested on the current that seemed to absorb it, reappeared in a swarm of tiny bubbles, then seemed to sink. "That's the way!" And the kids began emptying pounds and pounds.

"Look! Over there!" Michelino shouted, and pointed farther downstream.

After the bridge there were the falls. Where the stream began its descent, the bubbles were no longer visible; they reappeared farther down, but now they had become huge bubbles that swelled and pushed one another upwards from below, a wave of suds that rose and became gigantic, already it was as high as the falls, a whitish foam like a barber's mug lathered by his shaving-brush. It was as if all of those powders of rival brands had made a point of demonstrating their frothiness: and the river was brimming with suds at the piers, and the fishermen, who at the first light were already in the water wearing their hip-boots, pulled in their lines and ran off.

A little breeze stirred the morning air. A clump of bubbles broke from the water's surface, and flew off, lightly. It was dawn and the bubbles took on a pink hue. The children saw them go off, high over their heads, and cried: "Ooooo . . ."

The bubbles flew on, following the invisible tracks of the city's currents of air; they turned into the streets at roof-level, always avoiding bumps with cornices and drainpipes. Now the compactness of the bunch had dissolved: the bubbles, first one then another, had flown off on their own, and each following a route different because of altitude and speed and path; they wandered in mid-air. They had multiplied, it seemed; indeed, they really had, because the river continued spilling over with foam like a pan of milk on the stove. And the wind, the wind raised up froths and frills and clumps that stretched out into rainbow garlands (the rays of the oblique sun, having climbed over the roofs, had now taken possession of the city and the river), and invaded the sky above the wires and antennae.

Dark shadows of workers rushed to the factories on their chattering motorbikes and the blue-green swarm hovering over them followed as if each man were pulling behind him a bunch of balloons tied by a long string to his handle-bars.

It was some people on a tram who first took notice. "Look! Look! What's that up there?" The tram-driver stopped and got out: all the passengers got out and started looking into the sky, the bikes and motorbikes stopped and the cars and the news-vendors and the bakers and all the morning passers-by and among them Marcovaldo on his way to work, and all stuck their noses in the air, following the flight of the soap-bubbles.

urely it's not some atomic thing?" an old woman asked, and fear ran through the crowd, and one man, seeing a bubble about to light on him, ran off, yelling: "It's radioactive!"

But the bubbles continued to glisten, multi-hued and fragile and so light that one puff, whoosh, and they were gone; and soon, in the crowd, the alarm died as it had flared up. "Radioactive my foot! It's soap! Soap-bubbles like kids blow!" And a frantic gaiety seized them. "Look at this one! And that! And that!" because they saw some enormous ones, of incredible dimensions, flying over, and as these bubbles grazed each other, they merged, they became double and triple, and the sky, the roofs, the tall buildings, through these transparent cupolas, appeared in shapes and colors never seen before.

From their smoke-stacks the factories had begun belching forth black smoke, as they did every morning. And the swarms of bubbles encountered the smoke-clouds and the sky was divided between currents of black smoke and currents of rainbow foam, and in the eddying wind they seemed to fight, and for a moment, only one moment, it looked as if the tops of the smoke-stacks were conquered by the bubbles, but soon there was such a mixture—between the smoke that imprisoned the rainbow foam and the globes of soap that imprisoned a veil of grains of soot—that you couldn't understand anything. Until, at a certain point, after seeking and seeking in the sky, Marcovaldo couldn't see the bubbles any longer, but only smoke, smoke, smoke.

Author's Profile
ITALO CALVINO

*O*ne of post-World War II Italy's most famous writers, Italo Calvino achieved an international reputation for his novels and short stories in a writing career that lasted almost 40 years.

Born in Cuba on October 15, 1923, and raised in San Remo, Italy, Calvino spent his teenage years as a partisan in the Italian Resistance, fighting against the fascist government of Benito Mussolini and the German occupation troops of Adolph Hitler. Out of this early experience, he wrote his first novel, *The Path to the Nest of Spiders,* in 1947. Unlike other novels of the resistance, Calvino told his story in the voice of a young boy, forced to grow up quickly by the war. He had become, with this novel, a member of a new generation of Italian writers, the neo-realists, of whom he later wrote:

> *We had survived the war, and the youngest of us partisans did*
> *not feel crushed, conquered, or "burned," but victors, propelled*
> *by a driving task of the battle just completed.*

His other novels (some critics have called them "anti-novels" or new novels which experiment in new forms of storytelling) include *The Non-Existent Knight and the Cloven Viscount* (1959), *Invisible Cities* (1972), *If on a Winter's Night a Traveler* (1979), and *Mr. Palomar* (1983). However, it is likely that Calvino's true fame as a writer will endure because of the very fine collections of short stories that he continued to publish all through his career: *Difficult Loves* (1955), *Italian Fables* (1956), *Marcovaldo or The Seasons in the City* (1963), and *Cosmicomics* (1965).

Calvino's stories, in particular, veer back and forth between realism and fantasy and result in a blending of these two polar opposites. He once wrote in the introduction to his *Italian Fables,* "I believe that fables are true." And, therefore, reality becomes more fantasy or "fabulous" in his writing.

Calvino died after suffering a stroke in Siena, Italy, on September 19, 1985.

A Doctor's Visit

BY ANTON CHEKHOV

ANTICIPATING: 1. Describe the type of life or lifestyle that you think will make you content or happy.

2. React to Chekhov's famous statement about his childhood: ". . . in my childhood there was no childhood. . . ."

3. Write about an experience, good or bad, that you have had with a health care situation: with either a doctor, a nurse, or a hospital. Describe what your expectations were, what your actual experience was, and how your expectations remained the same or were altered by the experience.

The professor received a telegram from the Lyalikovs' factory; he was asked to come as quickly as possible. The daughter of some Madame Lyalikov, apparently the owner of the factory, was ill, and that was all that one could make out of the long, incoherent telegram. And the professor did not go himself, but sent instead his assistant, Korolyov. 🖋 It was two stations from Moscow, and there was a drive of three miles from the station. A carriage with three horses had been sent to the station to meet Korolyov; the coachman wore a hat with a peacock's feather on it, and answered every question in a loud voice like a soldier: "No, sir!" "Certainly, sir!" 🖋 It was Saturday evening; the sun was setting, the workpeople were coming in crowds from the factory to the station, and they bowed to the carriage in which Korolyov was driving. And he was charmed with the evening, the farmhouses and villas on the road, and the birch trees, and the quiet atmosphere all around, when the fields and woods and the sun seemed preparing, like the workpeople now on the eve of the holiday, to rest, and perhaps to pray. . . . 🖋

He was born and had grown up in Moscow; he did not know the country, and he had never taken any interest in factories, or been inside one, but he had happened to read about factories, and had been in the houses of manufacturers and had talked to them; and whenever he saw a factory far or near, he always thought how quiet and peaceable it was outside, but within there was always sure to be impenetrable ignorance and dull egoism on the side of the owners, wearisome, unhealthy toil on the side of the workpeople, squabbling, vermin, vodka. And now when the workpeople timidly and respectfully made way for the carriage, in their faces, their caps, their walk, he read physical impurity, drunkenness, nervous exhaustion, bewilderment.

They drove in at the factory gates. On each side he caught glimpses of the little houses of workpeople, of the faces of women, of quilts and linen on the railings. "Look out!" shouted the coachman, not pulling up the horses. It was a wide courtyard without grass, with five immense blocks of buildings with tall chimneys a little distance one from another, warehouses and barracks, and over everything a sort of gray powder as though from dust. Here and there, like oases in the desert, there were pitiful gardens, and the green and red roofs of the houses in which the managers and clerks lived. The coachman suddenly pulled up the horses, and the carriage stopped at the house, which had been newly painted gray; here was a flower garden, with a lilac bush covered with dust, and on the yellow steps at the front door there was a strong smell of paint.

"Please come in, Doctor," said women's voices in the passage and the entry, and at the same time he heard sighs and whisperings. "Pray walk in. . . . We've been expecting you so long . . . we're in real trouble. Here, this way."

Madame Lyalikov—a stout elderly lady wearing a black silk dress with fashionable sleeves, but, judging from her face, a simple uneducated woman—looked at the doctor in a flutter, and could not bring herself to hold out her hand to him; she did not dare. Beside her stood a personage with short hair and a pince-nez; she was wearing a blouse of many colors, and was very thin and no longer young. The servants called her Christina Dmit-ryevna, and Korolyov guessed that this was the governess. Probably, as the person of most education in the house, she had been charged to meet and receive the doctor, for she began immediately, in great haste, stating the causes of the illness, giving trivial and tiresome details, but without saying who was ill or what was the matter.

The doctor and the governess were sitting talking while the lady of the house stood motionless at the door, waiting. From the conversation Korolyov learned that the patient was Madame Lyalikov's only daughter and heiress, a girl of twenty, called Liza; she had been ill for a long time and had consulted various doctors, and the previous night she had suffered till morning from such violent palpitations of the heart that no one in the house had slept, and they had been afraid she might die.

"She has been, one may say, ailing from a child," said Christina Dmitryevna in a singsong voice, continually wiping her lips with her hand. "The doctors say it is nerves; when she was a little girl she was scrofulous, and the doctors drove it inwards, so I think it may be due to that."

hey went to see the invalid. Fully grown up, big and tall, but ugly like her mother, with the same little eyes and disproportionate breadth of the lower part of her face, lying with her hair in disorder, muffled up to the chin, she made upon Korolyov at the first minute the impression of a poor, destitute creature, sheltered and cared for here out of charity, and he could hardly believe this was the heiress of the five huge buildings.

"I am the doctor come to see you," said Korolyov. "Good evening."

He mentioned his name and pressed her hand, a large, cold, ugly hand; she sat up, and, evidently accustomed to doctors, let herself be sounded, without showing the least concern that her shoulders and chest were uncovered.

"I have palpitations of the heart," she said. "It was so awful all night. . . . I almost died of fright! Do give me something."

"I will, I will; don't worry yourself."

Korolyov examined her and shrugged his shoulders.

"The heart is all right," he said; "it's all going on satisfactorily; everything is in good order. Your nerves must have been playing pranks a little, but that's so common. The attack is over by now, one must suppose; lie down and go to sleep."

At that moment a lamp was brought into the bedroom. The patient screwed up her eyes at the light, then suddenly put her hands to her head and broke into sobs. And the impression of a destitute, ugly creature vanished, and Korolyov no longer noticed the little eyes or the heavy development of the lower part of the face. He saw a soft, suffering expression which was intelligent and touching: she seemed to him altogether graceful, feminine, and simple; and he longed to soothe her, not with drugs, not with advice, but with simple, kindly words. Her mother put her arms round her head and hugged her. What despair, what grief was in the old woman's face! She, her mother, had reared her and brought her up, spared nothing, and devoted her whole life to having her daughter taught French, dancing, music: had engaged a dozen teachers for her; had consulted the best doctors, kept a governess. And now she could not make out the reason of these tears, why there was all this misery, she could not understand, and was bewildered; and she had a guilty, agitated, despairing expression, as though she had omitted something very important, had left something undone, had neglected to call in somebody—and whom, she did not know.

"Lizanka, you are crying again . . . again," she said, hugging her daughter to her. "My own, my darling, my child, tell me what it is! Have pity on me! Tell me."

Both wept bitterly. Korolyov sat down on the side of the bed and took Liza's hand.

"Come, give over; it's no use crying," he said kindly. "Why, there is nothing in the world that is worth those tears. Come, we won't cry; that's no good. . . ."

And inwardly he thought:

"It's high time she was married. . . ."

"Our doctor at the factory gave her kalibromati," said the governess, "but I notice it only makes her worse. I should have thought that if she is given anything for the heart it ought to be drops. . . . I forget the name. . . . Convallaria, isn't it?"

And there followed all sorts of details. She interrupted the doctor, preventing his speaking, and there was a look of effort on her face, as though she supposed that, as the woman of most education in the house, she was duty bound to keep up a conversation with the doctor, and on no other subject but medicine.

Korolyov felt bored.

"I find nothing special the matter," he said, addressing the mother as he went out of the bedroom. "If your daughter is being attended by the factory doctor, let him go on attending her. The treatment so far has been perfectly correct, and I see no reason for changing your doctor. Why change? It's such an ordinary trouble; there's nothing seriously wrong."

He spoke deliberately as he put on his gloves, while Madame Lyalikov stood without moving, and looked at him with her tearful eyes.

 have half an hour to catch the ten o'clock train," he said. "I hope I am not too late."

"And can't you stay?" she asked, and tears trickled down her cheeks, again. "I am ashamed to trouble you, but if you would be so good. . . . For God's sake," she went on in an undertone, glancing toward the door, "do stay tonight with us! She is all I have . . . my only daughter. . . . She frightened me last night; I can't get over it. . . . Don't go away, for goodness' sake! . . ."

He wanted to tell her that he had a great deal of work in Moscow, that his family were expecting him home; it was disagreeable to him to spend the evening and the whole night in a strange house quite needlessly; but he looked at her face, heaved a sigh, and began taking off his gloves without a word.

All the lamps and candles were lighted in his honor in the drawing room and the dining room. He sat down at the piano and began turning over the music. Then he looked at the pictures on the walls, at the portraits. The pictures, oil paintings in gold frames, were views of the Crimea—a stormy sea with a ship, a Catholic monk with a wineglass; they were all dull, smooth daubs, with no trace of talent in them. There was not a single good-looking face among the portraits, nothing but broad cheekbones and astonished-looking eyes. Lyalikov, Liza's father, had a low forehead and a self-satisfied expression; his uniform sat like a sack on his bulky plebeian figure; on his breast was a medal and a Red Cross Badge. There was little sign of culture, and the luxury was senseless and haphazard, and was as ill fitting as that uniform. The floors irritated him with their brilliant polish, the lusters on the chandelier irritated him, and he was reminded for some reason of the story of the merchant who used to go to the baths with a medal on his neck. . . .

He heard a whispering in the entry; someone was softly snoring. And suddenly from outside came harsh, abrupt, metallic sounds, such as

Korolyov had never heard before, and which he did not understand now; they roused strange, unpleasant echoes in his soul.

"I believe nothing would induce me to remain here to live . . ." he thought, and went back to the music books again.

"Doctor, please come to supper!" the governess called him in a low voice.

He went into supper. The table was large and laid with a vast number of dishes and wines, but there were only two to supper: himself and Christina Dmitryevna. She drank Madeira, ate rapidly, and talked, looking at him through her pince-nez:

"Our workpeople are very contented. We have performances at the factory every winter; the workpeople act themselves. They have lectures with a magic lantern, a splendid tearoom, and everything they want. They are very much attached to us, and when they heard that Lizanka was worse they had a service sung for her. Though they have no education, they have their feelings too."

"It looks as though you have no man in the house at all," said Korolyov.

"Not one. Pyotr Nikanoritch died a year and a half ago, and left us alone. And so there are the three of us. In the summer we live here, and in winter we live in Moscow, in Polianka. I have been living with them for eleven years—as one of the family."

At supper they served sterlet, chicken rissoles, and stewed fruit; the wines were expensive French wines.

"Please don't stand on ceremony, Doctor," said Christina Dmitryevna, eating and wiping her mouth with her fist, and it was evident she found her life here exceedingly pleasant. "Please have some more."

After supper the doctor was shown to his room, where a bed had been made up for him, but he did not feel sleepy. The room was stuffy and it smelt of paint; he put on his coat and went out.

It was cool in the open air; there was already a glimmer of dawn, and all the five blocks of buildings, with their tall chimneys, barracks, and warehouses, were distinctly outlined against the damp air. As it was a holiday, they were not working and the windows were dark, and in only one of the buildings was there a furnace burning; two windows were crimson, and fire mixed with smoke came from time to time from the chimney. Far away beyond the yard the frogs were croaking and the nightingales singing.

Looking at the factory buildings and the barracks, where the workpeople were asleep, he thought again what he always thought when he saw a factory. They may have performances for the workpeople, magic lanterns, factory doctors, and improvements of all sorts, but, all the same, the workpeople he had met that day on his way from the station did not look in any way different from those he had known long ago in his childhood, before there were factory performances and improvements. As a doctor accustomed to judging correctly of chronic complaints, the radical cause of which was incomprehensible and incurable, he looked upon factories as something baffling, the cause of which also was obscure and not removable, and all the improvements in the life of the factory hands he looked upon not as superfluous, but as comparable with the treatment of incurable illnesses.

here is something baffling in it, of course . . ." he thought, looking at the crimson windows. "Fifteen hundred or two thousand workpeople are working without rest in unhealthy surroundings, making bad cotton goods, living on the verge of starvation, and only waking from this nightmare at rare intervals in the tavern; a hundred people act as overseers, and the whole life of that hundred is spent in imposing fines, in abuse, in injustice, and only two or three so-called owners enjoy the profits, though they don't work at all, and despise the wretched cotton. But what are the profits, and how do they enjoy them? Madame Lyalikov and her daughter are unhappy—it makes one wretched to look at them; the only one who enjoys her life is Christina Dmitryevna, a stupid, middle-aged maiden lady in pince-nez. And so it appears that all these five blocks of buildings are at work, and inferior cotton is sold in the Eastern markets, simply that Christina Dmitryevna may eat sterlet and drink Madeira."

Suddenly there came a strange noise, the same sound Korolyov had heard before supper. Someone was striking on a sheet of metal near one of the buildings; he struck a note, and then at once checked the vibrations, so that short, abrupt, discordant sounds were produced, rather like "Dair . . . dair . . . dair. . . ." Then there was half a minute of stillness, and from another building there came sounds equally abrupt and unpleasant, lower bass notes:

"Drin . . . drin . . . drin. . . ." Eleven times. Evidently it was the watchman striking the hour.

Near the third building he heard "Zhuk . . . zhuk . . . zhuk. . . ." And so near all the buildings, and then behind the barracks and beyond the gates. And in the stillness of the night it seemed as though these sounds were uttered by a monster with crimson eyes—the devil himself, who controlled the owners and the workpeople alike, and was deceiving both.

Korolyov went out of the yard into the open country.

"Who goes there?" someone called to him at the gates in an abrupt voice.

"It's just like being in prison," he thought, and made no answer.

Here the nightingales and the frogs could be heard more distinctly, and one could feel it was a night in May. From the station came the noise of a train; somewhere in the distance drowsy cocks were crowing; but, all the same, the night was still, the world was sleeping tranquilly. In a field not far from the factory there could be seen the framework of a house and heaps of building material: Korolyov sat down on the planks and went on thinking.

"The only person who feels happy here is the governess, and the factory hands are working for her gratification. But that's only apparent; she is only the figurehead. The real person, for whom everything is being done, is the devil."

And he thought about the devil, in whom he did not believe, and he looked round at the two windows where the fires were gleaming. It seemed to him that out of those crimson eyes the devil himself was looking at him—that unknown force that had created the mutual relation of the strong and the weak, that coarse blunder which one could never correct. The strong must hinder the weak from living—such was the law of nature; but only in a newspaper article or in a schoolbook was that intelligible and easily accepted. In the hotchpotch which was everyday life, in the tangle of trivialities out of which human relations were woven, it was no longer a law, but a logical absurdity, when the strong and the weak were both equally victims of their mutual relations, unwillingly submitting to some directing force, unknown, standing outside life, apart from man.

So thought Korolyov, sitting on the planks, and little by little he was possessed by a feeling that this unknown and mysterious force was really close by and looking at him. Meanwhile the east was growing paler, time passed rapidly; when there was not a soul anywhere near, as though everything were dead, the five buildings and their chimneys against the gray background of the dawn had a peculiar look—not the same as by day; one forgot altogether that inside there were steam motors, electricity, telephones, and kept thinking of lake dwellings, of the Stone Age, feeling the presence of a crude, unconscious force. . . .

And again there came the sound: "Dair . . . dair . . . dair . . . dair . . . " twelve times. Then there was stillness, stillness for half a minute, and at the other end of the yard there rang out:

"Drin . . . drin . . . drin. . . ."

orribly disagreeable," thought Korolyov.

"Zhuk . . . zhuk . . ." there resounded from a third place, abruptly, sharply, as though with annoyance—"Zhuk . . . zhuk. . . ."

And it took four minutes to strike twelve. Then there was a hush; and again it seemed as though everything were dead.

Korolyov sat a little longer, then went to the house, but sat up for a good while longer. In the adjoining rooms there was whispering, there was a sound of shuffling slippers and bare feet.

"Is she having another attack?" thought Korolyov.

He went out to have a look at the patient. By now it was quite light in the rooms, and a faint glimmer of sunlight, piercing through the morning mist, quivered on the floor and on the wall of the drawing room. The door of Liza's room was open, and she was sitting in a low chair beside her bed, with her hair down, wearing a dressing gown and wrapped in a shawl. The blinds were down on the windows.

"How do you feel?" asked Korolyov.

"Thank you."

He touched her pulse, then straightened her hair that had fallen over her forehead.

"You are not asleep," he said. "It's beautiful weather outside. It's spring. The nightingales are singing, and you sit in the dark and think of something."

She listened and looked into his face; her eyes were sorrowful and intelligent, and it was evident she wanted to say something to him.

"Does this happen to you often?" he said.

She moved her lips, and answered:

"Often, I feel wretched almost every night."

At that moment the watchman in the yard began striking two o'clock. They heard: "Dair . . . dair . . ." and she shuddered.

"Do those knockings worry you?" he asked.

"I don't know. Everything here worries me," she answered, and pondered. "Everything worries me. I hear sympathy in your voice; it seemed to me as soon as I saw you that I could tell you all about it."

"Tell me, I beg you."

"I want to tell you of my opinion. It seems to me that I have no illness, but that I am weary and frightened, because it is bound to be so and cannot be otherwise. Even the healthiest person can't help being uneasy if, for instance, a robber is moving about under his window. I am constantly being doctored," she went on, looking at her knees, and she gave a shy smile. "I am very grateful, of course, and I do not deny that the treatment is a benefit; but I should like to talk, not with a doctor, but with some intimate friend who would understand me and would convince me that I was right or wrong."

"Have you no friends?" asked Korolyov.

"I am lonely. I have a mother; I love her, but, all the same, I am lonely. That's how it happens to be. . . . Lonely people read a great deal, but say little and hear little. Life for them is mysterious; they are mystics and often see the devil where he is not. Lermontov's Tamara was lonely and she saw the devil."

"Do you read a great deal?"

"Yes. You see, my whole time is free from morning till night. I read by day, and by night my head is empty; instead of thoughts there are shadows in it."

"Do you see anything at night?" asked Korolyov.

"No, but I feel. . . ."

She smiled again, raised her eyes to the doctor, and looked at him so sorrowfully, so intelligently; and it seemed to him that she trusted him, and that she wanted to speak frankly to him, and that she thought the same as he did. But she was silent, perhaps waiting for him to speak.

And he knew what to say to her. It was clear to him that she needed as quickly as possible to give up the five buildings and the million if she had it—to leave that devil that looked out at night; it was clear to him, too, that she thought so herself, and was only waiting for someone she trusted to confirm her.

But he did not know how to say it. How? One is shy of asking men under sentence what they have been sentenced for; and in the same way it is awkward to ask very rich people what they want so much money for, why they make such a poor use of their wealth, why they don't give it up, even when they see in it their unhappiness; and if they begin a conversation about it themselves, it is usually embarrassing, awkward, and long.

ow is one to say it?" Korolyov wondered. "And is it necessary to speak?"

And he said what he meant in a roundabout way:

"You in the position of a factory owner and a wealthy heiress are dissatisfied; you don't believe in your right to it; and here now you can't sleep. That, of course, is better than if you were satisfied, slept soundly, and thought everything was satisfactory. Your sleeplessness does you credit; in any case, it is a good sign. In reality, such a conversation as this between us now would have been unthinkable for our parents. At night they did not talk, but slept sound; we, our generation, sleep badly, are restless, but talk a great deal, and are always trying to settle whether we are right or not. For our children or grandchildren that question—whether they are right or not—will have been settled. Things will be clearer for them than for us. Life will be good in fifty years' time; it's only a pity we shall not last out till then. It would be interesting to have a peep at it.

"What will our children and grandchildren do?" asked Liza.

"I don't know. . . . I suppose they will throw it all up and go away."

"Go where?"

"Where? . . . Why, where they like," said Korolyov; and he laughed. "There are lots of places a good, intelligent person can go to."

He glanced at his watch.

"The sun has risen, though," he said. "It is time you were asleep. Undress and sleep soundly. Very glad to have made your acquaintance," he went on, pressing her hand. "You are a good, interesting woman. Good night!"

He went to his room and went to bed.

In the morning they all came out on to the steps to see him off. Liza, pale and exhausted, was in a white dress as though for a holiday, with a flower in her hair; she looked at him, as yesterday, sorrowfully and intelligently, smiled and talked, and all with an expression as though she wanted to tell him something special, important—him alone. They could hear the larks trilling and the church bells pealing. The windows in the factory buildings were sparkling gaily, and, driving across the yard and afterwards along the road to the station, Korolyov thought neither of the workpeople nor of lake dwellings, nor of the devil, but thought of the time, perhaps close at hand, when life would be as bright and joyous as that still Sunday morning; and he thought how pleasant it was on such a morning in the spring to drive with three horses in a good carriage, and to bask in the sunshine.

Author's Profile
ANTON CHEKHOV

Anton Chekhov is considered a master of both the modern short story and the modern drama. Both his stories and his plays recount everyday events in which very little seems to happen. But in the nuances of those everyday events, Chekhov gives his readers and playgoers both a glimpse of a bygone age (late nineteenth century Russia) and an insight into human aspirations and suffering that is universal.

Anton Pavlovich Chekhov was born in Taganrog in southern Russia on January 29, 1860, the third of six children of a grocer who later went bankrupt. Raised in an environment of severe parental beatings and forced piety, Chekhov became an early enemy of all forms of violence and hypocrisy. He would later write of these times: ". . . in my childhood there was no childhood."

In 1879, he enrolled in medical school, supporting himself by tutoring other students and by selling short sketches to various humor magazines. By the time of his graduation from medical school in 1884, he had grown from writing brief sketches and jokes to full-fledged stories. Medicine competed with literature in his life, though Chekhov saw this competition in a typically humorous light in a letter of September 11, 1888, to his friend and editor A. S. Suvorin:

> *Medicine is my lawful, wedded wife, and literature is my mistress. When one isn't enough for me, I spend the night with the other. That may be a little improper, but then it's less dull, and in any case, neither one loses anything by my perfidity.*

In actuality, however, Chekhov's two careers complimented each other: Medicine gave him a rare insight into human behavior and literature, the opportunity to articulate this knowledge. His concern was always to portray the human situation as honestly as possible, with little of the lengthy moralizing or ideological commentary that was so popular in most of the writing of his time.

By the late 1880s, Chekhov was considered one of Russia's most important younger writers. In 1887, he won the prestigious Pushkin Prize for his story collection *At Twilight*. In 1890, he made an almost yearlong trip to the Russian penal colony on Sakhalin Island. He recorded his trip and his observation on the lives of the convicts and the conditions of their incarceration in *Sakhalin Island* (1894). Besides continuing to write such short stories as "Ward No. 6," "The Lady with the Dog," "The Darling," "The Bishop," and many others, Chekhov was also writing plays for Konstantin Stanislovsky's Moscow Art Theatre: *The Seagull* (1896), *Uncle Vanya* (1899), *Three Sisters* (1901), and *The Cherry Orchard* (1903).

Long afflicted with tuberculosis, Chekhov spent the last seven years of his life living in Yalta and journeying to warmer climates that offered some relief to his lungs. He married actress Olga Knipper in 1901, but they were forced to live apart, due to his failing health and the demands of her theatrical career in Moscow. He died on July 15, 1904, in Badenweiler, Germany.

Author Robert Payne, who has written about various Russian writers and has translated many of Chekhov's stories, summed him up:

> *Chekhov celebrated the human variety, and while his peasants and princes have vanished, they are closer to us than we know.*

> *That is why of all Russian writers Chekhov, the archconservative, is the most subversive. He is dynamite for children, for he proclaimed the utmost freedom and gave to the human heart the place of sovereign eminence. His stories are hosannas in praise of freedom, of the wanderings of the human heart in search of its own peace. And so, with the insidious power of genius, he prepares us for the revolutions of the future.*

Bargain

BY A. B. GUTHRIE, JR.

ANTICIPATING: **Consider what your life would be like if you were unable to read. What difficulties would you have on the job, around the house, in clubs you belong to, in your daily life?**

r. Baumer and I had closed the Moon Dance Mercantile Company and were walking to the post office, and he had a bunch of bills in his hand ready to mail. There wasn't anyone or anything much on the street because it was suppertime. A buckboard and a saddle horse were tied at Hirschs' rack, and a rancher in a wagon rattled for home ahead of us, the sound of his going fading out as he prodded his team. Freighter Slade stood alone in front of the Moon Dance Saloon, maybe wondering whether to have one more before going to supper. People said he could hold a lot without showing it except in being ornerier even than usual. Mr. Baumer didn't see him until he was almost on him, and then he stopped and fingered through the bills until he found the right one. He stepped up to Slade and held it out. Slade said, "What's this, Dutchie?"

Mr. Baumer had to tilt his head up to talk to him. "You know vat it is."

Slade just said, "Yeah?" You never could tell from his face what went on inside his skull. He had dark skin and shallow cheeks and a thick-growing mustache that fell over the corners of his mouth.

"It is a bill," Mr. Baumer said. "I tell you before it is a bill. For twenty-vun dollars and fifty cents."

"You know what I do with bills, don't you, Dutchie?" Slade asked.

Mr. Baumer didn't answer the question. He said, "For merchandise."

Slade took the envelope from Mr. Baumer's hand and squeezed it up in his fist and let it drop on the plank sidewalk. Not saying anything, he reached down and took Mr. Baumer's nose between the knuckles of his fingers and twisted it up into his eyes. That was all. That was all at the time. Slade half turned and slouched to the door of the bar and let himself in. Some men were laughing in there.

Mr. Baumer stooped and picked up the bill and put it on top of the rest and smoothed it out for mailing. When he straightened up I could see tears in his eyes from having his nose screwed around.

He didn't say anything to me, and I didn't say anything to him, being so much younger and feeling embarrassed for him. He went into the post office and slipped the bills in the slot, and we walked on home together. At the last, at the crossing where I had to leave him, he remembered to say, "Better study, Al. Is good to know to read and write and figure." I guess he felt he had to push me a little, my father being dead.

I said, "Sure. See you after school tomorrow"—which he knew I would anyway. I had been working in the store for him during the summer and after classes ever since pneumonia took my dad off.

Three of us worked there regularly, Mr. Baumer, of course, and me and Colly Coleman, who knew enough to drive the delivery wagon but wasn't much help around the store except for carrying orders out to the rigs at the hitchpost and handling heavy things like the whisky barrel at the back of the store which Mr. Baumer sold quarts and gallons out of.

The store carried quite a bit of stuff—sugar and flour and dried fruits and canned goods and such on one side and yard goods and coats and caps and aprons and the like of that on the other, besides kerosene and bran and buckets and linoleum and pitchforks in the storehouse at the rear—but it wasn't a big store like Hirsch Brothers up the street. Never would be, people guessed, going on to say, with a sort of slow respect, that it would have gone under long ago if Mr. Baumer hadn't been half mule and half beaver. He had started the store just two years before and, the way things were, worked himself close to death.

He was at the high desk at the end of the grocery counter when I came in the next afternoon. He had an eyeshade on and black sateen protectors on his forearms, and his pencil was in his hand instead of behind his ear and his glasses were roosted on the nose that Slade had twisted. He didn't hear me open and close the door or hear my feet as I walked back to him, and I saw he wasn't doing anything with the pencil but holding it over paper. I stood and studied him for a minute, seeing a small stooped man with a little paunch bulging through his unbuttoned vest. He was a man you wouldn't remember from meeting once. There was nothing in his looks to set itself in your mind unless maybe it was his chin, which was a small, pink hill in the gentle plain of his face.

While I watched him, he lifted his hand and felt carefully of his nose. Then he saw me. His eyes had that kind of mistiness that seems to go with age or illness, though he wasn't really old or sick, either. He brought his hand down quickly and picked up the pencil, but he saw I still was looking at the nose, and finally he sighed and said, "That Slade."

ust the sound of the name brought Slade to my eye. I saw him slouched in front of the bar, and I saw him and his string coming down the grade from the buttes, the wheel horses held snug and the rest lined out pretty, and then the string leveling off and Slade's whip lifting hair from a horse that wasn't up in the collar. I had heard it said that Slade could make a horse scream with that whip. Slade's name wasn't Freighter, of course. Our town had nicknamed him that because that was what he was.

"I don't think it's any good to send him a bill, Mr. Baumer," I said. "He can't even read."

"He could pay yet."

"He don't pay anybody," I said.

"I think he hate me," Mr. Baumer went on. "That is the thing. He hate me for coming not from this country. I come here, sixteen years old, and learn to read and write, and I make a business, and so I think he hate me."

"He hates everybody."

Mr. Baumer shook his head. "But not to pinch the nose. Not to call Dutchie."

The side door squeaked open, but it was only Colly Coleman coming in from a trip so I said, "Excuse me, Mr. Baumer, but you shouldn't have trusted him in the first place."

"I know," he answered, looking at me with his misty eyes. "A man make mistakes. I think some do not trust him, so he will pay me because I do. And I do not know him well then. He only came back to town three-four months ago, from being away since before I go into business."

"People who knew him before could have told you," I said.

"A man make mistakes," he explained again.

"It's not my business, Mr. Baumer, but I would forget the bill."

His eyes rested on my face for a long minute, as if they didn't see me but the problem itself. He said, "It is not twenty-vun dollars and fifty cents now, Al. It is not that any more."

"What is it?"

He took a little time to answer. Then he brought his two hands up as if to help him shape the words. "It is the thing. You see, it is the thing."

I wasn't quite sure what he meant.

He took his pencil from behind the ear where he had put it and studied the point of it. "That Slade. He steal whisky and call it evaporation. He sneak things from his load. A thief, he is. And too big for me."

I said, "I got no time for him, Mr. Baumer, but I guess there never was a freighter didn't steal whisky. That's what I hear."

It was true, too. From the railroad to Moon Dance was fifty miles and a little better—a two-day haul in good weather, heck knew how long in bad. Any freight string bound home with a load had to lie out at least one night. When a freighter had his stock tended to and maybe a little fire going against the dark, he'd tackle a barrel of whisky or of grain alcohol if he had one aboard, consigned to Hirsch Brothers or Mr. Baumer's or the Moon Dance Saloon or the Gold Leaf Bar. He'd drive a hoop out of place, bore a little hole with a nail or bit and draw off what he wanted. Then he'd plug the hole with a whittled peg and pound the hoop back. That was evaporation. Nobody complained much. With freighters you generally took what they gave you, within reason.

"Moore steals it, too," I told Mr. Baumer. Moore was Mr. Baumer's freighter.

"Yah," he said, and that was all, but I stood there for a minute, thinking there might be something more. I could see thought swimming in his eyes, above that little hill of chin. Then a customer came in, and I had to go wait on him.

Nothing happened for a month, nothing between Mr. Baumer and Slade, that is, but fall drew on toward winter and the first flight of ducks headed south and Mr. Baumer hired Miss Lizzie Webb to help with the just-beginning Christmas trade, and here it was, the first week in October, and he and I walked up the street again with the monthly bills. He always sent them out. I guess he had to. A bigger store, like Hirschs', would wait on the ranchers until their beef or wool went to market.

Up to a point things looked and happened almost the same as they had before, so much the same that I had the crazy feeling I was going through that time again. There was a wagon and a rig tied up at Hirschs' rack and a saddle horse standing hipshot in front of the harness shop. A few more people were on the street now, not many, and lamps had been lit against the shortened day.

t was dark enough that I didn't make out Slade right away. He was just a figure that came out of the yellow wash of light from the Moon Dance Saloon and stood on the board walk and with his head made the little motion of spitting. Then I recognized the lean, raw shape of him and the muscles flowing down into the sloped shoulders, and in the settling darkness I filled the picture in—the dark skin and the flat cheeks and the peevish eyes and the mustache growing rank.

There was Slade and here was Mr. Baumer with his bills and here I was, just as before, just like in the second go-round of a bad dream. I felt like turning back, being embarrassed and half scared by trouble even when it wasn't mine. Please, I said to myself, don't stop, Mr. Baumer! Don't bite off anything! Please, shortsighted the way you are, don't catch sight of him at all! I held up and stepped around behind Mr. Baumer and came up on the outside so as to be between him and Slade where maybe I'd cut off his view.

But it wasn't any use. All along I think I knew it was no use, not the praying or the walking between or anything. The act had to play itself out.

Mr. Baumer looked across the front of me and saw Slade and hesitated in his step and came to a stop. Then in his slow, business way, his chin held firm against his mouth, he began fingering through the bills, squinting to make out the names. Slade had turned and was watching him, munching on a cud of tobacco like a bull waiting.

"You look, Al," Mr. Baumer said without lifting his face from the bills. "I cannot see so good."

So I looked, and while I was looking Slade must have moved. The next I knew Mr. Baumer was staggering ahead, the envelopes spilling out of his hands. There had been a thump, the clap of a heavy hand swung hard on his back.

Slade said, "Haryu, Dutchie?"

Mr. Baumer caught his balance and turned around, the bills he had trampled shining white between them and, at Slade's feet, the hat that Mr. Baumer had stumbled out from under.

Slade picked up the hat and scuffed through the bills and held it out. "Cold to be goin' without a sky-piece," he said.

Mr. Baumer hadn't spoken a word. The lampshine from inside the bar caught his eyes, and in them it seemed to me a light came and went as anger and the uselessness of it took turns in his head.

Two men had come up on us and stood watching. One of them was Angus McDonald, who owned the Ranchers' Bank, and the other was Dr. King. He had his bag in his hand.

Two others were drifting up, but I didn't have time to tell who. The light came in Mr. Baumer's eyes, and he took a step ahead and swung. I could have hit harder myself. The first landed on Slade's cheek without hardly so much as jogging his head, but it let hell loose in the man. I didn't know he could move so fast. He slid in like a practiced fighter and let Mr. Baumer have it full in the face.

Mr. Baumer slammed over on his back, but he wasn't out. He started lifting himself. Slade leaped ahead and brought a boot heel down on the hand he was lifting himself by. I heard meat and bone under that heel and saw Mr. Baumer fall back and try to roll away.

Things had happened so fast that not until then did anyone have a chance to get between them. Now Mr. McDonald pushed at Slade's chest, saying, "That's enough, Freighter. That's enough now," and Dr. King lined up, too, and another man I didn't know, and I took a place, and we formed a kind of screen between them. Dr. King turned and bent to look at Mr. Baumer.

"Damn fool hit me first," Slade said.

"That's enough," Mr. McDonald told him again while Slade looked at all of us as if he'd spit on us for a nickel. Mr. McDonald went on, using a half-friendly tone, and I knew it was because he didn't want to take Slade on any more than the rest of us did. "You go on home and sleep it off, Freighter. That's the ticket."

lade just snorted.

From behind us Dr. King said, "I think you've broken this man's hand."

"Lucky for him I didn't kill him," Slade answered. "Damn Dutch penny-pincher!" He fingered the chew out of his mouth. "Maybe he'll know enough to leave me alone now."

Dr. King had Mr. Baumer on his feet. "I'll take him to the office," he said.

Blood was draining from Mr. Baumer's nose and rounding the curve of his lip and dripping from the sides of his chin. He held his hurt right hand in the other. But a thing was that he didn't look beaten even then, not the way a man who has given up looks beaten. Maybe that was why Slade said, with a show of that fierce anger, "You stay away from me! Hear? Stay clear away, or you'll get more of the same!"

Dr. King led Mr. Baumer away, Slade went back into the bar, and the other men walked off, talking about the fight. I got down and picked up the bills, because I knew Mr. Baumer would want me to, and mailed them at the post office, dirty as they were. It made me sorer, someway, that Slade's bill was one of the few that wasn't marked up. The cleanness of it seemed to say that there was no getting the best of him.

Mr. Baumer had his hand in a sling the next day and wasn't much good at waiting on the trade. I had to hustle all afternoon and so didn't have a chance to talk to him even if he had wanted to talk. Mostly he stood at his desk, and once, passing it, I saw he was practicing writing with his left hand. His nose and the edges of the cheeks around it were swollen some.

At closing time I said, "Look, Mr. Baumer, I can lay out of school a few days until you kind of get straightened out here."

"No," he answered as if to wave the subject away. "I get somebody else. You go to school. Is good to learn."

I had a half notion to say that learning hadn't helped him with Slade. Instead, I blurted out that I would have the law on Slade.

"The law?" he asked.

"The sheriff or somebody."

"No, Al," he said. "You would not."

I asked why.

"The law, it is not for plain fights," he said. "Shooting? Robbing? Yes, the law come quick. The plain fights, they are too many. They not count enough."

He was right. I said, "Well, I'd do something anyhow."

"Yes," he answered with a slow nod of his head. "Something you vould do, Al." He didn't tell me what.

Within a couple of days he got another man to clerk for him—it was Ed Hempel, who was always finding and losing jobs—and we made out. Mr. Baumer took his hand from the sling in a couple or three weeks, but with the tape on it still wasn't any use to him. From what you could see of the fingers below the tape it looked as if it never would be.

He spent most of his time at the high desk, sending me or Ed out on the errands he used to run, like posting and getting the mail. Sometimes I wondered if that was because he was afraid of meeting Slade. He could just as well have gone himself. He wasted a lot of hours just looking at nothing, though I will have to say he worked hard at learning to write left-handed.

Then, a month and a half before Christmas, he hired Slade to haul his freight for him.

Ed Hempel told me about the deal when I showed up for work. "Yessir," he said, resting his foot on a crate in the storeroom where we were supposed to be working. "I tell you he's throwed in with Slade. Told me this morning to go out and locate him if I could and bring him in. Slade was at the saloon, o' course, and says to hell with Dutchie, but I told him this was honest-to-God business, like Baumer had told me to, and there was a quart of whisky right there in the store for him if he'd come and get it. He was out of money, I reckon, because the quart fetched him."

"What'd they say?" I asked him.

"Search me. There was two or three people in the store and Baumer told me to wait on 'em, and he and Slade palavered back by the desk."

"How do you know they made a deal?"

d spread his hands out. " 'Bout noon, Moore came in with his string, and I heard Baumer say he was makin' a change. Moore didn't like it too good, either."

It was a hard thing to believe, but there one day was Slade with a pile of stuff for the Moon Dance Mercantile Company, and that was proof enough with something left for boot.

Mr. Baumer never opened the subject up with me, though I gave him plenty of chances. And I didn't feel like asking. He didn't talk much these days but went around absent-minded, feeling now and then of the fingers that curled yellow and stiff out of the bandage like the toes on the leg of a dead chicken. Even on our walks home he kept his thoughts to himself.

I felt different about him now, and was sore inside. Not that I blamed him exactly. A hundred and thirty-five pounds wasn't much to throw against two hundred. And who could tell what Slade would do on a bellyful of whisky? He had promised Mr. Baumer more of the same, hadn't he? But I didn't feel good. I couldn't look up to Mr. Baumer like I used to and still wanted to. I didn't have the beginning of an answer when men cracked jokes or shook their heads in sympathy with Mr. Baumer, saying Slade had made him come to time.

Slade hauled in a load for the store, and another, and Christmas time was drawing on and trade heavy, and the winter that had started early and then pulled back came on again. There was a blizzard and then a still cold and another blizzard and afterwards a sunshine that was ice-shine on the drifted snow. I was glad to be busy, selling overshoes and sheep-lined coats and mitts and socks as thick as saddle blankets and Christmas candy out of buckets and hickory nuts and the fresh oranges that the people in our town never saw except when Santa Claus was coming.

One afternoon when I lit out from class the thermometer on the school porch read 42° below. But you didn't have to look at it to know how cold the weather was. Your nose and fingers and toes and ears and the bones inside you told you. The snow cried when you stepped on it.

I got to the store and took my things off and scuffed my hands at the stove for a minute so's to get life enough in them to tie a parcel. Mr. Baumer—he was always polite to me—said, "Hello, Al. Not so much to do today. Too cold for customers." He shuddered a little, as if he hadn't got the chill off even yet, and rubbed his broken hand with the good one. "Ve need Christmas goods," he said, looking out the window to the furrows that wheels had made in the snow-banked street, and I knew he was thinking of Slade's string, inbound from the railroad, and the time it might take even Slade to travel those hard miles.

Slade never made it at all.

Less than an hour later our old freighter, Moore, came in, his beard white and stiff with frost. He didn't speak at first but looked around and clumped to the stove and took off his heavy mitts, holding his news inside him.

Then he said, not pleasantly, "Your new man's dead, Baumer."

"My new man?" Mr. Baumer said.

"Who the hell do you think? Slade. He's dead."

All Mr. Baumer could say was, "Dead!"

"Froze to death, I figger," Moore told him while Colly Coleman and Ed Hempel and Miss Lizzie and I and a couple of customers stepped closer.

"Not Slade," Mr. Baumer said. "He know too much to freeze."

"Maybe so, but he sure's God's froze now. I got him in the wagon."

We stood looking at one another and at Moore. Moore was enjoying his news, enjoying feeding it out bit by bit so's to hold the stage. "Heart might've give out for all I know."

The side door swung open, letting in a cloud of cold and three men who stood, like us, waiting on Moore. I moved a little and looked through the window and saw Slade's freight outfit tied outside with more men around it. Two of them were on a wheel of one of the wagons, looking inside.

"Had a extra man, so I brought your stuff in," Moore went on. "Figgered you'd be glad to pay for it."

"Not Slade," Mr. Baumer said again.

"You can take a look at him."

r. Baumer answered no.

"Someone's takin' word to Connor to bring his hearse. Anyhow I told 'em to. I carted old Slade this far. Connor can have him now."

Moore pulled on his mitts. "Found him there by the Deep Creek crossin', doubled up in the snow an' his fire out." He moved toward the door. "I'll see to the horses, but your stuff'll have to set there. I got more'n enough work to do at Hirschs'."

Mr. Baumer just nodded.

I put on my coat and went out and waited my turn and climbed on a wagon wheel and looked inside, and there was Slade piled on some bags of bran. Maybe because of being frozen, his face was whiter than I ever saw it, whiter and deader, too, though it never had been lively. Only the mustache seemed still alive, sprouting thick like greasewood from alkali. Slade was doubled up all right, as if he had died and stiffened leaning forward in a chair.

I got down from the wheel, and Colly and then Ed climbed up. Moore was unhitching, tossing off his pieces of information while he did so. Pretty soon Mr. Connor came up with his old hearse, and he and Moore tumbled Slade into it, and the team that was as old as the hearse made off, the tires squeaking in the snow. The people trailed on away with it, their breaths leaving little ribbons of mist in the air. It was beginning to get dark.

Mr. Baumer came out of the side door of the store, bundled up, and called to Colly and Ed and me. "We unload," he said. "Already is late. Al, better you get a couple lanterns now."

We did a fast job, setting the stuff out of the wagons on to the platform and then carrying it or rolling it on the one truck that the store owned and stowing it inside according to where Mr. Baumer's good hand pointed.

A barrel was one of the last things to go in. I edged it up and Colly nosed the truck under it, and then I let it fall back. "Mr. Baumer," I said, "we'll never sell all this, will we?"

"Yah," he answered. "Sure we sell it. I get it cheap. A bargain, Al, so I buy it."

I looked at the barrel head again. There in big letters I saw "Wood Alcohol—Deadly Poison."

"Hurry now," Mr. Baumer said. "Is late." For a flash and no longer I saw through the mist in his eyes, saw, you might say, that hilly chin repeated there. "Then ve go home, Al. Is good to know how to read."

❧ ❧ ❧

A. B. GUTHRIE, JR.

*P*ulitzer Prize-winner A. B. Guthrie, Jr., is noted for his epic frontier novels which portrayed the West as it really was and settlers as noble, hardworking folks. A Montanan who lived close to the land, Guthrie was most famous for the novel *The Way West*, published in 1949, which won the Pulitzer Prize for fiction in 1950.

Born Alfred Bertram Guthrie on January 13, 1901, he started as a newspaperman, which accounts for his lean, straightforward prose. One critic praised his writing as "a kind of dramatic reportage" and commended his "clean, informal, and direct" style.

Guthrie wrote six panoramic westerns, beginning with *The Big Sky* in 1947 and later *The Way West* in 1949. Another notable work was *These Thousand Hills*, written in 1956. He also wrote short stories, essays, and mystery novels with western settings. In addition, Guthrie made his way into the film industry, writing screenplays for two classic western movies, *Shane* (1953) and *The Kentuckian* (1955).

Guthrie was interested in everyday people: the shopkeeper, the rancher, the trail rider. Of his writing, Guthrie said, "I don't write 'gun and gallop' jobs and promote the myth of the Old West. I avoid the myth. You see, for every Wyatt Earp or Billy the Kid, there were thousands of people trying to get along—not ready with a gun or ready to spill blood." He died in 1991 at the age of ninety, in Choteau, Montana.

The Hack Driver

BY SINCLAIR LEWIS

ANTICIPATING: Most of us entered the world of work in a small way, as a babysitter, mowing lawns, caring for someone's pet, watering shrubs, or running errands. Write about your first job, even if it was just chores around the house. Or write about a job you had as a team member, like playing second base. Include details on who hired you, what tasks you were expected to perform, the people who worked along with you, how you felt about this new situation, and any problems you had.

 dare say there's no man of large affairs, whether he is bank president or senator or dramatist, who hasn't a sneaking love for some old rum-hound in a frightful hat, living back in a shanty and making his living by ways you wouldn't care to examine too closely. (It was the Supreme Court Justice speaking. I do not pretend to guarantee his theories or his story.) He may be a Maine guide, or the old garageman who used to keep the livery stable, or a perfectly useless innkeeper who sneaks off to shoot ducks when he ought to be sweeping the floors, but your pompous big-city man will contrive to get back and see him every year, and loaf with him, and secretly prefer him to all the highfalutin leaders of the city. 🖉 There's that much truth, at least, to this Open Spaces stuff you read in advertisements of wild and woolly Western novels. I don't know the philosophy of it; perhaps it means that we retain a decent simplicity, no matter how much we are tied to Things, to houses and motors and expensive wives. Or again it may give away the whole game of civilization; may mean that the apparently civilized man is at heart nothing but a hobo who prefers flannel shirts and bristly cheeks and cussing and dirty tin plates to all the trim, hygienic, forward-looking life our women-folks make us put on for them. 🖉

When I graduated from law school I suppose I was about as artificial and idiotic and ambitious as most youngsters. I wanted to climb, socially and financially. I wanted to be famous and dine at large houses with men who shuddered at the Common People who don't dress for dinner. You see, I hadn't learned that the only thing duller than a polite dinner is the conversation afterward, when the victims are digesting the dinner and accumulating enough strength to be able to play bridge. Oh, I was a fine young calf! I even planned a rich marriage. Imagine then how I felt when, after taking honors and becoming fifteenth assistant clerk in the magnificent law firm of Hodgins, Hodgins, Berkman and Taupe, I was set not at preparing briefs but at serving summonses! Like a cheap private detective! Like a mangy sheriff's officer! They told me I had to begin that way and, holding my nose, I feebly went to work. I was kicked out of actresses' dressing rooms, and from time to time I was righteously beaten by large and indignant litigants. I came to know, and still more to hate, every dirty and shadowy corner of the city. I thought of fleeing to my home town, where I could at once become a full-fledged attorney-at-law. I rejoiced one day when they sent me out forty miles or so to a town called New Mullion, to serve a summons on one Oliver Lutkins. This Lutkins had worked in the Northern Woods, and he knew the facts about a certain timberland boundary agreement. We needed him as a witness, and he had dodged service.

hen I got off the train at New Mullion, my sudden affection for sweet and simple villages was dashed by the look of the place, with its mud-gushing streets and its rows of shops either paintless or daubed with a sour brown. Though it must have numbered eight or nine thousand inhabitants, New Mullion was as littered as a mining camp. There was one agreeable-looking man at the station—the expressman. He was a person of perhaps forty, red-faced, cheerful, thick; he wore his overalls and denim jumper as though they belonged to him, he was quite dirty and very friendly and you knew at once he liked people and slapped them on the back out of pure easy affection.

"I want," I told him, "to find a fellow named Oliver Lutkins."

"Him? I saw him 'round here 'twan't an hour ago. Hard fellow to catch, though—always chasing around on some phony business or other.

Probably trying to get up a poker game in the back of Fritz Beinke's harness shop. I'll tell you, boy—Any hurry about locating Lutkins?"

"Yes. I want to catch the afternoon train back." I was as impressively secret as a stage detective.

"I'll tell you. I've got a hack. I'll get out the boneshaker and we can drive around together and find Lutkins. I know most of the places he hangs out."

He was so frankly friendly, he so immediately took me into the circle of his affection, that I glowed with the warmth of it. I knew, of course, that he was drumming up business, but his kindness was real, and if I had to pay hack fare in order to find my man, I was glad that the money would go to this good fellow. I got him down to two dollars an hour; he brought from his cottage, a block away, an object like a black piano-box on wheels.

He didn't hold the door open, certainly he didn't say "Ready, sir." I think he would have died before calling anybody "sir." When he gets to Heaven's gate he'll call St. Peter "Pete," and I imagine the good saint will like it. He remarked, "Well, young fellow, here's the handsome equipage," and his grin—well, it made me feel that I had always been his neighbor. They're so ready to help a stranger, those villagers. He had already made it his own task to find Oliver Lutkins for me.

He said, and almost shyly: "I don't want to butt in on your private business, young fellow, but my guess is that you want to collect some money from Lutkins—he never pays anybody a cent; he still owes me six bits on a poker game I was fool enough to get into. He ain't a bad sort of a Yahoo but he just naturally hates to loosen up on a coin of the realm. So if you're trying to collect any money off him, we better kind of you might say creep up on him and surround him. If you go asking for him—anybody can tell you come from the city, with that trick Fedora of yours—he'll suspect something and take a sneak. If you want me to, I'll go into Fritz Beinke's and ask for him, and you can keep out of sight behind me."

I loved him for it. By myself I might never have found Lutkins. Now, I was an army with reserves. In a burst I told the hack driver that I wanted to serve a summons on Lutkins; that the fellow had viciously refused to testify in a suit where his knowledge of a certain conversation would clear up everything. The driver listened earnestly—and I was still young enough to be grateful at being taken seriously by any man of forty. At the end he pounded my shoulder (very painfully) and chuckled: "Well, we'll spring a little surprise on Brer Lutkins."

"Let's start, driver."

"Most folks around here call me Bill. Or Magnuson. William Magnuson, fancy carting and hauling."

ll right, Bill. Shall we tackle this harness shop—Beinke's?"

"Yes, jus' likely to be there as anywheres. Plays a lot of poker and a great hand at bluffing—damn him!" Bill seemed to admire Mr. Lutkins's ability as a scoundrel; I fancied that if he had been sheriff he would have caught Lutkins with fervor and hanged him with affection.

At the somewhat gloomy harness shop we descended and went in. The room was odorous with the smell of dressed leather. A scanty sort of a man, presumably Mr. Beinke, was selling a horse collar to a farmer.

"Seen Nolly Lutkins around today? Friend of his looking for him," said Bill, with treacherous heartliness.

Beinke looked past him at my shrinking alien self; he hesitated and owned: "Yuh, he was in here a little while ago. Guess he's gone over to the Swede's to get a shave."

"Well, if he comes in, tell him I'm looking for him. Might get up a little game of poker. I've heard tell that Lutkins plays these here immoral games of chance."

"Yuh, I believe he's known to sit in on Authors," Beinke growled.

We sought the barber shop of "the Swede." Bill was again good enough to take the lead, while I lurked at the door. He asked not only the Swede but two customers if they had seen Lutkins. The Swede decidedly had not; he raged: "I ain't seen him, and I don't want to, but if you find him you can just collect the dollar thirty-five he owes me." One of the customers thought he had seen Lutkins "hiking down Main Street, this side of the hotel."

"Well, then," Bill concluded, as we labored up into the hack, "his credit at the Swede's being ausgewent, he's probably getting a scrape at Heinie Gray's. He's too darn lazy to shave himself."

At Gray's barber shop we missed Lutkins by only five minutes. He had just left—presumably for the poolroom. At the poolroom it appeared that he had merely bought a pack of cigarettes and gone on. Thus we pursued him, just behind him but never catching him, for an hour, till it was past one and I was hungry. Village born as I was, and in the city often lonely for good coarse country wit, I was so delighted by Bill's cynical opinions on the barbers and clergymen and doctors and draymen of New Mullion that I scarcely cared whether I found Lutkins or not.

"How about something to eat?" I suggested. "Let's go to a restaurant and I'll buy you a lunch."

"Well, ought to go home to the old woman. And I don't care much for these restaurants—ain't but four of 'em and they're all rotten. Tell you what we'll do. Like nice scenery? There's an elegant view from Wade's Hill. We'll get the old woman to put us up a lunch—she won't charge you but a half dollar, and it'd cost you that for a greasy feed at the cafe—and we'll go up there and have a Sunday-school picnic."

I knew that my friend Bill was not free from guile; I knew that his hospitality to the Young Fellow from the City was not altogether a matter of brotherly love. I was paying him for his time; in all I paid him for six hours (including the lunch hour) at what was then a terrific price. But he was no more dishonest than I, who charged the whole thing up to the Firm, and it would have been worth paying him myself to have his presence. His country serenity, his natural wisdom, was a refreshing bath to the city-twitching youngster. As we sat on the hilltop, looking across orchards and a creek which slipped among the willows, he talked of New Mullion, gave a whole gallery of portraits. He was cynical yet tender. Nothing had escaped him, yet there was nothing, no matter how ironically he laughed at it, which was beyond his understanding and forgiveness. In ruddy color he painted the rector's wife who when she was most in debt most loudly gave the responses at which he called the "Episcopalopian church." He commented on the boys who came home from college in "ice-cream pants," and on the lawyer who, after years of torrential argument with his wife, would put on either a linen collar or a necktie, but never both. He made them live. In that day I came to know New Mullion better than I did the city, and to love it better.

If Bill was ignorant of universities and of urban ways, yet much had he traveled in the realm of jobs. He had worked on railroad section gangs, in harvest fields and contractors' camps, and from his adventures he had brought back a philosophy of simplicity and laughter. He strengthened me. Nowadays, thinking of Bill, I know what people mean (though I abominate the simpering phrase) when they yearn over "real he-men."

We left that placid place of orchards and resumed the search for Oliver Lutkins. We could not find him. At last Bill cornered a friend of Lutkins and made him admit that "he'd guess Oliver'd gone out to his ma's farm, three miles north."

e drove out there, mighty with strategy.

"I know Oliver's ma. She's a terror. She's a cyclone," Bill sighed. "I took a trunk out for her once, and she pretty near took my hide off because I didn't treat it like it was a crate of eggs. She's somewheres about nine feet tall and four feet thick and quick's a cat, and she sure manhandles the Queen's English. I'll bet Oliver has heard that somebody's on his trail and he's sneaked out there to hide behind his ma's skirts. Well, we'll try bawling her out. But you better let me do it, boy. You may be great at Latin and geography, but you ain't educated in cussing."

We drove into a poor farmyard; we were faced by an enormous and cheerful old woman. My guardian stockily stood before her and snarled, "Remember me? I'm Bill Magnuson, the expressman. I want to find your son Oliver. Friend of mine from the city's got a present for him."

"I don't know anything about Oliver and I don't want to," she bellowed.

"Now you look here. We've stood for just about enough plenty nonsense. This young man is the attorney general's provost, and we got legal right to search any and all premises for the person of one Oliver Lutkins."

Bill made it seem terrific, and the Amazon seemed impressed. She retired into the kitchen and we followed. From the low old range, turned by years of heat into a dark silvery gray, she snatched a sadiron, and she marched on us, clamoring, "You just search all you want to—providin' you don't mind getting burnt to a cinder!" She bellowed, she swelled, she laughed at our nervous retreat.

"Let's get out of this. She'll murder us," Bill groaned and, outside: "Did you see her grin? She was making fun of us. Can you beat that for nerve?"

I agreed that it was lese majesty.

We did, however, make adequate search. The cottage had but one story. Bill went round it, peeking in at all the windows. We explored the barn and the stable; we were reasonably certain that Lutkins was not there. It was nearly time for me to catch the afternoon train, and Bill drove me to the station. On the way to the city I worried very little over my failure to find Lutkins. I was too absorbed in the thought of Bill Magnuson. Really, I considered returning to New Mullion to practice law. If I had found Bill so deeply and richly human might I not come to love the yet uncharted Fritz Beinke and the Swede barber and a hundred other slow-spoken, simple, wise neighbors? I saw a candid and happy life beyond the neat learnings of universities' law firms. I was excited, as one who has found a treasure.

But if I did not think much about Lutkins, the office did. I found them in a state next morning; the suit was ready to come to trial; they had to have Lutkins; I was a disgrace and a fool. That morning my eminent career almost came to an end. The Chief did everything but commit mayhem; he somewhat more than hinted that I would do well at ditch-digging. I was ordered back to New Mullion, and with me they sent an ex-lumber-camp clerk who knew Lutkins. I was rather sorry, because it would prevent my loafing again in the gorgeous indolence of Bill Magnuson.

When the train drew in at New Mullion, Bill was on the station platform, near his dray. What was curious was that the old dragon, Lutkins's mother, was there talking to him, and they were not quarreling but laughing.

From the car steps I pointed them out to the lumber-camp clerk, and in young hero-worship I murmured: "There's a fine fellow, a real man."

"Meet him here yesterday?" asked the clerk.

"I spent the day with him."

"He help you hunt for Oliver Lutkins?"

"Yes, he helped me a lot."

"He must have! He's Lutkins himself!"

But what really hurt was that when I served the summons Lutkins and his mother laughed at me as though I were a bright boy of seven, and with loving solicitude they begged me to go to a neighbor's house and take a cup of coffee.

"I told 'em about you, and they're dying to have a look at you," said Lutkins joyfully. "They're about the only folks in town that missed seeing you yesterday."

Author's Profile
SINCLAIR LEWIS

Sinclair Lewis is best known as the first American to win a Nobel Prize in literature. Born in Sauk Centre, Minnesota, in 1885, Lewis started his career as a freelance journalist after graduating from Yale in 1908. It was not until 1920 that his writing career began in earnest when *Main Street* was published. This story, set in the fictitious town of Gopher Prairie, is modeled after Lewis's hometown and its people. In this popular novel, Lewis exposes what he considered the smug mediocrity and narrow-mindedness of the townspeople.

Next came *Babbitt* in 1922, a story named for its main character, a self-deluding realtor and community "booster." Both *Main Street* and *Babbitt* were well-received and set the stage for his third big success, *Arrowsmith*, in 1925. This was a bitter documentation of the roadblocks placed in the path of an idealistic medical researcher by society. In 1926, Lewis was awarded the Pulitzer Prize for *Arrowsmith*, but he surprised the committee by turning it down.

He did accept the Nobel Prize in 1930 for overall achievement in the literary field. By then he had written *Elmer Gantry* (1927), a portrait of religious revivalists and their opportunism, and *Dodsworth* (1929), the story of a wealthy industrialist turned expatriate.

To this day, Lewis remains unsurpassed for his fictional documentation of the inanely optimistic, self-admiring citizen of the early decades of the twentieth century.

Lewis published ten novels in the ensuing years, but none was as successful as those produced during the 1920s. Unable to refine his style or deepen his insights to document the social changes brought on by a worldwide depression, atomic warfare, and political events, he eventually left the country. He arrived in Rome in 1949, where he stayed until his death on January 10, 1951, at the age of sixty-six.

Balthazar's Marvelous Afternoon

BY GABRIEL GARCIA MARQUEZ

ANTICIPATING: Think of some object you have designed and made yourself. Perhaps it was an item you made in pottery class, an article of clothing you sewed, a great recipe you tried, or a picture you drew. Discuss the project, how you planned it, what great care you took to make it, and how you felt when the project was finished.

he cage was finished. Balthazar hung it under the eave, from force of habit, and when he finished lunch everyone was already saying that it was the most beautiful cage in the world. So many people came to see it that a crowd formed in front of the house, and Balthazar had to take it down and close the shop. 🖉 "You have to shave," Ursula, his wife, told him. "You look like a Capuchin." 🖉 "It's bad to shave after lunch," said Balthazar. 🖉 He had two weeks' growth, short, hard, and bristly hair like the mane of a mule, and the general expression of a frightened boy. But it was a false expression. In February he was thirty; he had been living with Ursula for four years, . . . without having children, and life had given him many reasons to be on guard but none to be frightened. He did not even know that for some people the cage he had just made was the most beautiful one in the world. For him, accustomed to making cages since childhood, it had been hardly any more difficult than the others. 🖉

"Then rest for a while," said the woman. "With that beard you can't show yourself anywhere."

While he was resting, he had to get out of his hammock several times to show the cage to the neighbors. Ursula had paid little attention to it until then. She was annoyed because her husband had neglected the work of his carpenter's shop to devote himself entirely to the cage, and for two weeks had slept poorly, turning over and muttering incoherencies, and he hadn't thought of shaving. But her annoyance dissolved in the face of the finished cage. When Balthazar woke up from his nap, she had ironed his pants and a shirt; she had put them on a chair near the hammock and had carried the cage to the dining table. She regarded it in silence.

"How much will you charge?" she asked.

"I don't know," Balthazar answered. "I'm going to ask for thirty pesos to see if they'll give me twenty."

"Ask for fifty," said Ursula. "You've lost a lot of sleep in these two weeks. Furthermore, it's rather large. I think it's the biggest cage I've ever seen in my life."

Balthazar began to shave.

"Do you think they'll give me fifty pesos?"

"That's nothing for Mr. Chepe Montiel, and the cage is worth it," said Ursula. "You should ask for sixty."

The house lay in the stifling shadow. It was the first week of April and the heat seemed less bearable because of the chirping of the cicadas. When he finished dressing, Balthazar opened the door to the patio to cool off the house, and a group of children entered the dining room.

The news had spread. Dr. Octavio Giraldo, an old physician, happy with life but tired of his profession, thought about Balthazar's cage while he was eating lunch with his invalid wife. On the inside terrace, where they put the table on hot days, there were many flowerpots and two cages with canaries. His wife liked birds, and she liked them so much that she hated cats because they could eat them up. Thinking about her, Dr. Giraldo went to see a patient that afternoon, and when he returned he went by Balthazar's house to inspect the cage.

There were a lot of people in the dining room. The cage was on display on the table: with its enormous dome of wire, three stories inside, with passageways and compartments especially for eating and sleeping and swings in the space set aside for the birds' recreation, it seemed like a small-scale model of a gigantic ice factory. The doctor inspected it carefully, without touching it, thinking that in effect the cage was better than its reputation, and much more beautiful than any he had ever dreamed of for his wife.

"This is a flight of the imagination," he said. He sought out Balthazar among the group of people and, fixing his maternal eyes on him, added, "You would have been an extraordinary architect."

Balthazar blushed.

hank you," he said.

"It's true," said the doctor. He was smoothly and delicately fat, like a woman who had been beautiful in her youth, and he had delicate hands. His voice seemed like that of a priest speaking Latin. "You wouldn't even need to put birds in it," he said, making the cage turn in front of the audience's eyes as if he were auctioning it off. "It would be enough to hang it in the trees so it could sing by itself." He put it back on the table, thought a moment, looking at the cage, and said:

"Fine, then I'll take it."

"It's sold," said Ursula.

"It belongs to the son of Mr. Chepe Montiel," said Balthazar. "He ordered it specially."

The doctor adopted a respectful attitude.

"Did he give you the design?"

"No," said Balthazar. "He said he wanted a large cage, like this one, for a pair of troupials."

The doctor looked at the cage.

"But this isn't for troupials."

"Of course it is, Doctor," said Balthazar, approaching the table. The children surrounded him. "The measurements are carefully calculated," he said, pointing to the different compartments with his forefinger. Then he struck the dome with his knuckles, and the cage filled with resonant chords.

"It's the strongest wire you can find, and each joint is soldered outside and in," he said.

"It's even big enough for a parrot," interrupted one of the children.

"That it is," said Balthazar.

The doctor turned his head.

"Fine, but he didn't give you the design," he said. "He gave you no exact specifications, aside from making it a cage big enough for troupials. Isn't that right?"

"That's right," said Balthazar.

"Then there's no problem," said the doctor. "One thing is a cage big enough for troupials, and another is this cage. There's no proof that this one is the one you were asked to make."

"It's this very one," said Balthazar, confused. "That's why I made it."

The doctor made an impatient gesture.

"You could make another one," said Ursula, looking at her husband. And then, to the doctor: "You're not in any hurry."

"I promised it to my wife for this afternoon," said the doctor.

"I'm very sorry, Doctor," said Balthazar, "but I can't sell you something that's sold already."

The doctor shrugged his shoulders. Drying the sweat from his neck with a handkerchief, he contemplated the cage silently with the fixed, unfocused gaze of one who looks at a ship which is sailing away.

"How much did they pay you for it?"

Balthazar sought out Ursula's eyes without replying.

"Sixty pesos," she said.

The doctor kept looking at the cage. "It's very pretty." He sighed. "Extremely pretty." Then, moving toward the door, he began to fan himself energetically, smiling, and the trace of that episode disappeared forever from his memory.

"Montiel is very rich," he said.

In truth, José Montiel was not as rich as he seemed, but he would have been capable of doing anything to become so. A few blocks from there, in a house crammed with equipment, where no one had ever smelled a smell that couldn't be sold, he remained indifferent to the news of the cage. His wife, tortured by an obsession with death, closed the doors and windows after lunch and lay for two hours with her eyes opened to the shadow of the room, while José Montiel took his siesta. The clamor of many voices surprised her there. Then she opened the door to the living room and found a crowd in front of the house, and Balthazar with the cage in the middle of the crowd, dressed in white, freshly shaved, with that expression of decorous candor with which the poor approach the houses of the wealthy.

"What a marvelous thing!" José Montiel's wife exclaimed, with a radiant expression, leading Balthazar inside. "I've never seen anything like it in my life," she said, and added, annoyed by the crowd which piled up at the door:

"But bring it inside before they turn the living room into a grandstand."

Balthazar was no stranger to José Montiel's house. On different occasions, because of his skill and forthright way of dealing, he had been called in to do minor carpentry jobs. But he never felt at ease among the rich. He used to think about them, about their ugly and argumentative wives, about their tremendous surgical operations, and he always experienced a feeling of pity. When he entered their houses, he couldn't move without dragging his feet.

s Pepe home?" he asked.

He had put the cage on the dining-room table.

"He's at school," said José Montiel's wife. "But he shouldn't be long," and she added, "Montiel is taking a bath."

In reality, José Montiel had not had time to bathe. He was giving himself an urgent alcohol rub, in order to come out and see what was going on. He was such a cautious man that he slept without an electric fan so he could watch over the noises of the house while he slept.

"Adelaide!" he shouted. "What's going on?"

"Come and see what a marvelous thing!" his wife shouted.

José Montiel, obese and hairy, his towel draped around his neck, appeared at the bedroom window.

"What is that?"

"Pepe's cage," said Balthazar.

His wife looked at him perplexedly.

"Whose?"

"Pepe's," replied Balthazar. And then, turning toward José Montiel, "Pepe ordered it."

Nothing happened at that instant, but Balthazar felt as if someone had just opened the bathroom door on him. José Montiel came out of the bedroom in his underwear.

"Pepe!" he shouted.

"He's not back," whispered his wife, motionless.

Pepe appeared in the doorway. He was about twelve, and had the same curved eyelashes and was as quietly pathetic as his mother.

"Come here," José Montiel said to him. "Did you order this?"

The child lowered his head. Grabbing him by the hair, José Montiel forced Pepe to look him in the eye.

"Answer me."

The child bit his lip without replying.

"Montiel," whispered his wife.

José Montiel let the child go and turned toward Balthazar in a fury. "I'm very sorry, Balthazar," he said. "But you should have consulted me before going on. Only to you would it occur to contract with a minor." As he spoke, his face recovered its serenity. He lifted the cage without looking at it and gave it to Balthazar.

"Take it away at once, and try to sell it to whomever you can," he said. "Above all, I beg you not to argue with me." He patted him on the back and explained, "The doctor has forbidden me to get angry."

The child had remained motionless, without blinking, until Balthazar looked at him uncertainly with the cage in his hand. Then he emitted a guttural sound, like a dog's growl, and threw himself on the floor screaming.

José Montiel looked at him, unmoved, while the mother tried to pacify him. "Don't even pick him up," he said. "Let him break his head on the floor, and then put salt and lemon on it so he can rage to his heart's content." The child was shrieking tearlessly while his mother held him by the wrists.

"Leave him alone," José Montiel insisted.

Balthazar observed the child as he would have observed the death throes of a rabid animal. It was almost four o'clock. At that hour, at his house, Ursula was singing a very old song and cutting slices of onion.

"Pepe," said Balthazar.

He approached the child, smiling, and held the cage out to him. The child jumped up, embraced the cage which was almost as big as he was, and stood looking at Balthazar through the wirework without knowing what to say. He hadn't shed one tear.

"Balthazar," said José Montiel softly. "I told you already to take it away."

"Give it back," the woman ordered the child.

"Keep it," said Balthazar. And then, to José Montiel: "After all, that's what I made it for."

José Montiel followed him into the living room.

"Don't be foolish, Balthazar," he was saying, blocking his path. "Take your piece of furniture home and don't be silly. I have no intention of paying you a cent."

t doesn't matter," said Balthazar. "I made it expressly as a gift for Pepe. I didn't expect to charge anything for it."

As Balthazar made his way through the spectators who were blocking the door, José Montiel was shouting in the middle of the living room. He was very pale and his eyes were beginning to get red.

"Idiot!" he was shouting. "Take your trinket out of here. The last thing we need is for some nobody to give orders in my house. . . ."

In the pool hall, Balthazar was received with an ovation. Until that moment, he thought that he had made a better cage than ever before, that he'd had to give it to the son of José Montiel so he wouldn't keep crying, and that none of these things was particularly important. But then he realized that all of this had a certain importance for many people, and he felt a little excited.

"So they gave you fifty pesos for the cage."

"Sixty," said Balthazar.

"Score one for you," someone said. "You're the only one who has managed to get such a pile of money out of Mr. Chepe Montiel. We have to celebrate."

They bought him a beer, and Balthazar responded with a round for everybody. Since it was the first time he had ever been out drinking, by dusk he was completely drunk, and he was talking about a fabulous project of a thousand cages, at sixty pesos each, and then of a million cages, till he had sixty million pesos. "We have to make a lot of things to sell to the rich before they die," he was saying, blind drunk. "All of them are sick, and they're going to die. They're so screwed up they can't even get angry any more." For two hours he was paying for the jukebox, which played without interruption. Everybody toasted Balthazar's health, good luck, and fortune, and the death of the rich, but at mealtime they left him alone in the pool hall.

Ursula had waited for him until eight, with a dish of fried meat covered with slices of onion. Someone told her that her husband was in the pool hall, delirious with happiness, buying beers for everyone, but she didn't believe it, because Balthazar had never got drunk. When she went to bed, almost at midnight, Balthazar was in a lighted room where there were little tables, each with four chairs, and an outdoor dance floor, where the plovers were walking around. . . . He had spent so much that he had had to leave his watch in pawn, with the promise to pay the next day. A moment later, spread-eagled in the street, he realized that his shoes were being taken off, but he didn't want to abandon the happiest dream of his life. The women who passed on their way to five-o'clock Mass didn't dare look at him, thinking he was dead.

✶ ✶ ✶

Author's Profile
GABRIEL GARCIA MARQUEZ

*J*ournalist, short-story writer, and novelist, Gabriel Garcia Marquez (pronounced "Mar-kays") is considered by most critics to be the foremost living Latin American writer.

Garcia Marquez was born in Aracataca, Colombia, on March 6, 1928. Raised by his grandmother, who told him stories that were later to shape his fiction, he studied literature and later law at the University of Bogota until political violence closed this institution. In the 1950s, he began his writing career as a reporter and film critic for the Colombian newspaper *El Espectador*. He later described his writing at this paper for Peter Stone in a *Paris Review: Writers at Work* interview:

> . . . *I used to do at least three stories a week, two or three editorial notes every day, and I did movie reviews. Then at night, after everyone had gone home, I would stay behind writing my novels. I liked the noise of the Linotype machines, which sounded like rain. If they stopped, and I was left in silence, I wouldn't be able to work.*

In the 1950s and early 1960s, Garcia Marquez published his first novels and short stories: *Leaf Storm and Other Stories* (1955), *No One Writes to the Colonel and Other Stories* (1961), and *In Evil Hour* (1962). He spent five years writing and rewriting his 1967 novel *One Hundred Years of Solitude*, which was a worldwide critical and commercial success. This novel, a blending of realism and fantasy, tells the story of six generations of a family whose chronicle reflects the history of Colombia. Garcia Marquez later told Peter Stone how his grandmother's style of storytelling helped him develop his tone as a writer:

> *She told things that sounded supernatural and fantastic, but she told them with complete naturalness.*

> . . . *What was most important was the expression she had on her face. She did not change her expression at all when telling her stories, and everyone was surprised. In previous attempts to write*

One Hundred Years of Solitude, *I tried to tell the story without believing in it. I discovered that what I had to do was believe in them myself and write them with the same expression with which my grandmother told them: with a brick face.*

Later Garcia Marquez novels include *The Autumn of the Patriarch* (1975), *Chronicle of a Death Foretold* (1981), *Love in a Time of Cholera* (1982), and *The General in his Labyrinth* (1989). In 1982, the Swedish Academy awarded Garcia Marquez the Nobel Prize in literature, citing his "strong commitment on the side of the poor against domestic oppression and foreign exploitation."

Self-exiled from Colombia for 30 years due to his opposition to its government, Garcia Marquez continues to live and write in Mexico City.

Forty-Five a Month

BY R. K. NARAYAN

ANTICIPATING: **Describe a personal disappointment which occurred when you were very young. For example, you might choose to write about the bicycle that didn't appear on Christmas, a friend who moved away, a visitor who didn't arrive, a grandparent's death. Or describe a disappointment which you have experienced recently. Be sure to include how you felt and why.**

Shanta could not stay in her class any longer. She had done clay-modelling, music, drill, a bit of alphabets and numbers, and was now cutting coloured paper. She would have to cut till the bell rang and the teacher said, "Now you may all go home," or "Put away the scissors and take up your alphabets—" Shanta was impatient to know the time. She asked her friend sitting next to her, "Is it five now?" "Maybe," she replied. "Or is it six?" "I don't think so," her friend replied, "because night comes at six."

"Do you think it is five?"

"Yes."

"Oh, I must go. My father will be back at home now. He has asked me to be ready at five. He is taking me to the cinema this evening. I must go home." She threw down her scissors and ran up to the teacher. "Madam, I must go home."

"Why, Shanta Bai?"

"Because it is five o'clock now."

"Who told you it was five?"

"Kamala."

"It is not five now. It is—do you see the clock there? Tell me what the time is. I taught you to read the clock the other day." Shanta stood gazing at the clock in the hall, counted the figures laboriously and declared, "It is nine o'clock."

The teacher called the other girls and said, "Who will tell me the time from that clock?" Several of them concurred with Shanta and said it was nine o'clock, till the teacher said, "You are seeing only the long hand. See the short one, where is it?"

"Two and a half."

"So what is the time?"

"Two and a half."

"It is two forty-five, understand? Now you may all go to your seats—" Shanta returned to the teacher in about ten minutes and asked, "Is it five, madam, because I have to be ready at five. Otherwise my father will be very angry with me. He asked me to return home early."

"At what time?"

"Now." The teacher gave her permission to leave, and Shanta picked up her books and dashed out of the class with a cry of joy. She ran home, threw her books on the floor and shouted, "Mother, Mother," and Mother came running from the next house, where she had gone to chat with her friends.

Mother asked, "Why are you back so early?"

"Has Father come home?" Shanta asked. She would not take her coffee or tiffin but insisted on being dressed first. She opened the trunk and insisted on wearing the thinnest frock and knickers, while her mother wanted to dress her in a long skirt and thick coat for the evening. Shanta picked out a gorgeous ribbon from a cardboard soap box in which she kept pencils, ribbons and chalk bits. There was a heated argument between mother and daughter over the dress, and finally mother had to give in. Shanta put on her favourite pink frock, braided her hair and flaunted a green ribbon on her pigtail. She powdered her face and pressed a vermilion mark on her forehead. She said, "Now Father will say what a nice girl I am because I'm ready. Aren't you also coming, Mother?"

"Not today."

Shanta stood at the little gate looking down the street.

Mother said, "Father will come only after five; don't stand in the sun. It is only four o'clock."

The sun was disappearing behind the house on the opposite row, and Shanta knew that presently it would be dark. She ran in to her mother and asked, "Why hasn't Father come home yet, Mother?"

"How can I know? He is perhaps held up in the office."

Shanta made a wry face. "I don't like these people in the office. They are bad people—"

he went back to the gate and stood looking out. Her mother shouted from inside, "Come in, Shanta. It is getting dark, don't stand there." But Shanta would not go in. She stood at the gate and a wild idea came into her head. Why should she not go to the office and call out Father and then go to the cinema? She wondered where his office might be. She had no notion. She had seen her father take the turn at the end of the street every day. If one went there, perhaps one went automatically to Father's office. She threw a glance about to see if Mother was anywhere and moved down the street.

It was twilight. Everyone going about looked gigantic, walls of houses appeared very high and cycles and carriages looked as though they would bear down on her. She walked on the very edge of the road. Soon the lamps were twinkling, and the passers-by looked like shadows. She had taken two turns and did not know where she was. She sat on the edge of the road biting her nails. She wondered how she was to reach home. A servant employed in the next house was passing along, and she picked herself up and stood before him.

"Oh, what are you doing her all alone?" he asked. She replied, "I don't know. I came here. Will you take me to our house?" She followed him and was soon back in her house.

Venkat Rao, Shanta's father, was about to start for his office that morning when a *jutka* passed along the street distributing cinema handbills. Shanta dashed to the street and picked up a handbill. She held it up and asked, "Father, will you take me to the cinema today?" He felt unhappy at the question. Here was the child growing up without having any of the amenities and the simple pleasures of life. He had hardly taken her twice to the cinema. He had no time for the child. While children of her age in other houses had all the dolls, dresses and outing that they wanted, this child was growing up all alone like a barbarian more or less. He felt furious with his office. For forty rupees a month they seemed to have purchased him outright.

He reproached himself for neglecting his wife and child—even the wife could have her own circle of friends and so on; she was after all a grown-up, but what about the child? What a drab, colourless existence was hers! Every day they kept him at the office till seven or eight in the evening, and when he came home the child was asleep. Even on Sundays they wanted him at the office. Why did they think he had no personal life, a life of his own? They gave him hardly any time to take the child to the park or the pictures. He was going to show them that they weren't going to toy with him. Yes, he was prepared even to quarrel with the manager if necessary.

He said with resolve, "I will take you to the cinema this evening. Be ready at five."

"Really! Mother!" Shanta shouted. Mother came out of the kitchen.

"Father is taking me to the cinema this evening."

Shanta's mother smiled cynically. "Don't make false promises to the child—" Venkat Rao glared at her. "Don't talk nonsense. You think you are the only person who keeps promises—"

He told Shanta, "Be ready at five, and I will come and take you positively. If you are not ready, I will be very angry with you."

He walked to his office full of resolve. He would do his normal work and get out at five. If they started any old tricks of theirs, he was going to tell the boss, "Here is my resignation. My child's happiness is more important to me than these horrible papers of yours."

All day the usual stream of papers flowed onto his table and off it. He scrutinized, signed and drafted. He was corrected, admonished and insulted. He had a break of only five minutes in the afternoon for his coffee.

When the office clock struck five and the other clerks were leaving, he went up to the manager and said, "May I go, sir?" The manager looked up from his paper. "You!" It was unthinkable that the cash and account section should be closing at five. "How can you go?"

"I have some urgent private business, sir," he said, smothering the lines he had been rehearsing since the morning: "Herewith my resignation." He visualized Shanta standing at the door, dressed and palpitating with eagerness.

"There shouldn't be anything more urgent than the office work; go back to your seat. You know how many hours I work?" asked the manager. The manager came to the office three hours before opening time and stayed nearly three hours after closing, even on Sundays. The clerks commented among themselves. "His wife must be whipping him whenever he is seen at home; that is why the old owl seems so fond of his office."

"Did you trace the source of that ten-eight difference?" asked the manager.

"I shall have to examine two hundred vouchers. I thought we might do it tomorrow."

o, no, this won't do. You must rectify it immediately." Venkat Rao mumbled, "Yes, sir," and slunk back to his seat. The clock showed 5:30. Now it meant two hours of excruciating search among vouchers. All the rest of the office had gone. Only he and another clerk in his section were working, and of course, the manager was there. Venkat Rao was furious. His mind was made up. He wasn't a slave who had sold himself for forty rupees outright. He could make that money easily; and if he couldn't, it would be more honourable to die of starvation.

He took a sheet of paper and wrote: "Herewith my resignation. If you people think you have bought me body and soul for forty rupees, you are mistaken. I think it would be far better for me and my family to die of starvation than slave for this petty forty rupees on which you have kept me for years and years. I suppose you have not the slightest notion of giving me an increment. You give yourselves heavy slices frequently, and I don't see why you shouldn't think of us occasionally. In any case it doesn't interest me now, since this is my resignation. If I and my family perish of starvation, may our ghosts come and haunt you all your life—" He folded the letter, put it in an envelope, sealed the flap and addressed it to the manager. He left his seat and stood before the manager. The manager mechanically received the letter and put it on his pad.

"Venkat Rao," said the manager, "I'm sure you will be glad to hear this news. Our officer discussed the question of increments today, and I've recommended you for an increment of five rupees. Orders are not yet passed, so keep this to yourself for the present." Venkat Rao put out his hand, snatched the envelope from the pad and hastily slipped it in his pocket.

"What is that letter?"

"I have applied for a little casual leave, sir, but I think . . ."

"You can't get any leave for at least a fortnight to come."

"Yes, sir. I realize that. That is why I am withdrawing my application, sir."

"Very well. Have you traced that mistake?"

"I'm scrutinizing the vouchers, sir. I will find it out within an hour. . . ."

It was nine o'clock when he went home. Shanta was already asleep. Her mother said, "She wouldn't even change her frock, thinking that any moment you might be coming and taking her out. She hardly ate any food; and wouldn't lie down for fear of crumpling her dress. . . ."

Venkat Rao's heart bled when he saw his child sleeping in her pink frock, hair combed and face powdered, dressed and ready to be taken out. "Why should I not take her to the night show?" He shook her gently and called, "Shanta, Shanta." Shanta kicked her legs and cried, irritated at being disturbed. Mother whispered, "Don't wake her," and patted her back to sleep.

Venkat Rao watched the child for a moment. "I don't know if it is going to be possible for me to take her out at all—you see, they are giving me an increment—" he wailed.

🍂 🍂 🍂

Author's Profile
R. K. NARAYAN

R.K. Narayan is India's best-known novelist. His writings retell classic Indian epics and focus on the rich culture of his country. He has written more than 200 short stories and 13 novels.

Rasipuram Kirshnaswamy Narayan was born in Madras, India, on October 10, 1906, and was educated there and at Maharaja's College in Mysore. He writes in English and sets his fictional works in the imaginary town of Malgudi (said to be Mysore, India). The stories usually present an eccentric character's involvement in a bizarre predicament.

Narayan writes with clarity in English but carefully crafts the rhythms of the typical Indian. Among the memorable inhabitants of Malgudi are *Sami and Friends* (1935), *The Bachelor of Arts* (1937), *The English Teacher* (1945), *The Printer of Malgudi* (1949), *The Guide* (1958), *The Vendor of Sweets* (1967), *The Talkative Man* (1986), and *Nagaraj of the World of Nagaraj* (1990). Narayan also translated the *Mahabharata* into English and published an autobiography, *My Days*, in 1975.

In 1958, his novel *The Guide* won him the National Prize of the Indian Literary Academy. Six years later in 1964, then-Prime Minister Nehru presented him with the Padma Bhushan, one of four honors given annually for distinguished service of the highest order. In 1981, Narayan received honorable membership in the American Academy and Institute of Arts and Letters. He lives in Mysore, India.

The late and distinguished British novelist Graham Greene offered one of the most fitting tributes to Narayan:

> *Narayan wakes in me a spring of gratitude, for he has offered me a second home. Without him I could never have known what it is like to be an Indian.*

The Man To Send Rain Clouds
BY LESLIE SILKO

ANTICIPATING: Have you ever heard the children's rhyme, "Step on a crack, you'll break your mother's back"? This is a common superstition like knocking on wood for luck. What are some others? Write about customs in society, in your family, and in the world which you have heard about or that you practice.

ONE

They found him under a big cottonwood tree. His Levi jacket and pants were faded light-blue so that he had been easy to find. The big cottonwood tree stood apart from a small grove of winterbare cottonwoods which grew in the wide, sandy arroyo. He had been dead for a day or more, and the sheep had wandered and scattered up and down the arroyo. Leon and his brother-in-law, Ken, gathered the sheep and left them in the pen at the sheep camp before they returned to the cottonwood tree. Leon waited under the tree while Ken drove the truck through the deep sand to the edge of the arroyo. He squinted up at the sun and unzipped his jacket—it sure was hot for this time of year. But high and northwest the blue mountains were still deep in snow. Ken came sliding down the low, crumbling bank about fifty yards down, and he was bringing the red blanket. ✒ Before they wrapped the old man, Leon took a piece of string out of his pocket and tied a small gray feather in the old man's long white hair. Ken gave him the paint. Across the brown wrinkled forehead he drew a streak of white and along the high cheekbones he drew a strip of blue paint. He paused and watched Ken throw pinches of corn meal and pollen into the wind that fluttered the small gray feather. Then Leon painted with yellow under the old man's broad nose, and finally, when he had painted green across the chin, he smiled. 🌶 "Send us rain clouds, Grandfather." They laid the bundle in the back of the pickup and covered it up with a heavy tarp before they started back to the pueblo. 🌶

They turned off the highway onto the sandy pueblo road. Not long after they passed the store and post office they saw Father Paul's car coming toward them. When he recognized their faces he slowed his car and waved for them to stop. The young priest rolled down the car window.

"Did you find old Teofilo?" he asked loudly.

eon stopped the truck. "Good morning, Father. We were just out to the sheep camp. Everything is O.K. now."

"Thank God for that. Teofilo is a very old man. You really shouldn't allow him to stay at the sheep camp alone."

"No, he won't do that any more now."

"Well, I'm glad you understand. I hope I'll be seeing you at Mass this week—we missed you last Sunday. See if you can get old Teofilo to come with you." The priest smiled and waved at them as they drove away.

TWO

Louise and Teresa were waiting. The table was set for lunch, and the coffee was boiling on the black iron stove. Leon looked at Louise and then at Teresa.

"We found him under a cottonwood tree in the big arroyo near sheep camp. I guess he sat down to rest in the shade and never got up again." Leon walked toward the old man's bed. The red plaid shawl had been shaken and spread carefully over the bed, and a new brown flannel shirt and pair of stiff new Levis were arranged neatly beside the pillow. Louise held the screen door open while Leon and Ken carried in the red blanket. He looked small and shriveled, and after they dressed him in the new shirt and pants he seemed more shrunken.

It was noontime now because the church bells rang the Angelus. They ate the beans with hot bread, and nobody said anything until after Teresa poured the coffee.

Ken stood up and put on his jacket. "I'll see about the gravediggers. Only the top layer of soil is frozen. I think it can be ready before dark."

Leon nodded his head and finished his coffee. After Ken had been gone for a while, the neighbors and clanspeople came quietly to embrace Teofilo's family and to leave food on the table because the gravediggers would come to eat when they were finished.

THREE

The sky in the west was full of pale-yellow light. Louise stood outside with her hands in the pockets of Leon's green army jacket that was too big for her. The funeral was over, and the old men had taken their candles and medicine bags and were gone. She waited until the body was laid into the pickup before she said anything to Leon. She touched his arm, and he noticed that her hands were still dusty from the corn meal that she had sprinkled around the old man. When she spoke, Leon could not hear her.

"What did you say? I didn't hear you."

"I said that I had been thinking about something."

"About what?"

"About the priest sprinkling holy water for Grandpa. So he won't be thirsty."

Leon stared at the new moccasins that Teofilo had made for the ceremonial dances in the summer. They were nearly hidden by the red blanket. It was getting colder, and the wind pushed gray dust down the narrow pueblo road. The sun was approaching the long mesa where it disappeared during the winter. Louise stood there shivering and watching his face. Then he zipped up his jacket and opened the truck door. "I'll see if he's there."

FOUR

Ken stopped the pickup at the church, and Leon got out; and then Ken drove down the hill to the graveyard where people were waiting. Leon knocked at the old carved door with its symbols of the Lamb. While he waited he looked up at the twin bells from the king of Spain with the last sunlight pouring around them in their tower.

The priest opened the door and smiled when he saw who it was. "Come in! What brings you here this evening?"

The priest walked toward the kitchen, and Leon stood with his cap in his hand, playing with the earflaps and examining the living room—the brown sofa, the green armchair, and the brass lamp that hung down from the ceiling by links of chain. The priest dragged a chair out of the kitchen and offered it to Leon.

"No thank you, Father. I only came to ask you if you would bring your holy water to the graveyard."

he priest turned away from Leon and looked out the window at the patio full of shadows and the dining-room windows of the nuns' cloister across the patio. The curtains were heavy, and the light from within faintly penetrated; it was impossible to see the nuns inside eating supper. "Why didn't you tell me he was dead? I could have brought the Last Rites anyway."

Leon smiled. "It wasn't necessary, Father."

The priest stared down at his scuffed brown loafers and the worn hem of his cassock. "For a Christian burial it was necessary."

His voice was distant, and Leon thought that his blue eyes looked tired.

"It's O.K. Father, we just want him to have plenty of water."

The priest sank down into the green chair and picked up a glossy missionary magazine. He turned the colored pages full of lepers and pagans without looking at them.

"You know I can't do that, Leon. There should have been the Last Rites and a funeral Mass at the very least."

Leon put on his green cap and pulled the flaps down over his ears. "It's getting late, Father. I've got to go."

When Leon opened the door Father Paul stood up and said, "Wait." He left the room and came back wearing a long brown overcoat. He followed Leon out the door and across the dim churchyard to the adobe steps in the front of the church. They both stooped to fit through the low adobe entrance. And when they started down the hill to the graveyard only half of the sun was visible above the mesa.

The priest approached the grave slowly, wondering how they had managed to dig into the frozen ground; and then he remembered that this was New Mexico, and saw the pile of cold loose sand beside the hole. The people stood close to each other with little clouds of steam puffing from their faces. The priest looked at them and saw a pile of jackets, gloves, and scarves in the yellow, dry tumbleweeds that grew in the graveyard. He looked at the red blanket, not sure that Teofilo was so small, wondering if it wasn't some perverse Indian trick—something they did in March to ensure a good harvest—wondering if maybe old Teofilo was actually at sheep camp corraling the sheep for the night. But there he was, facing into a cold dry wind and squinting at the last sunlight, ready to bury a red wool blanket while the faces of his parishioners were in shadow with the last warmth of the sun on their backs.

His fingers were stiff, and it took him a long time to twist the lid off the holy water. Drops of water fell on the red blanket and soaked into dark icy spots. He sprinkled the grave and the water disappeared almost before it touched the dim, cold sand; it reminded him of something—he tried to remember what it was, because he thought if he could remember he might understand this. He sprinkled more water; he shook the container until it was empty, and the water fell through the light from sundown like August rain that fell while the sun was still shining, almost evaporating before it touched the wilted squash flowers.

The wind pulled at the priest's brown Franciscan robe and swirled away the corn meal and pollen that had been sprinkled on the blanket. They lowered the bundle into the ground, and they didn't bother to untie the stiff pieces of new rope that were tied around the ends of the blanket. The sun was gone, and over on the highway the eastbound lane was full of headlights. The priest walked away slowly. Leon watched him climb the hill, and when he had disappeared within the tall, thick walls, Leon turned to look up at the high blue mountains in the deep snow that reflected a faint red light from the west. He felt good because it was finished, and he was happy about the sprinkling of the holy water; now the old man could send them big thunderclouds for sure.

⚹ ⚹ ⚹

Author's Profile
LESLIE SILKO

Along with N. Scott Momaday and Louise Erdrich, Leslie Marmon Silko is considered one of the leading Native American writers of today.

Silko was born in Albuquerque, New Mexico, on March 5, 1948. She was raised in the Laguna Pueblo Reservation, where her grandmother and aunt instructed her in the Laguna traditions and myths which have greatly influenced her prose and poetry. Silko has Anglo, Laguna, Great Plains Indian, and Mexican ancestry. She graduated from the University of New Mexico in 1969 with a degree in English and then spent three semesters in law school before deciding to devote herself to a writing career. She has also been a teacher at the Navajo Community College, and at the Universities of Arizona and New Mexico.

Laguna Woman (1974), Silko's first book, is a poetry collection that incorporates many Laguna myths and ceremonies. One of her people's creation myths has the Indians crossing the Pacific Ocean 30,000 years ago to come to America. In her novel *Ceremony* (1977), her main character, Tayo, is a World War II veteran who, through his relationship with a tribal medicine woman, becomes a protector of nature. The Laguna reservation in New Mexico has been the scene of atomic bomb testing at nearby Los Alamos in the 1940s and uranium mining by the Anaconda Company in the 1950s. Tayo begins to see the protection of nature as a duty that unites all people. *Storyteller* (1981) is a collection of Silko's poetry and short fiction.

When Silko was honored by the prestigious MacArthur Foundation with a $176,000 award, she told *Time* that now she could be a "little less beholden to the everyday world."

Just Lather, That's All

BY HERNANDO TELLEZ

ANTICIPATING: Think about someone you know who truly takes pride in his/her job and who consequently is a model of a true professional. An alternative would be to select a performer (musician, athlete, artist) that you have either read about or seen an interview of. A third alternative would be to select a fictional character from a novel or a film. Describe this person in your journal, and give a specific example of this person in action, things that they either say or do which personify this pride and professionalism.

e said nothing when he entered. I was passing the best of my razors back and forth on a strop. When I recognized him I started to tremble. But he didn't notice. Hoping to conceal my emotion, I continued sharpening the razor. I tested it on the meat of my thumb and then held it up to the light. At that moment he took off the bullet-studded belt that his gun holster dangled from. He hung it up on a wall hook and placed his military cap over it. Then he turned to me, loosening the knot of his tie, and said, "It's hot as hell. Give me a shave." He sat in the chair. 🖋 I estimated he had a four-day beard. The four days taken up by the latest expedition in search of our troops. His face seemed reddened, burned by the sun. Carefully, I began to prepare the soap. I cut off a few slices, dropped them into the cup, mixed in a bit of warm water, and began to stir with the brush. Immediately the foam began to rise. "The other boys in the group should have this much beard, too." I continued stirring the lather. 🖋 "But we did all right, you know. We got the main ones. We brought back some dead, and we've got some others still alive. But pretty soon they'll all be dead." 🖋

"How many did you catch?" I asked.

"Fourteen. We had to go pretty deep into the woods to find them. But we'll get even. Not one of them comes out of this alive, not one."

e leaned back on the chair when he saw me with the lather-covered brush in my hand. I still had to put the sheet on him. No doubt about it, I was upset. I took a sheet out of a drawer and knotted it around my customer's neck. He wouldn't stop talking. He probably thought I was in sympathy with his party.

"The town must have learned a lesson from what we did the other day," he said.

"Yes," I replied, securing the knot at the base of his dark, sweaty neck.

"That was a fine show, eh?"

"Very good," I answered, turning back for the brush. The man closed his eyes with a gesture of fatigue and sat waiting for the cool caress of the soap. I had never had him so close to me. The day he ordered the whole town to file into the patio of the school to see the four rebels hanging there, I came face to face with him for an instant. But the sight of the mutilated bodies kept me from noticing the face of the man who had directed it all, the face I was now about to take into my hands. It was not an unpleasant face, certainly. And the beard, which made him seem a bit older than he was, didn't suit him badly at all. His name was Torres. Captain Torres. A man of imagination, because who else would have thought of hanging the naked rebels and then holding target practice on certain parts of their bodies? I began to apply the first layer of soap. With his eyes closed, he continued. "Without any effort I could go straight to sleep," he said, "but there's plenty to do this afternoon." I stopped the lathering and asked with a feigned lack of interest: "A firing squad?" "Something like that, but a little slower." I got on with the job of lathering his beard. My hands started trembling again. The man could not possibly realize it, and this was in my favor. But I would have preferred that he hadn't come. It was likely that many of our faction had seen him enter. And an enemy under one's roof imposes certain conditions. I would be obliged to shave that beard like any other one, carefully, gently, like that of any customer, taking pains to see that no single pore emitted a drop of blood. Being careful to see that the little tufts of hair did not lead the blade astray. Seeing that his skin ended up clean, soft, and healthy, so that passing the back of my hand over it I couldn't feel a hair. Yes, I was secretly a rebel, but I was a conscientious barber, and proud of the preciseness of my profession. And this four-day's growth of beard was a fitting challenge.

I took the razor, opened up the two protective arms, exposed the blade and began the job, from one of the sideburns downward. The razor responded beautifully. His beard was inflexible and hard, not too long, but thick. Bit by bit the skin emerged. The razor rasped along, making its customary sound as fluffs of lather mixed with bits of hair gathered along the blade. I paused a moment to clean it, then took up the strop again to sharpen the razor, because I'm a barber who does things properly. The man, who had kept his eyes closed, opened them now, removed one of his hands from under the sheet, felt the spot on his face where the soap had been cleared off, and said, "Come to the school today at six o'clock." "The same thing as other day?" I asked horrified. "It could be better," he replied. "What do you plan to do?" "I don't know yet. But we'll amuse ourselves." Once more he leaned back and closed his eyes. I approached him with the razor poised. "Do you plan to punish them all?" "All." The soap was drying on his face. I had to hurry. In the mirror I looked toward the street. It was the same as ever: the grocery store with two or three customers in it. Then I glanced at the clock: two-twenty in the afternoon. The razor continued on its downward stroke. Now from the other sideburn down. A thick, blue beard. He should have let it grow like some poets or priests do. It would suit him well. A lot of people wouldn't recognize him. Much to his benefit, I thought, as I attempted to cover the neck area smoothly. There, for sure, the razor had to be handled masterfully, since the hair, although softer, grew into little swirls. A curly beard. One of the tiny pores could be opened up and issue forth its pearl of blood. A good barber such as I prides himself on never allowing this to happen to a client. And this was a first-class client. How many of us had he ordered shot? How many of us had he ordered mutilated? It was better not to think about it. Torres did not know that I was his enemy. He did not know it nor did the rest. It was a secret shared by very few, precisely so that I could inform the revolutionaries of what Torres was doing in the town and of what he was planning each time he undertook a rebel-hunting excursion. So it was going to be very difficult to explain that I had him right in my hands and let him go peacefully—alive and shaved.

he beard was now almost completely gone. He seemed, younger, less burdened by years than when he had arrived. I suppose this always happens with men who visit barber shops. Under the stroke of my razor Torres was being rejuvenated—rejuvenated because I am a good barber, the best in the town, if I may say so. A little more lather here, under his chin, on his Adam's apple, on this big vein. How hot it is getting! Torres must be sweating as much as I. But he is not afraid. He is a calm man, who is not even thinking about what he is going to do with the prisoners this afternoon. On the other hand I, with this razor in my hands, stroking and re-stroking this skin, trying to keep blood from oozing from these pores, can't even think clearly. Damn him for coming, because I'm a revolutionary and not a murderer. And how easy it would be to kill him. And he deserves it. Does he? No! What the devil! No one deserves to have someone else make the sacrifice of becoming a murderer. What do you gain by it? Nothing. Others come along and still others, and the first ones kill the second ones and they the next ones and it goes on like this until everything is a sea of blood. I could cut this throat just so, zip! zip! I wouldn't give him time to complain and since he has his eyes closed he wouldn't see the glistening knife blade or my glistening eyes. But I'm trembling like a real murderer. Out of his neck a gush of blood would spout onto the sheet, on the chair, on my hands, on the floor. I would have to close the door. And the blood would keep inching along the floor, warm, ineradicable, uncontainable, until it reached the street, like a scarlet stream. I'm sure that one solid stroke, one deep incision, would prevent any pain. He wouldn't suffer. But what would I do with the body? Where would I hide it? I would have to flee, leaving all I have behind, and take refuge far away, far, far away. But they would follow until they found me. "Captain Torres' murderer. He slit his throat while he was shaving him—a coward." And then on the other side. "The avenger of us all. A name to remember. (And here they would mention my name.) He was the town barber. No one knew he was defending our cause."

And what of all this? Murderer or hero? My destiny depends on the edge of this blade. I can turn my hand a bit more, press a little harder on the razor, and sink it in. The skin would give way like silk, like rubber, like the strop. There is nothing more tender than human skin and the blood is always there, ready to pour forth. A blade like this doesn't fail. It is my best. But I don't want to be a murderer, no sir. You came to me for a shave. And I perform my work honorably. . . . I don't want blood on my hands. Just lather, that's all. You are an executioner and I am only a barber. Each person has his own place in the scheme of things. That's right. His own place.

Now his chin had been stroked clean and smooth. The man sat up and looked into the mirror. He rubbed his hands over his skin and felt it fresh, like new.

"Thanks," he said. He went to the hanger for his belt, pistol and cap. I must have been very pale; my shirt felt soaked. Torres finished adjusting the buckle, straightened his pistol in the holster and after automatically smoothing down his hair, he put on the cap. From his pants pocket he took out several coins to pay me for my services. And he began to head toward the door. In the doorway he paused for a moment, and turning to me he said: "They told me that you'd kill me. I came to find out. But killing isn't easy. You can take my word for it." And he headed on down the street.

✣ ✣ ✣

Author's Profile
HERNANDO TELLEZ

Though primarily known in the United States for this one frequently anthologized story, "Just Lather, That's All", Hernando Tellez is considered a major Latin American essayist.

Born in Bogota, Colombia, on March 22, 1908, Tellez attended a Christian Brothers school, where his rhetoric teacher, a priest who secretly wrote poetry, told him:

> *"Thank God, you are a terrible mathematics student. You have no recourse but to make a living through literature. Learn how to write."*

With this advice ringing in his ears, Tellez began his newspaper career at age sixteen, working for various small Columbian newspapers and magazines. At age twenty-one, he joined the staff of the Colombian newspaper *El Tiempo*, one of the largest papers in Latin America. Tellez started as a crime reporter, then became a political correspondent, and finally became editor of the literary supplement.

He began his political career in 1934 when he was elected to the City Council of Bogota. In 1937, he was named Colombian consul to France, a position he held until the outbreak of World War II in 1939. He returned to journalism briefly, becoming the deputy editor of the newspaper *El Liberal*, then became head of public relations for a corporation, briefly served in the Colombian Senate, and finally was editor of the magazine *Semana* in 1947.

In the 1940s, he began to publish collections of his newspaper and magazine literary, political, and social essays. His reputation for fiction rests primarily on his 1950 short story collection *Ashes for the Wind and Other Tales*, which includes "Just Lather, That's All."

Tellez died in 1966.

The Catbird Seat

BY JAMES THURBER

ANTICIPATING: Describe a situation in which you have had conflict with a peer, a fellow student, a co-worker, a team member, or someone in a club to which you belong. Tell how the conflict began and why things got continually worse. How did you resolve the problem? How do you wish you had solved it?

r. Martin bought the pack of Camels on Monday night in the most crowded cigar store on Broadway. It was theater time and seven or eight men were buying cigarettes. The clerk didn't even glance at Mr. Martin, who put the pack in his overcoat and went out. If any of the staff at F & S had seen him buy the cigarettes, they would have been astonished, for it was generally known that Mr. Martin did not smoke, and never had. No one saw him. It was just a week to the day since Mr. Martin had decided to rub out Mrs. Ulgine Barrows. The term "rub out" pleased him because it suggested nothing more than the correction of an error—in this case the error of Mr. Fitweiler. Mr. Martin had spent each night of the past week working out his plan and examining it. As he walked home now he went over it again. For the hundredth time he resented the element of imprecision, the margin of guesswork that entered into the business. The project as he had worked out was casual and bold, the risks were considerable. Something might go wrong anywhere along the line. And therein lay the cunning of his scheme. No one would ever see it in the cautious, painstaking hand of Erwin Martin, head of the filing department of F & S, of whom Mr. Fitweiler had once said, "Man is fallible but Martin isn't." No one would see his hand, that is, unless it were caught in the act.

Sitting in his apartment, drinking a glass of milk, Mr. Martin reviewed his case against Mrs. Ulgine Barrows, as he had every night for seven nights. He began at the beginning. Her quacking voice and braying laugh had first profaned the halls of F & S on March 7, 1941 (Mr. Martin had a head for dates). Old Roberts, the personnel chief, had introduced her as the newly appointed special adviser to the president of the firm, Mr. Fitweiler. The woman had appalled Mr. Martin instantly, but he hadn't shown it. He had given her his dry hand, a look of studious concentration, and a faint smile. "Well," she had said, looking at the papers on his desk, "are you lifting the oxcart out of the ditch?" As Mr. Martin recalled that moment, over his milk, he squirmed slightly. He must keep his mind on her crimes as a special adviser, not on her peccadillos as a personality. This he found difficult to do, in spite of entering an objection and sustaining it. The faults of the woman as a woman kept chattering on in his mind like an unruly witness. She had, for almost two years now, baited him. In the halls, in the elevator, even in his own office, into which she romped now and then like a circus horse, she was constantly shouting these silly questions at him. "Are you lifting the oxcart out of the ditch? Are you tearing up the pea patch? Are you hollering down the rain barrel? Are you scraping around the bottom of the pickle barrel? Are you sitting in the catbird seat?"

t was Joey Hart, one of Mr. Martin's two assistants, who had explained what the gibberish meant. "She must be a Dodger fan," he had said. "Red Barber announces the Dodger games over the radio and he uses those expressions—picked 'em up down South." Joey had gone on to explain one or two. "Tearing up the pea patch" meant going on a rampage; "sitting in the catbird seat" meant sitting pretty, like a batter with three balls and no strikes on him. Mr. Martin dismissed all this with an effort. It had been annoying, it had driven him near to distraction, but he was too solid a man to be moved to murder by anything so childish. It was fortunate, he reflected as he passed on to the important charges against Mrs. Barrows, that he had stood up under it so well. He had maintained always an outward appearance of polite tolerance. "Why, I even believe you like the woman," Miss Paird, his other assistant, had once said to him. He had simply smiled.

A gavel rapped in Mr. Martin's mind and the case proper was resumed. Mrs. Ulgine Barrows stood charged with willful, blatant, and persistent attempts to destroy the efficiency and system of F & S. It was competent, material, and relevant to review her advent and rise to power. Mr. Martin had got the story from Miss Paird, who seemed always able to find things out. According to her, Mrs. Barrows had met Mr. Fitweiler at a party, where she had rescued him from the embraces of a powerfully built drunken man who had mistaken the president of F & S for a famous retired Middle Western football coach. She had led him to a sofa and somehow worked upon him a monstrous magic. The aging gentleman had jumped to the conclusion there and then that this was a woman of singular attainments, equipped to bring out the best in him and in the firm. A week later he had introduced her into F & S as his special adviser. On that day confusion got its foot in the door. After Miss Tyson, Mr. Brundage, and Mr. Bartlett had been fired and Mr. Munson had taken his hat and stalked out, mailing in his resignation later, old Roberts had been emboldened to speak to Mr. Fitweiler. He mentioned that Mr. Munson's department had been "a little disrupted" and hadn't they perhaps better resume the old system there? Mr. Fitweiler had said certainly not. He had the greatest faith in Mrs. Barrows' ideas. "They require a little seasoning, a little seasoning, is all," he had added. Mr. Roberts had given it up. Mr. Martin reviewed in detail all the changes wrought by Mrs. Barrows. She had begun chipping at the cornices of the firm's edifice and now she was swinging at the foundation stones with a pickaxe.

Mr. Martin came now, in his summing up, to the afternoon of Monday, November 2, 1942—just one week ago. On that day, at 3 P.M., Mrs. Barrows had bounced into his office. "Boo!" she had yelled. "Are you scraping around the bottom of the pickle barrel?" Mr. Martin had looked at her from under his green eyeshade, saying nothing. She had begun to wander about the office, taking it in with her great, popping eyes. "Do you really need *all* these filing cabinets?" she had demanded suddenly. Mr. Martin's heart had jumped. "Each of these files," he had said, keeping his voice even, "plays an indispensable part in the system of F & S." She had brayed at him, "Well, don't tear up the pea patch!" and gone to the door. From there she had bawled, "But you sure have got a lot of fine scrap in here!" Mr. Martin could no longer doubt that the finger was on his beloved department. Her pickaxe was on the upswing, poised for the first blow. It had not come yet; he had received no blue memo from the enchanted Mr. Fitweiler bearing nonsensical instructions deriving from the obscene woman. But there was no doubt in Mr. Martin's mind that one would be forthcoming. He must act quickly. Already a precious week had gone by. Mr. Martin stood up in his living room, still holding his milk glass. "Gentlemen of the jury," he said to himself, "I demand the death penalty for this horrible person."

The next day Mr. Martin followed his routine, as usual. He polished his glasses more often and once sharpened an already sharp pencil, but not even Miss Paird noticed. Only once did he catch sight of his victim; she swept past him in the hall with a patronizing "Hi!" At five-thirty he walked home, as usual, and had a glass of milk, as usual. He had never drunk anything stronger in his life—unless you could count ginger ale. The late Sam Schlosser, the S of F & S, had praised Mr. Martin at a staff meeting several years before for his temperate habits. "Our most efficient worker neither drinks nor smokes," he had said. "The results speak for themselves." Mr. Fitweiler had sat by, nodding approval.

r. Martin was still thinking about that red-letter day as he walked over to the Schrafft's on Fifth Avenue near Forty-sixth Street. He got there, as he always did, at eight o'clock. He finished his dinner and the financial page of the *Sun* at a quarter to nine, as he always did. It was his custom after dinner to take a walk. This time he walked down Fifth Avenue at a casual pace. His gloved hands felt moist and warm, his forehead cold. He transferred the Camels from his overcoat to a jacket pocket. He wondered, as he did so, if they did not represent an unnecessary note of strain. Mrs. Barrows smoked only Luckies. It was his idea to puff a few puffs on a Camel (after the rubbing out), stub it out in the ashtray holding her lipstick-stained Luckies, and thus drag a small red herring across the trail. Perhaps it was not a good idea. It would take time. He might even choke, too loudly.

Mr. Martin had never seen the house on West Twelfth Street where Mrs. Barrows lived, but he had a clear enough picture of it. Fortunately, she had bragged to everybody about her ducky first-floor apartment in the perfectly darling three-story red brick. There would be no doorman or other attendants; just the tenants of the second and third floors. As he walked along, Mr. Martin realized that he would get there before nine-thirty. He had considered walking north on Fifth Avenue from Schrafft's to a point from which it would take him until ten o'clock to reach the house. At that hour people were less likely to be coming in or going out. But the procedure would have made an awkward loop in the straight thread of his casualness, and he had abandoned it. It was impossible to figure when people would be entering or leaving the house, anyway. There was a great risk at any hour. If he ran into anybody, he would simply have to place the rubbing out of Ulgine Barrows in the inactive file forever. The same thing would hold true if there were someone in her apartment. In that case he would just say that he had been passing by, recognized her charming house and thought to drop in.

It was eighteen minutes after nine when Mr. Martin turned into Twelfth Street. A man passed him, and a man and a woman talking. There was no one within fifty paces when he came to the house, halfway down the block. He was up the steps and in the small vestibule in no time, pressing the bell under the card that said "Mrs. Ulgine Barrows." When the clicking in the lock started, he jumped forward against the door. He got inside fast, closing the door behind him. A bulb in a lantern hung from the hall ceiling on a chain seemed to give a monstrously bright light. There was nobody on the stair, which went up ahead of him along the left wall. A door opened down the hall in the wall on the right. He went toward it swiftly, on tiptoe.

"Well, for God's sake, look who's here!" bawled Mrs. Barrows, and her braying laugh rang out like the report of a shotgun. He rushed past her like a football tackle, bumping her. "Hey, quit shoving!" she said, closing the door behind them. They were in her living room, which seemed to Mr. Martin to be lighted by a hundred lamps. "What's after you?" she said. "You're as jumpy as a goat." He found he was unable to speak. His heart was wheezing in his throat. "I—yes," he finally brought out. She was jabbering and laughing as she started to help him off with his coat. "No, no" he said. "I'll put it here." He took it off and put it on a chair near the door. "Your hat and gloves, too," she said. "You're in a lady's house." He put his hat on top of the coat. Mrs. Barrows seemed larger than he had thought. He kept his gloves on. "I was passing by," he said. I recognized—is there anyone here?" She laughed louder than ever. "No," she said, "we're all alone. You're as white as a

sheet, you funny man. Whatever *has* come over you? I'll mix you a toddy."
She started toward a door across the room. "Scotch and soda be all right? But
say, you don't drink, do you?" She turned and gave him her amused look. Mr.
Martin pulled himself together. "Scotch and soda will be all right," he heard
himself say. He could hear her laughing in the kitchen.

Mr. Martin looked quickly around the living room for the weapon.
He had counted on finding one there. There were andirons and a poker and
something in a corner that looked like an Indian club. None of them would
do. It couldn't be that way. He began to pace around. He came to a desk. On
it lay a metal paper knife with an ornate handle. Would it be sharp enough?
He reached for it and knocked over a small brass jar. Stamps spilled out of it
and it fell to the floor with a clatter. "Hey," Mrs. Barrows yelled from the
kitchen, "are you tearing up the pea patch?" Mr. Martin gave a strange laugh.
Picking up the knife, he tried its point against his left wrist. It was blunt. It
wouldn't do.

hen Mrs. Barrows reappeared, carrying two highballs, Mr.
Martin, standing there with his gloves on, became acutely
conscious of the fantasy he had wrought. Cigarettes in his
pocket, a drink prepared for him—it was all too grossly improbable. It was
more than that; it was impossible. Somewhere in the back of his mind a
vague idea stirred, sprouted. "For heaven's sake, take off those gloves," said
Mrs. Barrows. "I always wear them in the house," said Mr. Martin. The idea
began to bloom, strange and wonderful. She put the glasses on a coffee table
in front of a sofa and sat on the sofa. "Come over here, you odd little man,"
she said. Mr. Martin went over and sat beside her. It was difficult getting a
cigarette out of the pack of Camels, but he managed it. She held a match for
him, laughing. "Well," she said, handing him his drink, "this is perfectly marvelous. You with a drink and a cigarette."

Mr. Martin puffed, not too awkwardly, and took a gulp of the
highball. "I drink and smoke all the time," he said. He clinked his glass
against hers. "Here's nuts to that old windbag, Fitweiler," he said, and gulped
again. The stuff tasted awful, but he made no grimace. "Really, Mr. Martin,"
she said, her voice and posture changing, "you are insulting our employer."
Mrs. Barrows was now all special adviser to the president. "I am preparing a
bomb," said Mr. Martin, "which will blow the old goat higher than hell." He

had only had a little of the drink, which was not strong. It couldn't be that. "Do you take dope or something?" Mrs. Barrows asked coldly. "Heroin," said Mr. Martin. "I'll be coked to the gills when I bump that old buzzard off." "Mr. Martin!" she shouted, getting to her feet. "That will be all of that. You must go at once." Mr. Martin took another swallow of his drink. He tapped his cigarette out in the ashtray and put the pack of Camels on the coffee table. Then he got up. She stood glaring at him. He walked over and put on his hat and coat. "Not a word about this," he said, and laid an index finger against his lips. All Mrs. Barrows could bring out was "Really!" Mr. Martin put his hand on the doorknob. "I'm sitting in the catbird seat," he said. He stuck his tongue out at her and left. Nobody saw him go.

Mr. Martin got to his apartment, walking, well before eleven. No one saw him go in. He had two glasses of milk after brushing his teeth, and he felt elated. It wasn't tipsiness, because he hadn't been tipsy. Anyway, the walk had worn off all effects of the whiskey. He got in bed and read a magazine for a while. He was asleep before midnight.

Mr. Martin got to the office at eight-thirty the next morning, as usual. At a quarter to nine, Ulgine Barrows, who had never before arrived at work before ten, swept into his office. "I'm reporting to Mr. Fitweiler now!" she shouted. "If he turns you over to the police, it's no more than you deserve!" Mr. Martin gave her a look of shocked surprise. "I beg your pardon?" he said. Mrs. Barrows snorted and bounced out of the room, leaving Miss Paird and Joey Hart staring after her. "What's the matter with that old devil now?" asked Miss Paird. "I have no idea," said Mr. Martin, resuming his work. The other two looked at him and then at each other. Miss Paird got up and went out. She walked slowly past the closed door of Mr. Fitweiler's office. Mrs. Barrows was yelling inside, but she was not braying. Miss Paird could not hear what the woman was saying. She went back to her desk.

Forty-five minutes later, Mrs. Barrows left the president's office and went into her own, shutting the door. It wasn't until half an hour later that Mr. Fitweiler sent for Mr. Martin. The head of the filing department, neat, quiet, attentive, stood in front of the old man's desk. Mr. Fitweiler was pale and nervous. He took his glasses off and twiddled them. He made a small bruffing sound in his throat. "Martin," he said, "you have been with us more than twenty years." "Twenty-two, sir," said Mr. Martin. "In that time," pursued the president, "your work and your—uh—manner have been exemplary." "I trust so, sir," said Mr. Martin. "I have understood, Martin," said Mr. Fitweiler, "that you have never taken a drink or smoked." "That is correct, sir," said Mr. Martin. "Ah, yes." Mr. Fitweiler polished his glasses. "You may describe what you did after leaving the office yesterday, Martin," he said. Mr. Martin allowed less than a second for his bewildered pause. "Certainly, sir," he said. "I walked home. Then I went to Schrafft's for dinner. Afterward I walked home again. I went to bed early, sir, and read a magazine for a while. I was asleep before eleven." "Ah, yes," said Mr. Fitweiler again. He was silent for a moment, searching for the proper words to say to the head of the filing department. "Mrs. Barrows," he said finally, "Mrs. Barrows has worked hard, Martin, very hard. It grieves me to report that she has suffered a severe breakdown. It has taken the form of a persecution complex accompanied by distressing hallucinations. "I am very sorry, sir," said Mr. Martin. "Mrs. Barrows is under the delusion," continued Mr. Fitweiler, "that you visited her last evening and behaved yourself in an—uh—unseemly manner." He raised his hand to silence Mr. Martin's little pained outcry. "It is the nature of these psychological diseases," Mr. Fitweiler said, "to fix upon the least likely and most innocent party as the—uh—source of persecution. These matters are not for the lay mind to grasp, Martin. I've just had my psychiatrist, Dr. Fitch, on the phone. He would not, of course, commit himself, but he made enough generalizations to substantiate my suspicions. I suggested to Mrs. Barrows when she had completed her—uh—story to me this morning, that she visit Dr. Fitch, for I suspected a condition at once. She flew, I regret to say, into a rage, and demanded—uh—requested that I call you on the carpet. You may not know, Martin, but Mrs. Barrows had planned a reorganization of your department—subject to my approval, of course, subject to my approval. This brought you, rather than anyone else, to her mind—but again that is a phenomenon for Dr. Fitch and not for us. So, Martin, I am afraid Mrs. Barrows' usefulness here is at an end." "I am dreadfully sorry, sir," said Mr. Martin.

It was at this point that the door to the office blew open with the suddenness of a gas-main explosion and Mrs. Barrows catapulted through it. "Is the little rat denying it?" she screamed. "He can't get away with that!" Mr. Martin got up and moved discreetly to a point beside Mr. Fitweiler's chair.

"You drank and smoked at my apartment," she bawled at Mr. Martin, "and you know it! You called Mr. Fitweiler an old windbag and said you were going to blow him up when you got coked to the gills on your heroin!" She stopped yelling to catch her breath and a new glint came into her popping eyes. "If you weren't such a drab, ordinary little man," she said, "I'd think you'd planned it all. Sticking your tongue out, saying you were sitting in the catbird seat, because you thought no one would believe me when I told it! My God, it's really too perfect!" She brayed loudly and hysterically, and the fury was on her again. She glared at Mr. Fitweiler. "Can't you see how he has tricked us, you old fool? Can't you see his little game?" But Mr. Fitweiler had been surreptitiously pressing all the buttons under the top of his desk and employees of F & S began pouring into the room. "Stockton," said Mr. Fitweiler, "you and Fishbein will take Mrs. Barrows to her home. Mrs. Powell, you will go with them." Stockton, who had played a little football in high school, blocked Mrs. Barrows as she made for Mr. Martin. It took him and Fishbein together to force her out of the door into the hall, crowded with stenographers and office boys. She was still screaming imprecations at Mr. Martin, tangled and contradictory imprecations. The hubbub finally died out down the corridor.

"I regret that this has happened," said Mr. Fitweiler. "I shall ask you to dismiss it from your mind, Martin." "Yes, sir," said Mr. Martin, anticipating his chief's "That will be all" by moving to the door. "I will dismiss it." He went out and shut the door, and his step was light and quick in the hall. When he entered his department he had slowed down to his customary gait, and he walked quietly across the room to the W20 file, wearing a look of studious concentration.

✎ ✎ ✎

Author's Profile
JAMES THURBER

James Thurber described himself as a "professional writer, a semi-professional cartoonist and an amateur actor . . . also a reasonably competent babysitter." It is this eccentric slant on life which earned him enormous popularity and consideration as second only to Mark Twain as a humorist.

Thurber is the author of more than 20 books, hundreds of cartoon-like drawings, and numerous journalistic reports. He was born in Columbus, Ohio, on December 8, 1894, to a politician father, a mother overwhelmed by the newfangled inventions of the times, and a wildly erratic grandfather who believed that the Civil War was still raging. These and other family members appeared again and again in hilarious stories saturated with bewilderment, disarray, and general bedlam. Especially notable are "The Night the Bed Fell" and "The Night the Ghost Got In."

Thurber's early days were spent as a reporter for the *Columbus Dispatch* and the Paris edition of the *Chicago Tribune.* He later was asked to join *The New Yorker* magazine's staff during the 1920s, where he shared office space with essay writer E. B. White (who later became famous for his children's stories like *Charlotte's Web*). The two played off one another's personalities. White encouraged Thurber to use his drawings, and together they initiated the still-famous column, "Talk of the Town." Stories of his family filled different issues of the magazine and were eventually compiled into his classic work, *My Life and Hard Times,* published in 1933.

Blindness from a childhood eye injury set in during the early 1940s but did not deter him. In 1942, he published his best-known and best-loved story, "The Secret Life of Walter Mitty." During World War II, Thurber wrote and illustrated *The Last Flower,* an antiwar satire, and *The Male Animal,* a play coauthored by actor Elliott Nugent which enjoyed great success on Broadway. *The Thurber Album,* written in 1952, reveals his deep feelings for his family and his roots in America's early history.

Thurber, too, hit the bright lights, playing himself in the Broadway production of *A Thurber Carnival,* a revue of his comic and satiric sketches. A year later he underwent surgery for cerebral thrombosis and died of pneumonia on November 2, 1961.

His last years found him alienated from a world where:

. . . comedy didn't die, it just went crazy. It has identified itself with the very tension and terror it once did so much to alleviate.

This from a man who in his more optimistic youth said, "Every time is a time for comedy."

The Richer, The Poorer

BY DOROTHY WEST

ANTICIPATING: Read aloud and discuss the meaning of Robert Frost's poem "The Road Not Taken." What does this poem mean to you? Write in your journal how you feel about the roads, where each leads, and which one you will take.

Over the years Lottie had urged Bess to prepare for her old age. 🌶 Over the years Bess had lived each day as if there were no other. Now they were both past sixty, the time for summing up. Lottie had a bank account that had never grown lean. Bess had the clothes on her back, and the rest of her worldly possessions in a battered suitcase. 🌶 Lottie had hated being a child, hearing her parents' skimping and scraping. Bess had never seemed to notice. All she ever wanted was to go outside and play. She learned to skate on borrowed skates. She rode a borrowed bicycle. Lottie couldn't wait to grow up and buy herself the best of everything. 🌶

As soon as anyone would hire her, Lottie put herself to work. She minded babies, she ran errands for the old.

She never touched a penny of her money, though her child's mouth watered for ice cream and candy. But she could not bear to share with Bess, who never had anything to share with her. When the dimes began to add up to dollars, she lost her taste for sweets.

By the time she was twelve, she was clerking after school in a small variety store. Saturdays she worked as long as she was wanted. She decided to keep her money for clothes. When she entered high school, she would wear a wardrobe that neither she nor anyone else would be able to match.

But her freshman year found her unable to indulge so frivolous a whim, particularly when her admiring instructors advised her to think seriously of college. No one in her family had ever gone to college, and certainly Bess would never get there. She would show them all what she could do, if she put her mind to it.

She began to bank her money, and her bank became her most private and precious possession.

In her third year high she found a job in a small but expanding restaurant, where she cashiered from the busy hour until closing. In her last year high the business increased so rapidly that Lottie was faced with the choice of staying in school or working full-time.

She made her choice easily. A job in hand was worth two in the future.

Bess had a beau in the school band, who had no other ambition except to play a horn. Lottie expected to be settled with a home and family while Bess was still waiting for Harry to earn enough to buy a marriage license.

That Bess married Harry straight out of high school was not surprising. That Lottie never married at all was not really surprising either. Two or three times she was halfway persuaded, but to give up a job that paid well for a homemaking job that paid nothing was a risk she was incapable of taking.

Bess's married life was nothing for Lottie to envy. She and Harry lived like gypsies, Harry playing in second-rate bands all over the country, even getting himself and Bess stranded in Europe. They were often in rags and never in riches.

Bess grieved because she had no child, not having sense enough to know she was better off without one. Lottie was certainly better off without nieces and nephews to feel sorry for. Very likely Bess would have dumped them on her doorstep.

That Lottie had a doorstep they might have been left on was only because her boss, having bought a second house, offered Lottie his first house at a price so low and terms so reasonable that it would have been like losing money to refuse.

She shut off the rooms she didn't use, letting them go to rack and ruin. Since she ate her meals out, she had no food at home, and did not encourage callers, who always expected a cup of tea.

Her way of life was mean and miserly, but she did not know it. She thought she lived frugally in her middle years so that she could live in comfort and ease when she most needed peace of mind.

The years, after forty, began to race. Suddenly Lottie was sixty, and retired from her job by her boss's son, who had no sentimental feeling about keeping her on until she was ready to quit.

he made several attempts to find other employment, but her dowdy appearance made her look old and inefficient. For the first time in her life Lottie would gladly have worked for nothing, to have some place to go, something to do with her day.

Harry died abroad, in a third-rate hotel, with Bess weeping as hard as if he had left her a fortune. He had left her nothing but his horn. There wasn't even money for her passage home.

Lottie, trapped by the blood tie, knew she would not only have to send for her sister, but take her in when she returned. It didn't seem fair that Bess should reap the harvest of Lottie's lifetime of self-denial.

It took Lottie a week to get a bedroom ready, a week of hard work and hard cash. There was everything to do, everything to replace or paint. When she was through the room looked so fresh and new that Lottie felt she deserved it more than Bess.

She would let Bess have her room, but the mattress was so lumpy, the carpet so worn, the curtains so threadbare that Lottie's conscience pricked her. She supposed she would have to redo that room, too, and went about doing it with an eagerness that she mistook for haste.

When she was through upstairs, she was shocked to see how dismal downstairs looked by comparison. She tried to ignore it, but with nowhere to go to escape it, the contrast grew more intolerable.

She worked her way from kitchen to parlor, persuading herself she was only putting the rooms to right to give herself something to do. At night she slept like a child after a long and happy day of playing house. She was having more fun than she had ever had in her life. She was living each hour for itself.

There was only a day now before Bess would arrive. Passing her gleaming mirrors, at first with vague awareness, then with plainful clarity, Lottie saw herself as others saw her, and could not stand the sight.

She went on a spending spree from specialty shops to beauty salon, emerging transformed into a woman who believed in miracles.

She was in the kitchen basting a turkey when Bess rang the bell. Her heart raced, and she wondered if the heat from the oven was responsible.

She went to the door, and Bess stood before her. Stiffly she suffered Bess's embrace, her heart racing harder, her eyes suddenly smarting from the onrush of cold air.

"Oh Lottie, it's good to see you," Bess said, but saying nothing about Lottie's splendid appearance. Upstairs Bess, putting down her shabby suitcase, said, "I'll sleep like a rock tonight," without a word of praise for her lovely room. At the lavish table, top-heavy with turkey, Bess said, "I'll take light and dark both," with no marveling at the size of the bird, or that there was turkey for two elderly women, one of them too poor to buy her own bread.

With the glow of good food in her stomach, Bess began to spin stories. They were rich with places and people, most of them lowly, all of them magnificent. Her face reflected her telling, the joys and sorrows of her remembering, and above all, the love she lived by that enhanced the poorest place, the humblest person.

Then it was that Lottie knew why Bess had made no mention of her finery, or the shining room, or the twelve-pound turkey. She had not even seen them. Tomorrow she would see the room as it really looked, and Lottie as she really looked, and the warmed-over turkey in its second-day glory. Tonight she saw only what she had come seeking, a place in her sister's home and heart.

She said, "That's enough about me. How have the years used you?"

"It was me who didn't use them," said Lottie wistfully. "I saved for them. I forgot the best of them would go without my ever spending a day or a dollar enjoying them. That's my life story in those few words, a life never lived."

"Now it's too near the end to try."

Bess said, "To know how much there is to know is the beginning of learning to live. Don't count the years that are left us. At our time of life it's the days that count. You've too much catching up to do to waste a minute of a waking hour feeling sorry for yourself."

Lottie grinned, a real wide open grin, "Well, to tell the truth I felt sorry for you. Maybe if I had any sense I'd feel sorry for myself, after all. I know I'm too old to kick up my heels, but I'm going to let you show me how. If I land on my head, I guess it won't matter. I feel giddy already, and I like it."

❦ ❦ ❦

Author's Profile
DOROTHY WEST

*D*orothy West was born in Boston on June 2, 1907, the only child of ex-slave Isaac Christopher West and his wife, Rachel. Her father was a self-made man who provided a good living for his family as owner of several businesses, including a restaurant, a grocery store, and a wholesale fruit company. Her mother, one of 22 children, married this man much older than herself for the fine life he could provide for her and her extended family. Dorothy was a bright child who, at four years old, could do second grade lessons. She was well-educated in Boston and studied journalism and philosophy at Columbia University.

West became a writer at the age of seven when her story "Promise and Fulfillment" won a prize in the *Boston Post*. Future stories continued to win and eventually she was offered a trip to New York by *Opportunity* magazine just before she turned eighteen. The trip changed her life.

There she became involved with the Harlem Renaissance writers and intellectuals. She became good friends with Zora Neale Hurston and Langston Hughes, as well as Countee Cullen and Rachel Wright. To make ends meet during the Depression, West worked as an actor in the original stage production of *Porgy*. During the 1930s she travelled to Russia with Langston Hughes to make a film about African-American life. They became very close, and it is said she even proposed marriage to him.

Returning to America at the age of twenty-five, West founded the literary magazine *Challenge* to publish and promote young African-American writers. Due to financial problems and few submissions, it folded in 1937. She became a social worker but continued to write and publish. From 1940 to 1960 she produced 26 stories through the *New York Daily News*, though her friends looked down on this publication. In 1945, she started *The Living is Easy*, published in 1948, and reprinted in 1982 by the Feminist Press. Though in her mid-eighties, she is currently finishing her second novel, *The Wedding*, to be published by Doubleday.

West lives in Oak Bluffs, Massachusetts. Her literary career spans 50 years, and her writing explores the ironies of African-American urban lifestyles. She once said of her vocation, "I have no ability nor desire to be other than a writer, though the fact is, I whistle beautifully."

NON
FICT
ION

Personal Memoirs

Cotton-Picking Time
BY MAYA ANGELOU

ANTICIPATING: Choose a day in your life which started off well, but then something negative happened. Write a journal entry recounting your feelings as the day began and the changes in your feelings and attitude at the day's end.

ach year I watched the field across from the Store turn caterpillar green, then gradually frosty white. I knew exactly how long it would be before the big wagons would pull into the front yard and load on the cotton pickers at daybreak to carry them to the remains of slavery's plantations. 📖 During the picking season my grandmother would get out of bed at four o'clock (she never used an alarm clock) and creak down to her knees and chant in a sleep-filled voice, "Our Father, thank you for letting me see this New Day. Thank you that you didn't allow the bed I lay on last night to be my cooling board, nor my blanket my winding sheet. Guide my feet this day along the straight and narrow, and help me to put a bridle on my tongue. Bless this house, and everybody in it. Thank you, in the name of your Son, Jesus Christ, Amen." 📖 Before she had quite arisen, she called our names and issued orders, and pushed her large feet into homemade slippers and across the bare lye-washed wooden floor to light the coal-oil lamp. 📖

The lamplight in the Store gave a soft make-believe feeling to our world which made me want to whisper and walk about on tiptoe. The odors of onions and oranges and kerosene had been mixing all night and wouldn't be disturbed until the wooden slat was removed from the door and the early morning air forced its way in with the bodies of people who had walked miles to reach the pick-up place.

"Sister, I'll have two cans of sardines."

"I'm gonna work so fast today I'm gonna make you look like you standing still."

emme have a hunk uh cheese and some sody crackers."

"Just gimme a coupla them fat peanut paddies." That would be from a picker who was taking his lunch. The greasy brown paper sack was stuck behind the bib of his overalls. He'd use the candy as a snack before the noon sun called the workers to rest.

In those tender mornings the Store was full of laughing, joking, boasting and bragging. One man was going to pick two hundred pounds of cotton, and another three hundred. Even the children were promising to bring home fo' bits and six bits.

The champion picker of the day before was the hero of the dawn. If he prophesied that the cotton in today's field was going to be sparse and stick to the bolls like glue, every listener would grunt a hearty agreement.

The sound of the empty cotton sacks dragging over the floor and the murmurs of waking people were sliced by the cash register as we rang up the five-cent sales.

If the morning sounds and smells were touched with the supernatural, the late afternoon had all the features of the normal Arkansas life. In the dying sunlight the people dragged, rather than their empty cotton sacks.

Brought back to the Store, the pickers would step out of the backs of trucks and fold down, dirt-disappointed, to the ground. No matter how much they had picked, it wasn't enough. Their wages wouldn't even get them out of debt to my grandmother, not to mention the staggering bill that waited on them at the white commissary downtown.

The sounds of the new morning had been replaced with grumbles about cheating houses, weighted scales, snakes, skimpy cotton and dusty rows. In later years I was to confront the stereotyped picture of gay song-singing cotton pickers with such inordinate rage that I was told even by fellow Blacks that my paranoia was embarrassing. But I had seen the fingers cut by the mean little cotton bolls, and I had witnessed the backs and shoulders and arms and legs resisting any further demands.

Some of the workers would leave their sacks at the Store to be picked up the following morning, but a few had to take them home for repairs. I winced to picture them sewing the coarse material under a coal-oil lamp with fingers stiffening from the day's work. In too few hours they would have to walk back to Sister Henderson's Store, get vittles and load, again, onto the trucks. Then they would face another day of trying to earn enough for the whole year with the heavy knowledge that they were going to end the season as they started it. Without the money or credit necessary to sustain a family for three months. In cotton-picking time the late afternoons revealed the harshness of Black Southern life, which in the early morning had been softened by nature's blessing of grogginess, forgetfulness and the soft lamplight.

Author's Profile
MAYA ANGELOU

*P*oet, autobiographer, playwright, actress, director, singer, composer, and teacher are just a few of the words used to describe the life and work of Maya Angelou. She is universally considered to be one of the most passionate and articulate voices in African-American literature.

Born Marguerita Johnson in St. Louis, Missouri, on April 4, 1928, Angelou attended public schools in Arkansas and California, and then studied music, dance (with Martha Graham), and drama. She began her career as an actress and singer in such productions as *Porgy and Bess* (1954-1955), *Calypso Heatwave* (1957), and *The Blacks* (1960). She worked as an administrator and teacher in the 1960s and 1970s in between theatrical appearances.

Best known for her autobiography *I Know Why the Caged Bird Sings* (1971), she has produced other volumes of memoirs: *Gather Together in My Name* (1974), *Singin' and Swingin' and Gettin' Merry Like Christmas* (1976), *The Heart of a Woman* (1981), and *All God's Children Need Traveling Shoes* (1986). Her volumes of poetry include *Just Give Me a Cool Drink of Water 'fore I Die* (1971), *Oh Pray My Wings Are Gonna Fit Me Well* (1975), *And Still I Rise* (1978), and *Shaker, Why Don't You Sing?* (1983).

In January, 1993, she read her poem "On the Pulse of the Morning" at the inauguration of her fellow Arkansan President Bill Clinton. Recently, in an interview with C. J. Houtchens in *USA Weekend*, Angelou spoke of her career as a teacher and what she teaches in her classes:

> *I think I see all of us as teachers. We're all teachers, whether we like it or not, whether we claim that title and accept that responsibility or not. We all teach. Implicitly and explicitly, we teach. I am a teacher. I teach at Wake Forest University. I'm a serious teacher. And a good teacher.*
>
> *It's probably the same thing I teach in my poetry, and in my books and in the music I write. It's probably all the same, which is that you may encounter many defeats, but you must not be defeated . . . And, of course, linked to that, not as a clause but really as important a sentence as that first sentence, is the statement that human beings are more alike than we are unalike.*

My Lack of Gumption

BY RUSSELL BAKER

ANTICIPATING: 1. Describe a job that you have had that you truly hated. It can be a job either outside of your home or perhaps a chore that you have had to perform at home. Describe the job itself, some specific stories or memories that you have about it, and the end result of the job.

2. Describe what, at this point in your life, is the ideal job or career for you. Describe what you imagine it will be like, what the requirements or training would be like, and what attracts you to this career. Also, you can research this job, using either your library or career center or interviews, to add additional information on income, outlook, training, and working conditions.

 began working in journalism when I was eight years old. It was my mother's idea. She wanted me to "make something" of myself and, after a level-headed appraisal of my strengths, decided I had better start young if I was to have any chance of keeping up with the competition. The flaw in my character which she had already spotted was lack of "gumption." My idea of a perfect afternoon was lying in front of the radio rereading my favorite Big Little Book, *Dick Tracy Meets Stooge Viller*. My mother despised inactivity. Seeing me having a good time in repose, she was powerless to hide her disgust. "You've got no more gumption than a bump on a log," she said. "Get out in the kitchen and help Doris do those dirty dishes." My sister Doris, though two years younger than I, had enough gumption for a dozen people. She positively enjoyed washing dishes, making beds, and cleaning the house. When she was only seven she could carry a piece of short-weighted cheese back to the A&P, threaten the manager with legal action, and come back triumphantly with the full quarter-pound we'd paid for and a few ounces extra thrown in for forgiveness. Doris could have made something of herself if she hadn't been a girl. Because of this defect, however, the best she could hope for was a career as a nurse or schoolteacher, the only work that capable females were considered up to in those days. This must have saddened my mother, this twist of fate that had allocated all the gumption to the daughter and left her with a son who was content with Dick Tracy and Stooge Viller. If disappointed, though, she wasted no energy on self-pity. She would make me make something of myself whether I wanted to or not. "The Lord helps those who help themselves," she said. That was the way her mind worked.

She was realistic about the difficulty. Having sized up the material the Lord had given her to mold, she didn't overestimate what she could do with it. She didn't insist that I grow up to be President of the United States. ifty years ago parents still asked boys if they wanted to grow up to be President, and asked it not jokingly but seriously. Many parents who were hardly more than paupers still believed their sons could do it. Abraham Lincoln had done it. We were only sixty-five years from Lincoln. Many a grandfather who walked among us could remember Lincoln's time. Men of grandfatherly age were the worst for asking if you wanted to grow up to be President. A surprising number of little boys said yes and meant it.

I was asked many times myself. No, I would say, I didn't want to grow up to be President. My mother was present during one of these interrogations. An elderly uncle, having posed the usual question and exposed my lack of interest in the Presidency, asked, "Well, what do you want to be when you grow up?"

I loved to pick through trash piles and collect empty bottles, tin cans with pretty labels, and discarded magazines. The most desirable job on earth sprang instantly to mind. "I want to be a garbage man," I said.

My uncle smiled, but my mother had seen the first distressing evidence of a bump budding on a log. "Have a little gumption, Russell," she said.

Her calling me Russell was a signal of unhappiness. When she approved of me I was always "Buddy."

When I turned eight years old she decided that the job of starting me on the road toward making something of myself could no longer be safely delayed. "Buddy," she said one day, "I want you to come home right after school this afternoon. Somebody's coming and I want you to meet him."

When I burst in that afternoon she was in conference in the parlor with an executive of the Curtis Publishing Company. She introduced me. He bent low from the waist and shook my hand. Was it true as my mother had told him, he asked, that I longed for the opportunity to conquer the world of business?

My mother replied that I was blessed with a rare determination to make something of myself.

"That's right," I whispered.

"But have you got the grit, the character, the never-say-quit spirit it takes to succeed in business?"

My mother said I certainly did.

"That's right," I said.

He eyed me silently for a long pause, as though weighing whether I could be trusted to keep his confidence, then spoke man-to-man. Before taking a crucial step, he said, he wanted to advise me that working for the Curtis Publishing Company placed enormous responsibility on a young man. It was one of the great companies of America. Perhaps the greatest publishing house in the world. I had heard, no doubt, of the *Saturday Evening Post*?

Heard of it? My mother said that everyone in our house had heard of the *Saturday Post* and that I, in fact, read it with religious devotion.

Then doubtless, he said, we were also familiar with those two monthly pillars of the magazine world, the *Ladies Home Journal* and the *Country Gentleman*.

Indeed we were familiar with them, said my mother.

Representing the *Saturday Evening Post* was one of the weightiest honors that could be bestowed in the world of business, he said. He was personally proud of being part of that great corporation.

My mother said he had every right to be.

Again he studied me as though debating whether I was worthy of a knighthood. Finally: "Are you trustworthy?"

My mother said I was the soul of honesty.

hat's right," I said.

The caller smiled for the first time. He told me I was a lucky young man. He admired my spunk. Too many young men thought life was all play. Those young men would not go far in this world. Only a young man willing to work and save and keep his face washed and his hair neatly combed could hope to come out on top in a world such as ours. Did I truly and sincerely believe that I was such a young man?

"He certainly does," said my mother.

"That's right," I said.

He said he had been so impressed by what he had seen of me that he was going to make me a representative of the Curtis Publishing Company. On the following Tuesday, he said, thirty freshly printed copies of the *Saturday Evening Post* would be delivered at our door. I would place these magazines, still damp with the ink of the presses, in a handsome canvas bag, sling it over my shoulder, and set forth through the streets to bring the best in journalism, fiction, and cartoons to the American public.

He had brought the canvas bag with him. He presented it with reverence fit for a chasuble. He showed me how to drape the sling over my left shoulder and across the chest so that the pouch lay easily accessible to my right hand, allowing the best in journalism, fiction, and cartoons to be swiftly extracted and sold to a citizenry whose happiness and security depended upon us soldiers of the free press.

The following Tuesday I raced home from school, put the canvas bag over my shoulder, dumped the magazines in, and, tilting to the left to balance their weight on my right hip, embarked on the highway of journalism.

We lived in Belleville, New Jersey, a commuter town at the northern fringe of Newark. It was 1932, the bleakest year of the Depression. My father had died two years before, leaving us with a few pieces of Sears, Roebuck furniture and not much else, and my mother had taken Doris and me to live with one of her younger brothers. This was my Uncle Allen. Uncle Allen had made something of himself by 1932. As salesman for a soft-drink bottler in Newark, he had an income of $30 a week; wore pearl-gray spats, detachable collars, and a three-piece suit; was happily married; and took in threadbare relatives.

With my load of magazines I headed toward Belleville Avenue. That's where the people were. There were two filling stations at the intersection with Union Avenue, as well as an A&P, a fruit stand, a bakery, a barber shop, Zuccarelli's drugstore, and a diner shaped like a railroad car. For several hours I made myself highly visible, shifting position now and then from corner to corner, from shop window to shop window, to make sure everyone could see the heavy black lettering on the canvas bag that said *The Saturday Evening Post.* When the angle of the light indicated it was suppertime, I walked back to the house.

"How many did you sell, Buddy?" my mother asked.

"None."

"Where did you go?"

"The corner of Belleville and Union Avenues."

"What did you do?"

"Stood on the corner waiting for somebody to buy a *Saturday Evening Post.*"

"You just stood there?"

"Didn't sell a single one."

"For God's sake, Russell!"

Uncle Allen intervened. "I've been thinking about it for some time," he said, "and I've decided to take the *Post* regularly. Put me down as a regular customer." I handed him a magazine and he paid me a nickel. It was the first nickel I earned.

Afterwards my mother instructed me in salesmanship. I would have to ring doorbells, address adults with charming self-confidence, and break down resistance with a sales talk pointing out that no one, no matter how poor, could afford to be without the *Saturday Evening Post* in the home.

I told my mother I'd changed my mind about wanting to succeed in the magazine business.

"If you think I'm going to raise a good-for-nothing," she replied, "you've got another think coming." She told me to hit the streets with the canvas bag and start ringing doorbells the instant school was out next day. When I objected that I didn't feel any aptitude for salesmanship, she asked me how I'd like to lend her my leather belt so she could whack some sense into me. I bowed to superior will and entered journalism with a heavy heart.

My mother and I had fought this battle almost as long as I could remember. It probably started even before memory began, when I was a country child in northern Virginia and my mother, dissatisfied with my father's plain workman's life, determined that I could not grow up like him and his people, with calluses on their hands, overalls on their backs, and fourth-grade educations in their heads. She had fancier ideas of life's possibilities. Introducing me to the *Saturday Evening Post*, she was trying to wean me as early as possible from my father's world where men left with their lunch pails at sunup, worked with their hands until the grime ate into the pores, and died with a few sticks of mail-order furniture as their legacy. In my mother's vision of the better life there were desks and white collars, well-pressed suits, evenings of reading and lively talk, and perhaps—if a man were very, very lucky and hit the jackpot, really made something important of himself—perhaps there might be a fantastic salary of $5,000 a year to support a big house and a Buick with a rumble seat and a vacation in Atlantic City.

nd so I set forth with my sack of magazines. I was afraid of the dogs that snarled behind the doors of potential buyers. I was timid about ringing the doorbells of strangers, relieved when no one came to the door, and scared when someone did. Despite my mother's instructions, I could not deliver an engaging sales pitch. When a door opened I simply asked, "Want to buy a *Saturday Evening Post*?" In Belleville few persons did. It was a town of 30,000 people, and most weeks I rang a fair majority of its doorbells. But I rarely sold my thirty copies. Some weeks I canvassed the entire town for six days and still had four or five unsold magazines on Monday evening; then I dreaded the coming of Tuesday morning, when a batch of thirty fresh *Saturday Evening Posts* was due at the front door.

"Better get out there and sell the rest of those magazines tonight," my mother would say.

I usually posted myself then at a busy intersection where a traffic light controlled commuter flow from Newark. When the light turned red I stood on the curb and shouted my sales pitch at the motorists.

"Want to buy a *Saturday Evening Post*?"

One rainy night when car windows were sealed against me I came back soaked and with not a single sale to report. My mother beckoned to Doris.

"Go back down there with Buddy and show him how to sell these magazines," she said.

Brimming with zest, Doris, who was then seven years old, returned with me to the corner. She took a magazine from the bag, and when the light turned red she strode to the nearest car and banged her small fist against the closed window. The driver, probably startled at what he took to be a midget assaulting his car, lowered the window to stare, and Doris thrust a *Saturday Evening Post* at him.

"You need this magazine," she piped, "and it only costs a nickel."

Her salesmanship was irresistible. Before the light had changed half a dozen times she disposed of the entire batch. I didn't feel humiliated. To the contrary, I was so happy I decided to give her a treat. Leading her to the vegetable store on Belleville Avenue, I bought three apples, which cost a nickel, and gave her one.

"You shouldn't waste money," she said.

"Eat your apple." I bit into mine.

"You shouldn't eat before supper," she said. "It'll spoil your appetite."

Back at the house that evening, she dutifully reported me for wasting a nickel. Instead of a scolding, I was rewarded with a pat on the back for having the good sense to buy fruit instead of candy. My mother reached into her bottomless supply of maxims and told Doris, "An apple a day keeps the doctor away."

By the time I was ten I had learned all my mother's maxims by heart. Asking to stay up past normal bedtime, I knew that a refusal would be explained with, "Early to bed and early to rise, makes a man healthy, wealthy, and wise." If I whimpered about having to get up early in the morning, I could depend on her to say, "The early bird gets the worm."

The one I most despised was, "If at first you don't succeed, try, try again." This was the battle cry with which she constantly sent me back into the hopeless struggle whenever I moaned that I had rung every doorbell in town and knew there wasn't a single potential buyer left in Belleville that week. After listening to my explanation, she handed me the canvas bag and said, "If at first you don't succeed . . ."

Three years in that job, which I would gladly have quit after the first day except for her insistence, produced at least one valuable result. My mother finally concluded that I would never make something of myself by pursuing a life in business and started considering careers for me that demanded less competitive zeal.

One evening when I was eleven I brought home a short "composition" on my summer vacation which the teacher had graded with an A. Reading it with her own schoolteacher's eye, my mother agreed that it was top-drawer seventh grade prose and complimented me. Nothing more was said about it immediately, but a new idea had taken life in her mind. Halfway through supper she suddenly interrupted the conversation.

uddy," she said, "maybe you could be a writer."

I clasped the idea to my heart. I had never met a writer, had shown no previous urge to write, and hadn't a notion how to become a writer, but I loved stories and thought that making up stories must surely be almost as much fun as reading them. Best of all, though, and what really gladdened my heart, was the ease of the writer's life. Writers did not have to trudge through the town peddling from canvas bags, defending themselves against angry dogs, being rejected by surly strangers. Writers did not have to ring doorbells. So far as I could make out, what writers did couldn't even be classified as work.

I was enchanted. Writers didn't have to have any gumption at all. I did not dare tell anybody for fear of being laughed at in the schoolyard, but secretly I decided that what I'd like to be when I grew up was a writer.

📖 📖 📖

Author's Profile
RUSSELL BAKER

*O*ne of America's premier humor writers, Russell Baker's thrice weekly "Observer" has been a fixture for *New York Times'* readers for more than 30 years. Groucho Marx once sent him a picture of the Marx Brothers with the inscription, "You're the reason I read the *New York Times.*" In recent years, Baker has written two well-received volumes of his autobiography.

Russell Wayne Baker was born in Virginia on August 14, 1925, was raised by his widowed and stalwart mother, Lucy Elizabeth Baker, and was graduated from Johns Hopkins University in 1947. After graduation, Baker spent six years (1947-1953) as a staff writer for the *Baltimore Sun* and then joined the *New York Times*, where he spent the next eight years covering the White House, various Congressional committees, and the State Department. By the early 1960s, he had become bored with straight reporting; as he later told reporter John Skow:

> I had done enough reporting. It came to seem that this wasn't a worthy way for a grown man to spend his life. You have good seats, yes, but you're always on the sidelines. You're not making anything.

In 1962, he began writing his "Observer" columns three times a week on the editorial page of the *New York Times*. He requested free rein to tackle any subject, and told his bosses that he would write in "short sentences" and in "plain English" to reduce the suffering of those *Times'* readers who were "suffocating" on the newspaper's usual "polysyllabic Latinate English." In this vein, he wrote pieces that ridiculed showy language in government, the short-comings of politicians, and lapses of good taste on the part of the public.

Baker became the first humor writer to win a Pulitzer Prize for commentary in 1979. In the 1980s, he wrote two volumes of his autobiography: *Growing Up* (1982) and *The Good Times* (1989). *Growing Up* won him the Pulitzer Prize for autobiography/biography in 1982.

In 1993, although continuing with his "Observer" columns and other articles and books, Baker succeeded Alistair Cooke as the on-air host of Public Television's *Masterpiece Theatre*.

From Man to Boy

BY JOHN R. COLEMAN

ANTICIPATING: Think about a time when you were called a name you didn't deserve. Write about it in your journal. Try to recall the details of the incident and why you were called this name. Discuss how you felt and how you reacted.

Tuesday, March 27

One of the waitresses I find hard to take asked me at one point today, "Are you the boy who cuts the lemons?" 📖 "I'm the man who does," I replied. 📖 "Well, there are none cut." There wasn't even a hint that she heard my point. 📖 Dana, who has cooked here for twelve years or so, heard that exchange. 📖 "It's no use, Jack," he said when she was gone. "If she doesn't know now, she never will." There was a trace of a smile on his face, but it was a sad look all the same. 📖

In that moment, I learned the full thrust of those billboard ads of a few years ago that said, "BOY. Drop out of school and that's what they'll call you the rest of your life." I had read those ads before with a certain feeling of pride; education matters, they said, and that gave a lift to my field. Today I saw them saying something else. They were untrue in part; it turns out that you'll get called "boy" if you do work that others don't respect even if you have a Ph.D. It isn't education that counts, but the job in which you land. And the ads spoke too of a sad resignation about the world. They assumed that some people just won't learn respect for others, so you should adapt yourself to them. Don't try to change them. Get the right job and they won't call *you* boy any more. They'll save it for the next man.

It isn't just people like this one waitress who learn slowly, if at all. Haverford College has prided itself on being a caring, considerate community in the Quaker tradition for many long years. Yet when I came there I soon learned that the cleaning women in the dormitories were called "wombats" by all the students. No one seemed to know where the name came from or what connection, if any, it had with the dictionary definition. *The American College Dictionary* says a wombat is "any of three species of burrowing marsupials of Australia . . . somewhat resembling ground hogs." The name was just one of Haverford's unexamined ways of doing things.

It didn't take much persuasion to get the name dropped. Today there are few students who remember it at all. But I imagine the cleaning women remember it well.

Certainly I won't forget being called a boy today.

Author's Profile
JOHN R. COLEMAN

John R. Coleman was born in 1921 in Ontario, Canada, and became an American citizen in 1954. After graduating from the University of Toronto and the University of Chicago where he earned a Ph.D. in 1950, his distinguished career started at Massachusetts Institute of Technology where he was an instructor in the late 1940s in the economics department. He worked at the Ford Foundation, taught for CBS College of the Air, was president of a college, served on boards of several major companies, and wrote extensively in the field of economics.

At his inauguration at Haverford College, Coleman said college students should combine travel and work experiences with their formal education. He believed that a "lockstep" education did not allow them to mature and become aware of the world.

When New York City construction workers attacked student peace demonstrators and the building trades council paraded against the peace movement in the early 1970s, Coleman was distressed by this lack of understanding in these groups. Consequently, in the spring of 1973, Coleman left the world of academia and became a blue-collar worker. He dug sewers and ditches in Atlanta, made sandwiches and salads in Boston, and collected garbage in a suburb of Washington, D.C. All the while, he continued his monthly meetings with the board of directors of a large Philadelphia bank.

Writing *Blue-Collar Journal* as a firsthand account of the world of work, Coleman said his experiences as a blue-collar laborer had given him a perspective on his white-collar life. "I'm learning more about what we have in common than about what drives us apart. We are all somewhat mixed-up and some of us in both worlds are happy about even that fact." His book was well-received.

True Stories and Other Dreams

BY JUDY COLLINS

ANTICIPATING: Describe what you think life on the road is like for a rock band or a singer or a truck driver or a construction worker or any other profession where travel is required. Describe a mythical typical day in this lifestyle: travel, readiness, working, recreation, wind-down, sleep, and problems.

Monday, February 18, 1985/En route, Fargo to New York

t snowed in St. Paul the other night, and when I left on the airplane the weather reports for the whole country were filled with warnings for flurries and inches. I got to Fargo with time to spare, and met up with my band. Weather has seldom stopped me, and I think in twenty-five years I have missed very few concerts. (God must really want me to work.) 📖 The concert last night was in a hall that was built in 1915. Huge and barnlike, it is the scene of community functions in Fargo: the Chamber Orchestra, the school shows, the wrestling team— the Judy Collins concert. We dress in the motel across an alley covered with snow, so I tramp over ice and drifts from hotel to stage door, back and forth at intermission, my heels teetering on the slick, crusted surfaces. The concert is great, I feel nourished by the evening. 📖 "Why do you still do it? Why do you keep on traveling, keep on singing? What do you get out of a night of singing? Bette Midler says it's for the money," he says. The interviewer for an Ohio television station points a microphone in my face and waits for an answer. 📖

"It's for the heart, and it's great to make a living doing what you love to do," I say.

"Is it only a living, then?" asks the young, eager interviewer.

When did making a living and having a good job get a bad name? This young man, with his unblemished face, seems to harbor some hostility for work, as though—if one were really with it—one should have been able to find some way not to have to do it. I love to sing. I love performing. Singing is my life's blood. It gives me pleasure, it makes me happy; it's more than a job—it's a life in process. Work is vital. It gives me purpose, calls on me to do my best. You don't have to be paid for work. I work for free, and for fun too.

"How do you feel about being called a singer's singer, Ms. Collins?"

"I guess it is a compliment," I say.

 wonder if my destiny is always to be a singer's singer as I try to change, transform, and struggle to break through into new things. I feel that inner push again. It is a familiar companion, this urge to go on to something new, something different. It crunches at me from within, like an awkward new life, demanding attention, demanding that I listen.

The concert in Fargo is with my trio, and when we arrive at the hall it is late in the afternoon, all of us having come in on the plane, gone to the hotel to check in and unpack. I do my workout and rest for an hour. My work day continues with the sound check at four-thirty.

I go to the dressing room with Maria Pizzuro, my travel assistant, where we touch up my makeup, adjust my hat, and pull out my book of lyrics. Then I go to look for the stage, which can be a journey unto itself.

Sometimes the halls are gymnasiums, or tents, or cathedrals. Some of the best sound I have heard comes out of school auditoriums. At times I dress in a trailer and at times in the opulence of carpeted rooms with full-length mirrors. Tonight's hall is perfect, set in the classic design with the dressing rooms in the right places. At the sound check I talk to the sound man who is working on the show. After I am comfortable with the sound of my voice (I carry my own microphones, having learned over the years never to trust what might be supplied locally), my lighting director and I talk to the personnel at the hall, and I joke with my musicians as we try a new song on-stage, to see how it all sounds. Above us the local Fargo crew climbs over the light bars, balancing among the violet and green gels that dangle like spaceships over our heads.

After the sound check and local press interviews, I go back to the dressing room, where Maria has set up our home on the road. It is two-and-a-half hours before the show, and we have much to do. Out of the aluminum Halliburton cases, opened up on the floor of the dressing room, has come everything a touring singer could possibly need: needle and thread, gaffer's tape, regular and decaf instant coffee, iron, safety pins, mouthwash, iodine, scissors, slippers, Wash 'n Dri's, Kleenex, steamer, mirror, guitar picks, toothpicks, lipstick, tweezers, Swiss army knife, bottle opener, aspirin, Q-tips, straws, press photos, business cards, black pen for signing autographs, shampoo. I head for the shower that opens off the dressing room.

"Maria," I call, raising my voice to carry over the sound of the running water, "is the nailbrush there?" Maria brings it, handing it to me through the steam-covered glass shower door. I think I could ask Maria if there was a prefab log cabin in the Halliburton, and she would pull it out. When I have finished washing my hair, my dinner has arrived, and while I eat, Maria sets my hair in thirty rollers. I devour baked chicken and steamed vegetables (I have never gotten over being famished on the road) and drink sparkling water. Then I put cream on my face and do my yoga while Maria leaves to have her own dinner. I am alone to continue the quieting that has begun. When she returns, I am sitting in the chair under the hair dryer, meditating, and she begins my makeup. Peace. Centering. On the door, a sign in Spanish and English says DO NOT DISTURB. I am in another world. Maria does her work with competence, and a knock comes at the door, forty minutes before show-time. Maria has transformed me, the meditation has centered me. The band comes in and we have a production meeting, determine the sequence of the songs, joke a little, connecting before we go out on the stage to connect.

"Shall we do the order from the last concert?" I ask Shelton Becton, my pianist. He is a slim black man of indeterminate age, handsome and extremely talented, who can play Chopin, Marvin Hamlisch, or Collins with equal skill.

"I think we ought to add that new song of yours, 'Dreamin.' It sounded good in the rehearsals, and we haven't done it on-stage."

"Fine, let's try it. And I want to ask you about the tempo last night on 'Clowns.' I thought I dragged it a bit. I'll pull it up a little." Warren Odze, my drummer for years, runs his hands through his black curly hair.

"The order was good last night. Let's put 'Dreamin' in, but let's keep the flow of it the same. It felt right."

We settle on a new set. Mike Sapsis, my road manager, writes it down, copying everyone, and as they leave the room, Zev Katz, my bass player, tells a joke. I respond with one I heard recently from David Braun about Gloria Steinem. . . . My band is a fine group of musicians. Tonight Shelton Becton and Warren Odze are teasing Zev Katz about something that seems to be confidential. I think musicians on the road must be just a little mad. I think I'm a little mad. It's a fragmented life, the life of a gypsy. These musicians are talented, and I tell them so. They leave at seven-thirty, and I begin warming up my voice. I do scales, I say clear vowels, run the voice up and down, a clear *Ah*. I warm up for a half-hour, and by the end of that time I have on my lipstick and my stage clothes, my hair combed out. My energy is high and I am eager to be on stage, doing tonight what I have trained all my life to do.

he moment when I step from the wings onto the stage is a sacred time, a spiritual journey in which I plunge into an air of lightness, made of the energy of myself and the audience. The audience wants everything, and they deserve everything. They have been there for me from the first night at Michael's Pub, sitting in the dark, waiting to have their lives changed, touched. They have sat in the dark and stood in the rain, marched with me, cried and laughed with me; they greet what I bring them with willingness, never holding back when I have changed again and gone in a new direction. They have grown up and had children and brought their children to hear me—an audience dressed in blue jeans, dressed in silk. They have supported me, bought my records, written letters to me saying that I have changed their lives. They have changed mine. One must not take a night of singing for granted, for the gods may be jealous and take it away. I have my set of rituals and prayers: God, make me good, bless my audience, let me be an instrument. I bring everything I have studied to be and everything I am onto the stage. I am as vulnerable and as prepared as I can possibly be.

When I walk out onto the stage, the audience is usually invisible beyond the footlights: in the shock of light they see me, but I cannot see them. I depend upon hearing and feeling who they are and what they are willing to bring to me tonight. I learned from my father on those nights when I watched him on-stage in cities like Fargo and Butte and Carson City how to sense an audience without seeing them. I learned how to perform at the feet of a master dreamer and gypsy, and now I, too, go on, hauling my bags and my guitar and myself from hotel room to hotel room, from city to city, living out his dream for the joy of these moments on-stage when the actual becomes the mystical.

I stand on the stage in bright, bright light. I am singing "Shoot First," a song I wrote with Dave Grusin about violence and a child's game played in the park by two children. There is electronic music in the background, sirens and bombs, and then a lament by Thomas Moore, "The Minstrel Boy." If the audience is to go through an inner transformation during each song, I must go through it myself, and it is at this point that we are the same, the audience and I. Even from behind the bright lights, I can begin to see the faces, the eyes, the smiles, and I take energy from every pair of eyes. In the carbon arc light I am by myself, and the audience is out there, but we are together, united. I must make the song as fresh and familiar as though the audience knew it by heart, yet was hearing it for the very first time.

When I sing "My Father," sitting at the piano, very often my eyes are closed, and I think of the vivid details of the song—the Seine, the girls dancing in the light of a dying summer day, chiffon curtains ironed by my mother's hand blowing into the room, drifting in and out, breathing through the windows.

Tonight I am energized. Light as an eagle, I am flying. On-stage, in the bright light of the carbon arc, sometimes I am Piaf, scrawny arms and a black silhouette; sometimes I am Peter Allen in sequins and silk; sometimes John McCormack's spirit comes over me, a clear Irish tenor in tails. I am all of them, none of them; I am myself. I am a singer alone on an empty stage—no guitar, no mike stand—singing a song a capella from the whalers of the Scottish coast. I sing about the work they did, and the voices of the singing humpbacked whales, played on a tape, fill the auditorium. (In their poignant, calling voices you can hear the slap of the tails on the water and the wind in the big sails of the little ships that followed the Greenland, right, and humpbacked whales from Bermuda to Alaska and back again to Newfoundland.) Now, I am a lovestruck girl with just a guitar telling a story about a rodeo rider and how I would follow him anywhere. Then I sing "Marieke" in Flemish and French. At the piano I then accompany myself and sing in English the story of houses and lovers, then a song by Randy Newman. I love being funny on-stage. I love making people laugh and cry. I am the clown, I am the hero, I am all of these, none of these, I am the music. . . .

Off-stage, lights off, the show over, snowdrift and ice slush under my black high heel shoes (Where are my purple boots now that I need them!), we pack up the gear and change clothes. Maria has everything together now, Halliburtons packed, clothes in the hanging bags. The promoter comes to pick up the Halliburtons. He is absolutely deadpan and sad as he tells me it was a "lovelyshow." I wish he had let me revel in my own excitement instead of almost deflating me with his sullen mood. I am flying, and he sounds like he is on Quaaludes. Tomorrow he has a wrestling team coming in to Fargo.

Back at the Holiday Inn, one of the old motels with a courtyard square in the center, the swimming pool is full of snow, the doors to the rooms opening onto the snow-patched path. In the trees, sleeping birds are stacked, piled, layered. They are roused and begin to chirp and flutter as we pass them on the way to our rooms. I dump my sheepskin coat and my heavy purse, kiss Maria goodnight, and then I'm on the phone, cotton in my other hand, taking off makeup while I dial New York and Connecticut and wonder where is Louis, why isn't he in? It's late, what can he possibly be doing? I know he went out to dinner tonight with David Braun and Irene Cara. Did he fall in love with Irene Cara—fly the coop?

I try the number again and reach him before I go to sleep. It's so good to hear his voice.

Octopussy on the tube, then a chapter of St. Augustine in paperback. Life on the road. . . .

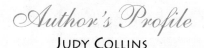

JUDY COLLINS

*T*hough best known as a folk singer, Judy Collins has also been a songwriter, social activist, film producer, and director. Her career has lasted more than 30 years.

Born in Seattle, Washington, on May 1, 1939, Judy Majorie Collins studied classical piano under Dr. Antonia Brica in Denver, Colorado, as a teenager. She switched her musical focus to folk songs in the late 1950s. Since the early 1960s, she has recorded more than 20 albums of folk and protest songs and romantic ballads, many of her own composition. At the same time, she was actively involved in African-American voter registration in the South and in the Vietnam War protest movement.

Collins produced and codirected a documentary, *Antonia: Portrait of a Woman* (1974), a tribute to Dr. Brica, her childhood piano teacher. The film was awarded a Blue Ribbon by the American Film Festival and was also nominated for an Academy Award. In 1987, she published her autobiography, *Trust Your Heart.*

Collins continues to write songs and perform. She also maintains her activism on a number of social issues.

Darkness At Noon

BY HAROLD KRENTS

ANTICIPATING: Write an account of a time in your life when you were misjudged. Were you ever treated as if you were incapable of doing something when that was not the case? Were you passed over for a part in a play? Were you put down because of your size or age? Describe how you felt and what your reaction was.

lind from birth, I have never had the opportunity to see myself and have been completely dependent on the image I create in the eye of the observer. To date it has not been narcissistic. 📖 There are those who assume that since I can't see, I obviously also cannot hear. Very often people will converse with me at the top of their lungs, enunciating each word very carefully. Conversely, people will also often whisper, assuming that since my eyes don't work, my ears don't either. 📖 For example, when I go to the airport and ask the ticket agent for assistance to the plane, he or she will invariably pick up the phone, call a ground hostess and whisper: "Hi, Jane, we've got a 76 here." I have concluded that the word "blind" is not used for one of two reasons: Either they fear that if the dread word is spoken, the ticket agent's retina will immediately detach, or they are reluctant to inform me of my condition of which I may not have been previously aware. 📖

On the other hand, others know that of course I can hear, but believe that I can't talk. Often, therefore, when my wife and I go out to dinner, a waiter or waitress will ask Kit if "*he* would like a drink" to which I respond that "indeed *he* would."

This point was graphically driven home to me while we were in England. I had been given a year's leave of absence from my Washington law firm to study for a diploma in law degree at Oxford University. During the year I became ill and was hospitalized. Immediately after admission, I was wheeled down to the X-ray room. Just at the door sat an elderly woman—elderly I would judge from the sound of her voice. "What is his name?" the woman asked the orderly who had been wheeling me.

"What's your name?" the orderly repeated to me.

"Harold Krents," I replied.

"Harold Krents," he repeated.

"When was he born?"

"When were you born?"

"Nov. 5, 1944," I responded.

"Nov. 5, 1944," the orderly intoned.

This procedure continued for approximately five minutes at which point even my saint-like disposition deserted me. "Look," I finally blurted out, "this is absolutely ridiculous. Okay, granted I can't see, but it's got to have become pretty clear to both of you that I don't need an interpreter."

"He says he doesn't need an interpreter," the orderly reported to the woman.

The toughest misconception of all is the view that because I can't see, I can't work. I was turned down by over forty law firms because of my blindness, even though my qualifications included a cum laude degree from Harvard College and a good ranking in my Harvard Law School class.

The attempt to find employment, the continuous frustration of being told that it was impossible for a blind person to practice law, the rejection letters, not based on my lack of ability but rather on my disability, will always remain one of the most disillusioning experiences of my life.

Fortunately, this view of limitation and exclusion is beginning to change. On April 16, the Department of Labor issued regulations that mandate equal-employment opportunities for the handicapped. By and large, the business community's response to offering employment to the disabled has been enthusiastic.

I therefore look forward to the day, with the expectation that it is certain to come, when employers will view their handicapped workers as a little child did me years ago when my family still lived in Scarsdale.

I was playing basketball with my father in our backyard according to procedures we had developed. My father would stand beneath the hoop, shout, and I would shoot over his head at the basket attached to our garage.

Our next-door neighbor, aged five, wandered over into our yard with a play-mate. "He's blind," our neighbor whispered to her friend in a voice that could be heard distinctly by Dad and me. Dad shot and missed. I did the same. Dad hit the rim. I missed entirely. Dad shot and missed the garage entirely. "Which one is blind?" whispered back the little friend.

I would hope that in the near future when a plant manager is touring the factory with the foreman and comes upon a handicapped and nonhandi-capped person working together, his comment after watching them work will be, "Which one is disabled?"

Author's Profile
HAROLD KRENTS

Harold Krents (1943-1987) was blind from childhood. He was educated at Harvard, both for undergraduate studies and in the school of law, graduating in 1970. He did graduate work at Oxford University as well. Returning to the United States, he was admitted to the Bar of New York State, practicing law in New York and Washington, D.C. In 1972, he wrote his autobiography, *To Race the Wind* (Putnam), which was later adapted for a television movie.

Krents was an avid advocate of rights for the disabled, serving on the President's Committee on Employment of the Handicapped. He also served as a consultant to the Vera Institute of Justice until shortly before his death. In 1975, he helped establish an organization to work for the legal rights of the handicapped, Mainstream, Inc.

Krents said, "I am the prototype for the main character of Leonard Gershe's play *Butterflies Are Free.*" The play tells the story of a young blind man living alone in a big city. In 1987, Krents died of a brain tumor in New York at the age of 44.

Shooting An Elephant

BY GEORGE ORWELL

ANTICIPATING: Discuss or write about a time when you had to do something that you really didn't want to do. Tell the story, but be sure to include any lessons or insights that you gained as a result of this incident.

I n Moulmein, in lower Burma, I was hated by large numbers of people—the only time in my life that I have been important enough for this to happen to me. I was sub-divisional police officer of the town, and in an aimless, petty kind of way anti-European feeling was very bitter. No one had the guts to raise a riot, but if a European woman went through the bazaars alone somebody would probably spit betel juice over her dress. As a police officer I was an obvious target and was baited whenever it seemed safe to do so. When a nimble Burman tripped me up on the football field and the referee (another Burman) looked the other way, the crowd yelled with hideous laughter. This happened more than once. In the end the sneering yellow faces of young men that met me everywhere, the insults hooted after me when I was at a safe distance, got badly on my nerves. The young Buddhist priests were the worst of all. There were several thousands of them in the town and none of them seemed to have anything to do except stand on street corners and jeer at Europeans. All this was perplexing and upsetting. For at that time I had already made up my mind that imperialism was an evil thing and the sooner I chucked up my job and got out of it the better. Theoretically—and secretly, of course—I was all for the Burmese and all against their oppressors, the British. As for the job I was doing, I hated it more bitterly than I can perhaps make clear. In a job like that you see the dirty work of Empire at close quarters. The wretched prisoners huddling in the stinking cages of the lock-ups, the gray, cowed faces of the long-term convicts, the scarred buttocks of the men who had been flogged with bamboos—all these oppressed me with an intolerable sense of guilt. But I could get nothing into perspective. I was young and ill educated and I had had to think out my problems in the utter silence that is imposed on every Englishman in the East. I did not even know that the British Empire is dying, still less did I know that it is a great deal better than the younger empires that are going to supplant it. All I knew was that I was stuck between my hatred of the empire I served and my rage against the evil-spirited little beast who tried to make my job impossible. With one part of my mind I thought of the British Raj as an unbreakable tyranny, as something clamped down, in *saecula saeculorum*, upon the will of prostrate peoples; with another part I thought that the greatest joy in the world would be to drive a bayonet into a Buddhist priest's gut. Feelings like these are the normal by-products of imperialism; ask any Anglo-Indian official, if you catch him off duty. 📖 One day something happened which in a roundabout way was enlightening. It was a tiny incident in itself, but it gave me a better glimpse than I had had before of the real nature of imperialism—the real motives for which despotic governments act. Early one morning the sub-inspector at a police station the other end of the town rang me up on the 'phone and said that an elephant was ravaging the bazaar. Would I please come and do something about it? I did not know what I could do, but I wanted to see what was happening and I got on to a pony and started out. I took my rifle, an old .44 Winchester and much too small to kill an elephant, but I thought the noise might be useful *in terrorem*. Various Burmans stopped me on the way and told me about the elephant's doing. It was not, of course, a wild elephant, but a tame one which had gone "must." It had been chained up, as tame elephants always are when their attack of "must" is due, but on the previous night it had broken its chain and escaped. Its mahout, the only person who can manage it when it was in that state, had set out in pursuit, but had taken the wrong direction and was now twelve hours' journey away, and in the morning the elephant had suddenly appeared in the town. The Burmese population had no weapons and were quite helpless against it. It had already destroyed somebody's bamboo hut, killed a cow and raided some fruit-stalls and devoured the stock; also it had met the municipal rubbish van and, when the driver jumped out and took to his heels, had turned the van over and inflicted violences upon it.

 he Burmese sub-inspector and some Indian constables were waiting for me in the quarter where the elephant had been seen. It was a very poor quarter, a labyrinth of squalid bamboo huts, thatched with palm-leaf, winding all over a steep hill-side. I remember that it was a cloudy, stuffy morning at the beginning of the rains. We began questioning the people as to where the elephant had gone and, as usual, failed to get any definite information. That is invariably the case in the East; a story always sounds clear enough at a distance, but the nearer you get to the scene of the events the vaguer it becomes. Some of the people said that the elephant had gone in one direction, some said that he had gone in another, some professed not even to have heard of any elephant. I had almost made up my mind that the whole story was a pack of lies, when we heard yells a little distance away. There was a loud, scandalized cry of "Go away, child! Go away this instant!" and an old woman with a switch in her hand came round the corner of a hut, violently shooing away a crowd of naked children. Some more women followed, clicking their tongues and exclaiming; evidently there was, something that the children ought not to have seen. I rounded the hut and saw a man's dead body sprawling in the mud. He was an Indian, a black Dravidian coolie, almost naked, and he could not have been dead many minutes. The people said that the elephant had come suddenly upon him round the corner of the hut, caught him with its trunk, put its foot on his back and ground him into the earth. This was the rainy season and the ground was soft, and his face had scored a trench a foot deep and a couple of yards long. He was lying on his belly with arms crucified and head sharply twisted to one side. His face was coated with mud, the eyes wide open, the teeth bared and grinning with an expression of unendurable agony. (Never tell me, by the way, that the dead look peaceful. Most of the corpses I have seen looked devilish.) The friction of the great beast's foot had stripped the skin from his back as neatly as one skins a rabbit. As soon as I saw the dead man I sent an orderly to a friend's house nearby to borrow an elephant rifle. I had already sent back the pony, not wanting it to go mad with fright and throw me if it smelt the elephant.

The orderly came back in a few minutes with a rifle and five cartridges, and meanwhile some Burmans had arrived and told us that the elephant was in the paddy fields below, only a few hundred yards away. As I started forward practically the whole population of the quarter flocked out of the houses and followed me. They had seen the rifle and were all shouting excitedly that I was going to shoot the elephant. They had not shown much interest in the elephant when he was ravaging their homes, but it was different now that he was going to be shot. It was a bit of fun to them, as it would be to an English crowd; besides they wanted the meat. It made me vaguely uneasy. I had no intention of shooting the elephant—I had merely sent for the rifle to defend myself if necessary—and it is always unnerving to have a crowd following you. I marched down the hill, looking and feeling a fool, with the rifle over my shoulder and an ever-growing army of people jostling at my heels. At the bottom, when you got away from the huts, there was a metalled road and beyond that a miry waste of paddy fields a thousand yards across, not yet ploughed but soggy from the first rains and dotted with coarse grass. The elephant was standing eight yards from the road, his left side toward us. He took not the slightest notice of the crowd's approach. He was tearing up bunches of grass, beating them against his knees to clean them, and stuffing them into his mouth.

I had halted on the road. As soon as I saw the elephant I knew with perfect certainty that I ought not to shoot him. It is a serious matter to shoot a working elephant—it is comparable to destroying a huge and costly piece of machinery—and obviously one ought not to do it if it can possibly be avoided.

And at that distance, peacefully eating, the elephant looked no more dangerous than a cow. I thought then and I think now that his attack of "must" was already passing off; in which case he would merely wander harmlessly about until the mahout came back and caught him. Moreover, I did not in the least want to shoot him. I decided that I would watch him for a little while to make sure that he did not turn savage again, and then go home.

ut at that moment I glanced round at the crowd that had followed me. It was an immense crowd, two thousand at the least and growing every minute. It blocked the road for a long distance on either side. I looked at the sea of yellow faces above the garish clothes—faces all happy and excited over this bit of fun, all certain that the elephant was going to be shot. They were watching me as they would watch a conjurer about to perform a trick. They did not like me, but with the magical rifle in my hands I was momentarily worth watching. And suddenly I realized that I should have to shoot the elephant after all. The people expected it of me and I had got to do it; I could feel their two thousand wills pressing me forward, irresistibly. And it was at this moment, as I stood there with the rifle in my hands, that I first grasped the hollowness, the futility of the white man's dominion in the East. Here was I, the white man with his gun, standing in front of the unarmed native crowd—seemingly the leading actor of the piece; but in reality I was only an absurd puppet pushed to and fro by the will of those yellow faces behind. I perceived in this moment that when the white man turns tyrant it is his own freedom that he destroys. He becomes a sort of hollow, posing dummy, the conventionalized figure of a sahib. For it is the condition of his rule that he shall spend his life in trying to impress the "natives," and so in every crisis he has got to do what the "natives" expect of him. He wears a mask, and his face grows to fit it. I had got to shoot the elephant. I had committed myself to doing it when I sent for the rifle. A sahib has got to act like a sahib; he has got to appear resolute, to know his own mind and do definite things. To come all that way, rifle in hand, with two thousand people marching at my heels, and then to trail feebly away, having done nothing—no, that was impossible. The crowd would laugh at me. And my whole life, every white man's life in the East, was one long struggle not to be laughed at.

But I did not want to shoot the elephant. I watched him beating his bunch of grass against his knees with that preoccupied grandmotherly air that elephants have. It seemed to me that it would be murder to shoot him. At that age I was not squeamish about killing animals, but I had never shot an elephant and never wanted to. (Somehow it always seems worse to kill a *large* animal.) Besides, there was the beast's owner to be considered. Alive, the elephant was worth at least a hundred pounds; dead, he would only be worth the value of his tusks, five pounds, possibly. But I had got to act quickly. I turned to some experienced-looking Burmans who had been there when we arrived, and asked them how the elephant had been behaving. They all said the same thing: he took no notice of you if you left him alone, but he might charge if you went too close to him.

It was perfectly clear to me what I ought to do. I ought to walk up to within, say, twenty-five yards of the elephant and test his behavior. If he charged, I could shoot; if he took no notice of me, it would be safe to leave him until the mahout came back. But also I knew that I was going to do no such thing. I was a poor shot with a rifle and the ground was soft mud into which one would sink at every step. If the elephant charged and I missed him, I should have about as much chance as a toad under a steam-roller. But even then I was not thinking particularly of my own skin, only of the watchful yellow faces behind. For at that moment, with the crowd watching me, I was not afraid in the ordinary sense, as I would have been if I had been alone. A white man mustn't be frightened in front of "natives"; and so, in general, he isn't frightened. The sole thought in my mind was that if anything went wrong those two thousand Burmans would see me pursued, caught, trampled on, and reduced to a grin-ning corpse like that Indian up the hill. And if that happened it was quite proba-ble that some of them would laugh. That would never do. There was only one alternative. I shoved the cartridges into the magazine and lay down on the road to get a better aim.

The crowd grew very still, and a deep, low, happy sigh, as of peo-ple who see the theater curtain go up at last, breathed from innumerable throats. They were going to have their bit of fun after all. The rifle was a beautiful Ger-man thing with cross-hair sights. I did not then know that in shooting an elephant one would shoot to cut an imaginary bar running from ear-hole to ear-hole. I ought, therefore, as the elephant was sideways on, to have aimed straight at his ear-hole; actually I aimed several inches in front of this, thinking the brain would be further forward.

When I pulled the trigger I did not hear the bang or feel the kick—one never does when a shot goes home—but I heard the devilish roar of glee that went up from the crowd. In that instant, in too short a time, one would have thought, even for the bullet to get there, a mysterious, terrible change had come over the elephant. He neither stirred nor fell, but every line of his body had altered. He looked suddenly stricken, shrunken, immensely old, as though the frightful impact of the bullet had paralyzed him without knocking him down. At last, after what seemed a long time—it might have been five seconds, I dare say—he sagged flabbily to his knees. His mouth slobbered. An enormous senility seemed to have settled upon him. One could have imagined him thousands of years old. I fired again into the same spot. At the second shot he did not collapse but climbed with desperate slowness to his feet and stood weakly upright, with legs sagging and head drooping. I fired a third time. That was the shot that did for him. You could see the agony of it jolt his whole body and knock the last remnant of strength from his legs. But in falling he seemed for a moment to rise, for as his hind legs collapsed beneath him he seemed to tower upward like a huge rock toppling, his trunk reaching skyward like a tree. He trumpeted, for the first and only time. And then down he came, his belly toward me, with a crash that seemed to shake the ground even where I lay.

 got up. The Burmans were already racing past me across the mud. It was obvious that the elephant would never rise again, but he was not dead. He was breathing very rhythmically with long rattling gasps, his ground mound of a side painfully rising and falling. His mouth was wide open—I could see far down into caverns of pale pink throat. I waited a long time for him to die, but his breathing did not weaken. Finally I fired my two remaining shots into the spot where I thought his heart must be. The thick blood welled out of him like red velvet, but still he did not die. His body did not even jerk when the shots hit him, the tortured breathing continued without a pause. He was dying, very slowly and in great agony, but in some world remote from me where not even a bullet could damage him further. I felt that I had got to put an end to that dreadful noise. It seemed dreadful to see the great beast lying there, powerless to move and yet powerless to die, and not even to be able to finish him. I sent back for my small rifle and poured shot after shot into his heart and down his throat. They seemed to make no impression. The tortured gasps continued as steadily as the ticking of a clock.

In the end I could not stand it any longer and went away. I heard later that it took him half an hour to die. Burmans were bringing dahs and baskets even before I left, and I was told they had stripped his body almost to the bones by the afternoon.

Afterward, of course, there were endless discussions about the shooting of the elephant. The owner was furious, but he was only an Indian and could do nothing. Besides, legally I had done the right thing, for a mad elephant has to be killed, like a mad dog, if its owner fails to control it. Among the Europeans opinion was divided. The older men said I was right, the younger men said it was a damn shame to shoot an elephant for killing a coolie, because an elephant was worth more than any damn Coringhee coolie. And afterward I was very glad that the coolie had been killed; it put me legally in the right and it gave me a sufficient pretext for shooting the elephant. I often wondered whether any of the others grasped that I had done it solely to avoid looking like a fool.

Author's Profile
George Orwell

George Orwell, the pen name of Eric Blair, has emerged as one of the most original and eloquent voices of modern times, both in his criticism of authoritarian governments and in his demand for clarity and accuracy in written and spoken language.

Born in Motihari, India, in 1903, George Orwell was the son of British-born members of the Indian Civil Service. Orwell was educated at Britain's Eton College and later joined the Indian Imperial Police in Burma in the early 1920s. Burma was to provide important material for both his 1936 essay "Shooting an Elephant" and his 1934 novel *Burmese Days*.

After leaving Burma, he recorded his life of self-imposed poverty in his nonfiction book *Down and Out in Paris and London* (1933). Also during the 1930s, Orwell published a number of novels, including *A Clergyman's Daughter* (1935) and *Coming Up for Air* (1939). He criticized political and academic writing in the essay "Politics and the English Language" (1936). He studied and objectively described the lives of poverty-stricken English miners in *The Road to Wigan Pier* (1937), and a year later recounted his experiences fighting against Franco's fascist forces in the Spanish Civil War in *Homage to Catalonia* (1938). In the 1940s, he published the works for which he is best remembered today: the novels *Animal Farm* (1945) and *1984* (1949).

Orwell was a strong critic of dictatorial governments, whether of the communist left in Russia or the fascist right in Germany and Spain, and of pompous and fuzzy bureaucratic jargon, all of which he sternly ridiculed in his novels and essays. Writing in *Time* (November 28, 1984), Paul Gray further noted about Orwell:

> *His greatest accomplishment was to remind people that they could think for themselves, at a time in this century when humanity seemed to prefer taking marching orders. He steadfastly valued ideals over ideology.*

Orwell died of tuberculosis on January 21, 1950, in London.

The Indian Basket

BY MICKEY ROBERTS

ANTICIPATING: Write and/or discuss a trade you have made, either in the past as a child or more recently. Maybe you traded some item for another or traded space like a bedroom with a brother or sister. How did you measure the values of each? What kind of deal did you make? How difficult was the decision? Do you feel the trade was fair on both sides?

he year was 1988, a bitterly cold morning in early winter. I held the small Indian basket, beautiful and artistic in the distinctive Native American tradition. It was clearly no copy of an Indian basket—it was the real thing and I did not have to be told that it was authentic. The basket was laid out on a table at a garage sale and the ticket said it was for sale for $250. I inquired of the owner as to who had made the basket and was told it was made by "The Thompson River Tribe." The owner went on to say the basket was well worth the money, for the Indians no longer made these works of art. I did not satisfy an urge to ask if tribes made baskets, for, being fair to the man, he could not have known the name of the Indian artist when it had never been asked for in the first place!

As I stood holding the basket, I remembered a bitterly cold day in the year 1939. It was the beginning of the winter season. We walked the streets of Bellingham— my mother, my great-grandmother, and me. We were selling Indian baskets. I was a very small girl and I kept saying I wanted to go home but my mother kept saying, ". . . just one more house."

We all carried baskets—large ones, small ones, round ones, square ones. Some of them were rectangular, with perfectly fitted covers, which were designed to be used as picnic baskets. How many hours of hard labor these baskets represented for my grandmother who could speak only in her native tongue! My grandmother had worked hard all her life and she had raised many children and had also raised my mother, who was her granddaughter. Somehow she had survived the changes that life had forced upon her with the changing life in a different culture.

At each house my mother would ask the occupant to look at the Indian baskets and suggest a price of a few articles of used clothing. If the woman of the house decided to look at the baskets and bring out some clothing she didn't want, the bargaining would begin. As in the case of our tribe's treaty, two generations earlier, the main decision would be at the discretion of the newcomer, and many hours of labor would go for a few shirts or dresses.

These days the price of Indian baskets is very high, and they are mostly owned by non-Indians. These treasures, obtained at less than bargain basement prices, are now being sold at premium prices, if they are obtainable at all. They are collector's items, but the name of the person who labored to make them is rarely known.

As we peddled our treasures in those early years, we probably appeared to be a pitiful people. We were, however, living in as dignified a manner as possible while selling a part of our culture for a few articles of used clothing.

We really hadn't much left to give.

Author's Profile
Mickey Roberts

Mickey Roberts is a freelance writer of Indian history from the state of Washington. A descendant of one of the original Nooksack Indian families, she continues to live on ancestral lands which have never been owned outside the tribe.

As director of the Nooksack Community Center, Roberts established a landbase which allowed the tribe to gain federal recognition in 1971. She also participated in the writing of the Nooksack tribe's constitution. She is presently working on a local tribal history and has published two short stories.

Roberts and her husband adopted and raised four Korean and Indian children. She considers this the principal achievement in her life. She expects to spend the rest of her life compiling her research and writing about her rich cultural heritage.

The Boy and the Bank Officer

BY PHILIP ROSS

ANTICIPATING: As a young person, have you ever experienced a negative attitude from a store clerk? Have you been ignored as a customer because you were young? Describe the situation and how you felt at the time.

 have a friend who hates banks with a special passion. "A bank is just a store like a candy store or a grocery store," he says, "except that a bank's merchandise happens to be money which is yours in the first place. If banks were required to sell wallets and money belts, they might act less like churches." I began thinking about my friend the other day as I walked into a small, overlighted branch office on the West Side. I had come to open a checking account. It was lunch time, and the only officer on duty was a fortyish black man with short, pressed hair; a pencil mustache; and a neatly pressed brown suit. Everything about him suggested a carefully groomed authority, an eager determination to define himself through his vaulted surroundings.

This officer was standing across a small counter from a young white boy who was wearing a crew-neck sweater, khakis, and loafers. He had sandy hair, and I think I was especially aware of him because he looked like he belonged more on the campus of a New England prep school than in a West Side bank.

The boy continued to hold my attention because of what happened next.

He was clutching an open savings-account book and wearing an expression of open dismay. "But I don't understand," he was saying to the officer. "I opened the account myself, so why can't I withdraw any money?"

"I've already explained to you," the officer told him, "that bank regulations prohibit someone who is fourteen years old from withdrawing any funds without a letter from his parents."

"But that doesn't seem fair," the boy said, his voice breaking. "It's my money. I put it in. It's my account."

"I know it is," the officer said, "but those are the rules. Now if you'll excuse me."

He turned to me with a smile. "May I help you, sir?"

I didn't think twice. "I was going to open a new account," I said, "but after seeing what's going on here, I think I've changed my mind."

"Excuse me?" he said.

"Look," I said, "if I understand what's going on here correctly, what you're saying is that this boy is old enough to deposit his money in your bank but he's not old enough to withdraw it. And since there doesn't seem to be any question as to whether it's his money or his account, the bank's so-called policy is patently ridiculous."

"It may seem ridiculous to you," he replied in a voice rising slightly in irritation, "but that is the bank's policy, and I have no alternative but to abide by the rules."

The boy had stood hopefully next to me during this exchange, but now I was reduced to his helplessness. Suddenly I noticed that the open savings book he continued to grasp showed a balance of about $100. It also showed that there had been a series of small deposits and withdrawals.

I had my opening.

"Have you withdrawn money before by yourself?" I asked the boy.

"Yes," he said.

I moved in for the kill.

"How do you explain that away?" I zeroed in on the officer. "Why did you let him withdraw money before but not now?"

He looked exasperated. "Because the tellers were not aware of his age before, and now they are. It's really very simple."

I turned to the boy with a pained shrug. "You're really getting ripped off," I said. "You ought to get your parents to come in here and protest."

The boy looked destroyed. Silently, he put his savings book in a rear pocket and walked out of the bank.

The officer turned to me. "You know," he said, "you really shouldn't have interfered."

"Shouldn't have interfered?" I shouted. "Well, it damn well seemed to me that he needed someone to represent his interests."

"Someone was representing his interests," he said softly.

"And who might that be?"

"The bank."

I couldn't believe what this idiot was saying. "Look," I concluded, "we're just wasting each other's time. But maybe you'd like to explain exactly how the bank was representing that boy's interests?"

ertainly," he said. "We were informed this morning that some neighborhood punk has been shaking this boy down for more than a month. The other guy was forcing him to take money out every week and hand it over. The poor kid was apparently too scared to tell anyone. That's the real reason he was so upset. He was afraid of what the other guy would do to him. Anyway, the police are on the case and they'll probably make an arrest today."

Uh.

"You mean there is no rule about being too young to withdraw funds from a savings account?"

"Not that I ever heard of. Now, sir, what can we do for you?"

Author's Profile
PHILIP ROSS

A former reporter and now freelance writer, Philip Ross finds his nonfiction subjects on the streets of New York and New Jersey.

Born in New York on June 29, 1939, Ross graduated from Princeton University in 1961, and received his master's degree a year later from Columbia. He worked as a reporter in New Jersey and New York from 1962 to 1965, as a freelance writer from 1965 to 1972, and in public relations for the Children's Television Workshop from 1972 to 1973. Since 1973, he has been a full-time writer, working on screenplays and television scripts.

In 1976, Ross wrote *The Bribe*, an account of his younger brother Burt, who as mayor of Fort Lee, New Jersey, was offered a $500,000 bribe to obtain special permission for the construction of a shopping center in a noncommercially zoned area. Burt Ross reported the bribery attempt to the F.B.I. He cooperated in an F.B.I. "sting" operation that led to the conviction of seven businessmen with ties to organized crime.

When asked why he chose freelance writing as a career, Ross remarked, "I write because it's what I seem to do best. It's a tough way to make a living."

Of Dry Goods and Black Bow Ties

BY YOSHIKO UCHIDA

ANTICIPATING: Write about a sudden change in your life or a sudden loss of a person or item you treasure. Tell the details of the situation and your feelings about the loss.

ong after reaching the age of sixty, when my father was persuaded at last to wear a conservative four-in-hand tie, it was not because of his family's urging, but because Mr. Shimada (I shall call him that) had died. Until then, for some forty years, my father had always worn a plain black bow tie, a formality which was required on his first job in America and which he had continued to observe as faithfully as his father before him had worn his samurai sword. My father came to America in 1906 when he was not yet twenty-one. Sailing from Japan on a small six-thousand-ton ship which was buffeted all the way by rough seas, he landed in Seattle on a bleak January day. He revived himself with the first solid meal he had enjoyed in many days, and then allowed himself one day of rest to restore his sagging spirits. Early on the second morning, wearing a stiff new bowler, he went to see Mr. Shozo Shimada to whom he carried a letter of introduction. At that time, Shozo Shimada was Seattle's most successful Japanese business man. He owned a chain of dry goods stores which extended not only from Vancouver to Portland, but to cities in Japan as well. He had come to America in 1880, penniless but enterprising, and sought to work as a laborer. It wasn't long, however, before he saw the futility in trying to compete with American laborers whose bodies were twice his in muscle and bulk. He knew he would never go far as a laborer, but he did possess another skill that could give him a start toward better things. He knew how to sew. It was a matter of expediency over masculine pride. He set aside his shovel, and hung a dressmaker's sign in his window. He was in business. 📖

In those days, there were some Japanese women in Seattle who had neither homes nor sewing machines, and were delighted to find a friendly Japanese person to do some sewing for them. They flocked to Mr. Shimada with bolts of cloth, elated to discover a dressmaker who could speak their native tongue and, although a male, sew western-styled dresses for them.

Mr. Shimada acquainted himself with the fine points of turning a seam, fitting sleeves, and coping with the slippery folds of silk, and soon the women told their friends and gave him enough business to keep him thriving and able to establish a healthy bank account. He became a trusted friend and confidant to many of them and soon they began to bring him what money they earned for safekeeping.

"Keep our money for us, Shimada-san," they urged, refusing to go to American banks whose tellers spoke in a language they could not understand.

At first the money accumulated slowly and Mr. Shimada used a pair of old socks as a repository, stuffing them into a far corner of his drawer beneath his union suits. But after a time, Mr. Shimada's private bank began to overflow and he soon found it necessary to replenish his supply of socks.

He went to a small dry goods store downtown, and as he glanced about at the buttons, threads, needles and laces, it occurred to him that he owed it to the women to invest their savings in a business venture with more future than the dark recesses of his bureau drawer. That night he called a group of them together.

"Think, ladies." he began. "What are the two basic needs of the Japanese living in Seattle? Clothes to wear and food to eat," he answered himself. "Is that not right? Every man must buy a shirt to put on his back and pickles and rice for his stomach."

The women marveled at Mr. Shimada's cleverness as he spread before them his fine plans for a Japanese dry goods store that would not only carry everything available in an American dry goods store, but Japanese foodstuff as well. That was the beginning of the first Shimada Dry Goods Store on State Street.

By the time my father appeared, Mr. Shimada had long since abandoned his sewing machine and was well on his way to becoming a business tycoon. Although he had opened cautiously with such stock items as ginghams, flannel, handkerchiefs, socks, shirts, overalls, umbrellas and ladies' silk and cotton stockings, he now carried tins of salt rice crackers, bottles of soy sauce, vinegar, ginger root, fish-paste cakes, bean paste, Japanese pickles, dried mushrooms, salt fish, red beans, and just about every item of canned food that could be shipped from Japan. In addition, his was the first Japanese store to install a U.S. Post Office Station, and he thereby attained the right to fly an American flag in front of the large sign that bore the name of his shop.

When my father first saw the big American flag fluttering in front of Mr. Shimada's shop, he was overcome with admiration and awe. He expected that Mr. Shozo Shimada would be the finest of Americanized Japanese gentlemen, and when he met him, he was not disappointed.

lthough Mr. Shimada was not very tall, he gave the illusion of height because of his erect carriage. He wore a spotless black alpaca suit, an immaculate white shirt and a white collar so stiff it might have overcome a lesser man. He also wore a black bow tie, black shoes that buttoned up the side and a gold watch whose thick chain looped grandly on his vest. He was probably in his fifties then, a ruddy-faced man whose hair, already turning white, was parted carefully in the center. He was an imposing figure to confront a young man fresh from Japan with scarcely a future to look forward to. My father bowed, summoned as much dignity as he could muster, and presented the letter of introduction he carried to him.

Mr. Shimada was quick to sense his need. "Do you know anything about bookkeeping?" he inquired.

"I intend to go to night school to learn this very skill," my father answered.

Mr. Shimada could assess a man's qualities in a very few minutes. He looked my father straight in the eye and said, "Consider yourself hired." Then he added, "I have a few basic rules. My employees must at all times wear a clean white shirt and a black bow tie. They must answer the telephone promptly with the words, 'Good morning or good afternoon, Shimada's Dry Goods,' and they must always treat each customer with respect. It never hurts to be polite," he said thoughtfully. "One never knows when one might be indebted to even the lowliest of beggars."

My father was impressed with these modest words from a man of such success. He accepted them with a sense of mission and from that day was committed to white shirts and black bow ties, and treated every customer, no matter how humble, with respect and courtesy. When, in later years, he had his own home, he never failed to answer the phone before it could ring twice if at all possible.

My father worked with Mr. Shimada for ten years, becoming first the buyer for his Seattle store and later, manager of the Portland branch. During this time Mr. Shimada continued on a course of exhilarated expansion. He established two Japanese banks in Seattle, bought a fifteen-room house outside the dreary confines of the Japanese community and dressed his wife and daughter in velvets and ostrich feathers. When his daughter became eighteen, he sent her to study in Paris, and the party he gave on the eve of her departure, hiring musicians, as well as caterers to serve roast turkey, venison, baked ham and champagne, seemed to verify rumors that he had become one of the first Japanese millionaires of America.

In spite of his phenomenal success, however, Mr. Shimada never forgot his early friends nor lost any of his generosity, and this, ironically enough, was his undoing. Many of the women for whom he had once sewn dresses were now well established, and they came to him requesting loans with which they and their husbands might open grocery stores and laundries and shoe repair shops. Mr. Shimada helped them all and never demanded any collateral. He operated his banks on faith and trust and gave no thought to such common prudence as maintaining a reserve.

When my father was called to a new position with a large Japanese firm in San Francisco, Mr. Shimada came down to Portland to extend personally his good wishes. He took Father to a Chinese dinner and told him over the peanut duck and chow mein that he would like always to be considered a friend.

"If I can ever be of assistance to you," he said, "don't ever hesitate to call." And with a firm shake of the hand, he wished my father well.

That was in 1916. My father wrote regularly to Mr. Shimada telling him of his new job, of his bride, and later, of his two children. Mr. Shimada did not write often, but each Christmas he sent a box of Oregon apples and pears, and at New Year's a slab of heavy white rice paste from his Seattle shop.

In 1929 the letters and gifts stopped coming, and Father learned from friends in Seattle that both of Mr. Shimada's banks had failed. He immediately dispatched a letter to Mr. Shimada, but it was returned unopened. The next news he had was that Mr. Shimada had had to sell all of his shops. My father was now manager of the San Francisco branch of his firm. He wrote once more asking Mr. Shimada if there was anything he could do to help. The letter did not come back, but there was no reply, and my father did not write again. After all, how do you offer help to the head of a fallen empire? It seemed almost irreverent.

It was many years later that Mr. Shimada appeared one night at our home in Berkeley. In the dim light of the front porch my mother was startled to see an elderly gentleman wearing striped pants, a morning coat and a shabby black hat. In his hand he carried a small black satchel. When she invited him inside, she saw that the morning coat was faded, and his shoes badly in need of a shine.

 am Shimada," he announced with a courtly bow, and it was my mother who felt inadequate to the occasion. She hurriedly pulled off her apron and went to call my father. When he heard who was in the living room, he put on his coat and tie before going out to greet his old friend.

Mr. Shimada spoke to them about Father's friends in Seattle and about his daughter who was now married and living in Denver. He spoke of a typhoon that had recently swept over Japan, and he drank the tea my mother served and ate a piece of her chocolate cake. Only then did he open his black satchel.

"I thought your girls might enjoy these books," he said, as he drew out a brochure describing *The Book of Knowledge*.

"Fourteen volumes that will tell them of the wonders of this world." He spread his arms in a magnificent gesture that recalled his eloquence of the past. "I wish I could give them to your children as a personal gift," he added softly.

Without asking the price of the set, my father wrote a check for one hundred dollars and gave it to Mr. Shimada.

Mr. Shimada glanced at the check and said, "You have given me fifty dollars too much." He seemed troubled for only a moment, however, and quickly added, "Ah, the balance is for a deposit, is it? Very well, yours will be the first deposit in my next bank."

"Is your home still in Seattle then?" Father asked cautiously.

"I am living there, yes," Mr. Shimada answered.

And then, suddenly overcome with memories of the past, he spoke in a voice so low he could scarcely be heard.

"I paid back every cent," he murmured. "It took ten years, but I paid it back. All of it. I owe nothing."

"You are a true gentleman, Shimada-san," Father said. "You always will be." Then he pointed to the black tie he wore, saying, "You see, I am still one of the Shimada men."

That was the last time my father saw Shozo Shimada. Some time later he heard that he had returned to Japan as penniless as the day he set out for America.

It wasn't until the Christmas after we heard of Mr. Shimada's death that I ventured to give my father a silk four-in-hand tie. It was charcoal gray and flecked with threads of silver. My father looked at it for a long time before he tried it on, and then fingering it gently, he said, "Well, perhaps it is time now that I put away my black bow ties."

Author's Profile
YOSHIKO UCHIDA

*P*rimarily known for her children's books, Yoshiko Uchida (pronounced "Oo-chee-dah") wrote juvenile and adult stories and articles which dealt with the Japanese-American experience in the United States.

Born in Alameda, California, on November 24, 1921, Uchida graduated with honors from the University of California at Berkeley in 1942. When her family was sent to a relocation center for Japanese-Americans during World War II, she became an elementary teacher at the camp. She received her master's degree in education from Smith College in 1944. Later, she worked as a secretary in order to have time to write after work.

Uchida's first book, *The Dancing Kettle and Other Japanese Folk Tales* (1949), was a series of stories she adapted for Americans, as was *The Magic Listening Cap—More Folk Tales from Japan* (1955). Other stories included *Friendship* (1957), *The Sea of Gold and Other Tales from Japan* (1965), and *The Birthday Visitor* (1975). She chronicled her family's World War II camp experiences in *Desert Exile: The Uprooting of a Japanese-American Family* (1981).

In a letter to the editors of the reference book *Contemporary Authors*, Uchida wrote:

> . . . I hope to give your Asian Americans a sense of their past and to reinforce their self-esteem and self-knowledge. At the same time, I want to dispel the stereotypic image still held by many non-Asians about the Japanese and write about them as real people . . . I want to celebrate our common humanity, for the basic elements of humanity are present in all our strivings.

Uchida died in Berkeley, California, on June 21, 1992.

Job Description

Perfection Is an Insult to the Gods
BY TRACY KIDDER

ANTICIPATING: Consider in your life what you do, either at work or leisure, that demands near perfection. Do you build models, sew, fly fish, bowl, or play an instrument? Do you perform chemistry experiments, dissect insects, balance books, count change, set type, tune engines, or balance tires? Write about a task you perform which demands exacting procedures.

ichard sits on a stack of two-by-tens, the one on which Jim presented his framing plan. The big pile of wood gives off a delicate aroma, like a woods with a pine-needle carpet. The stack makes a clean, fragrant, somewhat expensive picnic table for Richard. Sitting on it, feet dangling over the edge, he shakes his head over that day's Lindy cake, in order to ensure his partners' jealousy, and dislodges the pencil from behind his ear. It vanishes down a crack between the boards. "Whoops," says Richard, peering after it. "This pile just ate my pencil." The next day at lunchtime, Richard finds his pencil, on the ground, between two twelve-foot-long two-by-tens, which are all that remain of the pile.

Finish work never seems to end, but the frames of houses go up swiftly. And time passes quickly for Apple Corps when they're framing.

Ned stands on soggy, sandy ground and measures the distances between the bolts that protrude, threads up, out of the top of the foundation's gray walls, and Richard bores the necessary holes in a length of the two-by-six, pressure-treated southern pine. The board slips down right over the bolts. "The first piece of wood. Yaaay!" cries Richard. They install another piece of sill, then another, and then Ned says, "Wait a minute." The sills are sticking out over the edges of the foundation a little too far. Ned and Richard investigate. They measure the two-by-six lengths of pine, which are supposed to be five-and-a-half inches wide. These are five and five-eighths. Maybe they were sawn wrong. More likely, they sat outside and absorbed an eighth of an inch of water. Richard pulls the wood off the bolts. "We can't make this house thirty feet and a quarter inches right at the *start*," he says. They begin again. "It's just work," says Ned.

Observing this scene from the other side of the foundation, Jim nods approval. He says the difference between amateur and professional carpenters lies in the facts that pros make few mistakes and when they err they make corrections at once. Thus they prevent both brooding and remorse. Half an hour later, Jim drives a nail that splits a fresh piece of lumber, one he's spent some time cutting and installing. "This piece of wood just split from end to end," he says. He stares at the ruined board. Then he beats on it with his large framing hammer. But hadn't he said that a pro doesn't brood over an error? "That's right. But I never said you don't let it upset you." He wallops and wallops the board, tearing it along the grain. Jim smiles. He tosses the ruined wood aside. "I never said *that*. Send this back to the factory."

t's clear they do not like to leave mistakes behind. When Ned bends a nail, he withdraws that nail, pounds it straight again, and hammers it back in. Nails are cheap. Time costs the carpenters much more. But Ned seems interested not merely in correcting errors. He wants to erase them.

Each carpenter owns a short-handled crowbar with a rounded claw, known as a cat's paw. There's nothing like a cat's paw for extracting nails from mistakes. "What would a carpenter do without a cat's paw, Ned?"

"Buy one," Ned replies.

None of them carries his cat's paw, but each knows where it is. If he makes a mistake, he has to go and get the tool. They prepare for errors. They don't assume that errors will occur. When one of them does make a mistake, he usually blames it on whichever of the team happens to be absent or out of earshot at the moment.

"Oh, no!"

"Blame it on Jim."

For now, Jim usually gets the blame. Almost hourly it seems, he leaps over the trench near the foundation and trudges off up the hill, briefcase in hand, toward the phone in Jules Wiener's red horse barn, so he can call the lumberyard or a subcontractor or one of the utilities or Jonathan. Jim rarely accepts abuse without retorting, though. He makes a practice of signing his partners' mistakes. "Richard was here," he'll write in pencil on the wood at the sight of a withdrawn nail. In Apple Corps parlance, a carpenter gone sloppy is "a beaver," "a jabronie," or "a Hoople," and "thrashing" is the disjointed set of bad procedures that leads to "cobby" work or, worst of all, "a cob job." The last is a very old term. In one of its earliest meanings, *cob* meant a lump of something, and in medieval England to "build in cob" meant to make a house out of lumps of clay, earth, even manure. It was not thought to be a form of high-quality construction. "Cob job" probably came across the ocean with the first New England carpenters and has survived in such sanctuaries of the old-fashioned as the hilltowns. The term is more usual there than in the valley. The carpenters don't remember exactly when they first heard the expression, and they do not know its history, but it has the right pejorative sound for the kind of act that none wishes to be truly guilty of committing. When one of Apple Corps accuses another of thrashing or beavering or cobbing up some piece of work, he usually does so falsely, sometimes even in order to praise, but they also seem to be warning each other and themselves of the nearness of sin.

Usually, if one of them wants praise, he has to administer it himself. When Richard fixes a cobby piece of work, he "tunes it up" or he "fusses with it," and what comes out well is "custom," and for all of them a very good result is "perfect," "perfect enough," or "perfect or equal." And in nearly every case, a satisfactorily completed piece of the job is good enough for whatever town they happen to be working in, in this case, "good enough for Amherst."

"Close enough for Amherst," Ned pauses over his hammer to say. "It's a joke, but it's also a way of keeping perspective. Don't lose the building for the stick. You're always making value judgments, you know, about what's straight or plumb, but sooner or later you gotta nail it. You've got to have confidence it's right enough, or if it's not, that you can fix it."

On the second day of framing, the fourth partner, Alex Ghiselin, joins them. They set up, as they will every morning, a small factory beside the foundation:

generator, extension cords, ladders, sawhorses, electric and hand-driven saws. "Tooling up," as they call it, they buckle on belts and make themselves into roving hardware displays, hammers and numerous pouches hanging from their waists, red handkerchiefs in their back pockets, pencils behind their ears. Proper and efficient framing is the art of thinking ahead with clarity, of seeing the end in the beginning, and they have made the exercise of forethought, which is the opposite of thrashing, part of their daily routine in all departments of house-raising.

Alex is their cutter nonpareil. He likes nothing better than to get from Richard an order for thirty two-by-tens, all fifteen feet, five and three-eighths inches long. Alex writes down the numbers. He sets up the company's radial arm saw and the portable bench Jim once built for it. Then Alex measures that prescribed distance down the bench from the saw's blade and nails down a piece of wood at the spot. The end of each successive two-by-ten he'll place against this stop. It takes him a couple of minutes to set up the jig, but once it's done he can cut one board after another and measure only occasionally to make sure that nothing has moved.

henever they can, the carpenters assemble a portion of the frame out on the open ground, where they don't have to hang off ladders and there's room to swing their hammers freely. Then, standing on the foundation's walls and on stepladders, they install the construction, a section of floor joists, say, into its place within the frame. Most of the failures of most spare-time carpenters stem from misplaced haste. They haven't got much time. They want to see results at once. Apple Corps spends time now to save time later. It's a form of deferred gratification, which, the psychologists say, is the essence of true adulthood. Apple Corps has acquired the knack for looking calmly on the future. They always pause to remove any nails from boards they cast aside. The practice cuts down on tetanus shots. It was not always this way, but most of them have worked together for ten years now, and they have learned consideration.

Erecting girders, from stepladders set on the basement floor, Richard and Alex struggle to speak geometry. "Move it five-sixteenths that way. No, out that way, toward Pelham. No, up. Whoops. No, down. This sounds like *Sesame Street*," says Richard.

Richard climbs out of the cellar. He studies and restudies Jim's intricate framing plan. He does so out loud: "Oh, I'm being confused right now. That seems rather odd. Unh-hunh. Ohhhh. I see. I see what happened. Oh-Kay! Yup, right where it should be. Excellent. Just where it should be. Okay. Good." He adds, addressing Alex, "A *custom*-fit girder." Richard emits a guttural sound, which could imply some twisted pleasure.

"Nicely done," says Alex.

"Custom," says Richard. "I think we're winning."

When he is going well, Alex cuts lumber quickly and to within a thirty-second of an inch of the specified lengths. They attempt to keep their frame within about a sixteenth of an inch of perfection, which is about as accurate as their tape measures are, and more precise, in fact, than wood and weather allow. They work in sunshine and a few days into the framing, they even get their shirts off for a while. On the next day, a cold drizzle falls. Jim, who is responsible for worrying, measures the first floor's frame at the end of one sunny day and finds it jibes exactly with the numbers on his plan. Two rainy days later, he measures it again and finds that the bottom deck has grown a quarter of an inch along one wall and not at all along the others. They can easily rectify the discrepancy in the next level of the frame. Jim expected this to happen. He is not disappointed. He says again, "Perfection is an insult to the gods." They often speak about the fact of imperfection. The words must have a consoling ring for them.

Author's Profile
TRACY KIDDER

Tracy Kidder is a respected nonfiction writer whose books have ranged from murder to computers to construction to teaching. He thoroughly researches each writing project, spending large amounts of time almost becoming one with his subject.

Born in New York City on November 12, 1945, Kidder graduated from Harvard University in 1967, served in U.S. Army Intelligence in Vietnam and rose to the rank of lieutenant, and was awarded a Master of Fine Arts (M.F.A.) degree from the University of Iowa in 1974. Briefly experimenting with fiction, he won an Atlantic First Award from *Atlantic Monthly* for his short story "The Death of Major Great."

Since the early 1980s, he has worked in nonfiction. *The Road to Yuba City: A Journey into the Juan Corona Murders* (1974) tells the story of a Mexican labor contractor convicted of murdering 25 of his workers. *The Soul of a New Machine* (1981) chronicles the 18-month attempt of engineers at Data General Corporation to build a super mini-computer. *Among School Children* (1989) describes one year in the career of Holyoke, Massachusetts, elementary school teacher Chris Zajac and her attempts to deal with the different abilities, and social and ethnic backgrounds of her students.

In *House* (1985), Kidder tells the story of the building of a house in Massachusetts. In great detail, he describes the goals and aspirations of the home buyer, the architect, and the builders, and the relationships each establishes with the other two members of this complex triangle.

To Bid the World Farewell

BY JESSICA MITFORD

ANTICIPATING: Discuss or write about an activity that you feel qualified to describe. It can range from cooking a hamburger to changing a car's battery to putting a golf ball to flossing one's teeth. Try to describe this to someone who has no idea what this process involves. One simple rule: Take nothing for granted. List and describe both the equipment needed and the steps in the process.

mbalming is indeed a most extraordinary procedure, and one must wonder at the docility of Americans who each year pay hundreds of millions of dollars for its perpetuation, blissfully ignorant of what it is all about, what is done, how it is done. Not one in ten thousand has any idea of what actually takes place. Books on the subject are extremely hard to come by. They are not to be found in most libraries or bookshops. 📖 In an era when huge television audiences watch surgical operations in the comfort of their living rooms, when, thanks to the animated cartoon, the geography of the digestive system has become familiar territory even to the nursery school set, in a land where the satisfaction of curiosity about almost all matters is a national pastime, the secrecy surrounding embalming can, surely, hardly be attributed to the inherent gruesomeness of the subject. Custom in this regard has within this century suffered a complete reversal. In the early days of American embalming, when it was performed in the home of the deceased, it was almost mandatory for some relative to stay by the embalmer's side and witness the procedure. Today, family members who might wish to be in attendance would certainly be dissuaded by the funeral director. All others, except apprentices, are excluded by law from the preparation room. 📖 A close look at what does actually take place may explain in large measure the undertaker's intractable reticence concerning a procedure that has become his major *raison d'être*. Is it possible he fears that public information about embalming might lead patrons to wonder if they really want this service? If the funeral men are loath to discuss the subject outside the trade, the reader may, understandably, be equally loath to go on reading at this point. For those who have the stomach for it, let us part the formaldehyde curtain. . . . 📖

The body is first laid out in the undertaker's morgue—or rather, Mr. Jones is reposing in the preparation room—to be readied to bid the world farewell.

he preparation room in any of the better funeral establishments has the tiled and sterile look of a surgery, and indeed the embalmer-restorative artist who does his chores there is beginning to adopt the term "dermasurgeon" (appropriately corrupted by some mortician-writers as "demisurgeon") to describe his calling. His equipment, consisting of scalpels, scissors, augers, forceps, clamps, needles, pumps, tubes, bowls and basins, is crudely imitative of the surgeon's as is his technique, acquired in a nine- or twelve-month post-high-school course in an embalming school. He is supplied by an advanced chemical industry with a bewildering array of fluids, sprays, pastes, oils, powders, creams, to fix or soften tissue, shrink or distend it as needed, dry it here, restore the moisture there. There are cosmetics, waxes and paints to fill and cover features, even plaster of Paris to replace entire limbs. There are ingenious aids to prop and stabilize the cadaver: a Vari-Pose Head Rest, the Edwards Arm and Hand Positioner, the Repose Block (to support the shoulders during the embalming), and the Throop Foot Positioner, which resembles an old-fashioned stocks.

Mr. John H. Eckels, president of the Eckels College of Mortuary Science, thus describes the first part of the embalming procedure: "In the hands of a skilled practitioner, this work may be done in a comparatively short time and without mutilating the body other than by slight incision—so slight that it scarcely would cause serious inconvenience if made upon a living person. It is necessary to remove the blood, and doing this not only helps in the disinfecting, but removes the principal cause of disfigurements due to discoloration."

Another textbook discusses the all-important time element: "The earlier this is done, the better, for every hour that elapses between death and embalming will add to the problems and complications encountered. . . ." Just how soon should one get going on the embalming? The author tells us, "On the basis of such scanty information made available to this profession through its rudimentary and haphazard system of technical research, we must conclude that the best results are to be obtained if the subject is embalmed before life is completely extinct—that is, before cellular death has occurred. In the average case, this would mean within an hour after somatic death." For those who feel that there is something a little rudimentary, not to say haphazard, about this advice, a comforting thought is offered by another writer. Speaking of fears entertained in early days of premature burial, he points out, "One of the effects of embalming by chemical injection, however, has been to dispel fears of live burial." How true; once the blood is removed, chances of live burial are indeed remote.

To return to Mr. Jones, the blood is drained out through the veins and replaced by embalming fluid pumped in through the arteries. As noted in *The Principles and Practices of Embalming*, "every operator has a favorite injection and drainage point—a fact which becomes a handicap only if he fails or refuses to forsake his favorites when conditions demand it." Typical favorites are the carotid artery, femoral artery, jugular vein, subclavian vein. There are various choices of embalming fluid. If Flextone is used, it will produce a "mild, flexible rigidity. The skin retains a velvety softness, the tissues are rubbery and pliable. Ideal for women and children." It may be blended with B. and G. Products Company's Lyf-Lyk tint, which is guaranteed to reproduce "nature's own skin texture . . . the velvety appearance of living tissue." Suntone comes in three separate tints: Suntan; Special Cosmetic Tint, a pink shade "especially indicated for young female subjects"; and Regular Cosmetic Tint, moderately pink.

About three to six gallons of a dyed and perfumed solution of formaldehyde, glycerin, borax, phenol, alcohol and water is soon circulating through Mr. Jones, whose mouth has been sewn together with a "needle directed upward between the upper lip and gum and brought out through the left nostril," with the corners raised slightly "for a more pleasant expression." If he should be bucktoothed, his teeth are cleaned with Bon Ami and coated with colorless nail polish. His eyes, meanwhile, are closed with flesh-tinted eye caps and eye cement.

The next step is to have at Mr. Jones with a thing called a trocar. This is a long, hollow needle attached to a tube. It is jabbed into the abdomen, poked around the entrails and chest cavity, the contents of which are pumped out and replaced with "cavity fluid." This done, and the hole in the abdomen sewed up, Mr. Jones's face is heavily creamed (to protect the skin from burns which may be caused by leakage of the chemicals), and he is covered with a sheet and left unmolested for a while. But not for long—there is more, much more, in store for him. He has been embalmed, but not yet restored, and the best time to start the restorative work is eight to ten hours after embalming, when the tissues have become firm and dry.

he object of all this attention to the corpse, it must be remembered, is to make it presentable for viewing in an attitude of healthy repose. "Our customs require the presentation of our dead in the semblance of normality . . . unmarred by the ravages of illness, disease or mutilation," says Mr. J. Sheridan Mayer in his *Restorative Art*. This is rather a large order since few people die in the full bloom of health, unravaged by illness and unmarked by some disfigurement. The funeral industry is equal to the challenge: "In some cases the gruesome appearance of a mutilated or disease-ridden subject may be quite discouraging. The task of restoration may seem impossible and shake the confidence of the embalmer. This is the time for intestinal fortitude and determination. Once the formative work is begun and affected tissues are cleaned or removed, all doubts of success vanish. It is surprising and gratifying to discover the results which may be obtained."

The embalmer, having allowed an appropriate interval to elapse, returns to the attack, but now he brings in to play the skill and equipment of sculptor and cosmetician. Is a hand missing? Casting one in plaster of Paris is a simple matter. "For replacement purposes, only a cast of the back of the hand is necessary; this is within the ability of the average operator and is quite adequate." If a lip or two, a nose or an ear should be missing, the embalmer has at hand a variety of restorative waxes with which to model replacements. Pores and skin texture are simulated by stippling with a little brush, and over this cosmetics are laid on. Head off? Decapitation cases are rather routinely handled. Ragged edges are trimmed, and head joined to torso with a series of splints, wires and sutures. It is a good idea to have a little something at the neck—a scarf or high collar—when time for viewing comes. Swollen mouth? Cut out tissues as needed from inside the lips. If too much is removed, the surface contour can easily be restored by padding with cotton. Swollen necks and cheeks are reduced by removing tissue through vertical incisions made down each side of the neck. "When the deceased is casketed, the pillow will hide the suture incisions . . . as an extra precaution against leakage, the suture may be painted with liquid sealer."

The opposite condition is more likely to present itself—that of emaciation. His hypodermic syringe now loaded with massage cream, the embalmer seeks out and fills the hollowed and sunken areas by injection. In this procedure the backs of the hands and fingers and the under-chin area should not be neglected.

Positioning the lips is a problem that recurrently challenges the ingenuity of the embalmer. Closed too tightly, they tend to give a stern, even disapproving expression. Ideally, embalmers feel, the lips should give the impression of being ever so slightly parted, the upper lip protruding slightly for a more youthful appearance. This takes some engineering, however, as the lips tend to drift apart. Lip drift can sometimes be remedied by pushing one or two straight pins through the inner margin of the lower lip and then inserting them between the two front upper teeth. If Mr. Jones happens to have no teeth, the pins can just as easily be anchored in his Armstrong Face Former and Denture Replacer. Another method to maintain lip closure is to dislocate the lower jaw, which is then held in its new position by a wire run through holes which have been drilled through the upper and lower jaws at the midline. As the French are fond of saying, *il faut souffrir pour être belle.*

If Mr. Jones has died of jaundice, the embalming fluid will very likely turn him green. Does this deter the embalmer? Not if he has intestinal fortitude. Masking pastes and cosmetics are heavily laid on, burial garments and casket interiors are color-correlated with particular care, and Jones is displayed beneath rose-colored lights. Friends will say, "How *well* he looks." Death by carbon monoxide, on the other hand, can be rather a good thing from the embalmer's viewpoint: "One advantage is the fact that this type of discoloration is an exaggerated form of a natural pink coloration." This is nice because the healthy glow is already present and needs but little attention.

The patching and filling completed, Mr. Jones is now shaved, washed and dressed. Cream-based cosmetic, available in pink, flesh, suntan, brunette and blonde, is applied to his hands and face, his hair is shampooed and combed (and, in the case of Mrs. Jones, set), his hands manicured. For the horny-handed son of toil special care must be taken; cream should be applied to remove ingrained grime, and the nails cleaned. "If he were not in the habit of having them manicured in life, trimming and shaping is advised for better appearance—never questioned by kin."

ones is now ready for casketing (this is the present participle of the verb "to casket"). In this operation his right shoulder should be depressed slightly "to turn the body a bit to the right and soften the appearance of lying flat on the back." Positioning the hands is a matter of importance, and special rubber positioning blocks may be used. The hands should be cupped slightly for a more lifelike, relaxed appearance. Proper placement of the body requires a delicate sense of balance. It should lie as high as possible in the casket, yet not so high that the lid, when lowered, will hit the nose. On the other hand, we are cautioned, placing the body too low "creates the impression that the body is in a box."

Jones is next wheeled into the appointed slumber room where a last few touches may be added—his favorite pipe placed in his hand or, if he was a great reader, a book propped into position. (In the case of the little Master Jones a Teddy bear may be clutched.) Here he will hold open house for a few days, visiting hours 10 A.M. to 9 P.M.

Author's Profile
JESSICA MITFORD

The daughter of British nobleman Lord Redesdale, Jessica Mitford was born in Gloucestershire, England, on September 11, 1917, one of seven children born to a talented and eccentric family. Raised in a rather restrictive upper-class environment, she ran away from home at the age of nineteen and eloped with a nephew of Prime Minister Winston Churchill's. Left a widow early in World War II, she secured employment in Washington, D.C., in the Office of Price Administration, met and married her second husband, attorney Robert E. Treuhaft, and became an American citizen in 1943.

After the war, they made their home in Oakland, California, and Mitford became active in the Civil Rights movement on the West Coast. Her first book, the autobiographical *Lifeitselfmanship*, was published in 1960. After her lawyer husband expressed great concern that many of his clients' small estates went to pay the costs of their funerals, she researched and wrote her 1963 best-selling *The American Way of Death*, a scathing indictment of the American funeral industry, its high costs, and practices.

Later books include *The Trial of Dr. Spock* (1969), an account of the trial of anti-Vietnam War activists; *Kind and Usual Punishment, the Prison Business* (1973), a study of the corruption and brutality of the American prison system; and *The American Way of Birth* (1992), a critique of health costs in this country.

Mitford continues to live and work in Oakland, California.

Sarcophagus

BY RICHARD SELZER

ANTICIPATING: 1. Describe an experience you or someone close to you has had either with a doctor or with a hospital situation. Describe what brought you or the person to this need for medical care. Describe the doctors, nurses, and other health care specialists and how they treated you or the person. Describe the aftermath of this situation and the feelings and/or memories you have about it.

2. Describe a time when a job you were doing went terribly wrong. Describe the scene of this problem, what you were doing, what precisely went wrong and why, and the aftermath of this situation.

We are six who labor here in the night. No . . . seven! For the man horizontal upon the table strives as well. But we do not acknowledge his struggle. It is our own that preoccupies us. 📖 I am the surgeon. 📖 David is the anesthesiologist. You will see how kind, how soft he is. Each patient is, for him, a preparation respectfully controlled. Blood pressure, pulse, heartbeat, flow of urine, loss of blood, temperature, whatever is measurable, David measures. And he is a titrator, adding a little gas, drug, oxygen, fluid, blood in order to maintain the dynamic equilibrium that is the only state compatible with life. He is in the very center of the battle, yet he is one step removed; he has not known the patient before this time, nor will he deal with the next of kin. But for him, the occasion is no less momentous. 📖

Heriberto Paz is an assistant resident in surgery. He is deft, tiny, mercurial. I have known him for three years. One day he will be the best surgeon in Mexico.

Evelyn, the scrub nurse, is a young Irish woman. For seven years we have worked together. Shortly after her immigration, she led her young husband into my office to show me a lump on his neck. One year ago he died of

Hodgkin's disease. For the last two years of his life, he was paralyzed from the waist down. Evelyn has one child, a boy named Liam.

Brenda is a black woman of forty-five. She is the circulating nurse, who will conduct the affairs of this room, serving our table, adjusting the lights, counting the sponges, ministering to us from the unsterile world.

Roy is a medical student who is beginning his surgical clerkship. He has been assigned to me for the next six weeks. This is his first day, his first operation.

David is inducing anesthesia. In cases where the stomach is not empty through fasting, the tube is passed into the windpipe while the patient is awake. Such an "awake" intubation is called crashing. It is done to avoid vomiting and the aspiration of stomach contents into the lungs while the muscles that control coughing are paralyzed.

We stand around the table. To receive a tube in the windpipe while fully awake is a terrifying thing.

"Open your mouth wide," David says to the man. The man's mouth opens slowly to its fullest, as though to shriek. But instead, he yawns. We smile down at him behind our masks.

"OK. Open again. Real wide."

David sprays the throat of the man with a local anesthetic. He does this three times. Then, into the man's mouth, David inserts a metal tongue depressor which bears a light at the tip. It is called a laryngoscope. It is to light up the throat, reveal the glottic chink through which the tube must be shoved. All this while, the man holds his mouth agape, submitting to the hard pressure of the laryngoscope. But suddenly, he cannot submit. The man on the table gags, struggles to free himself, to spit out the instrument. In his frenzy his lip is pinched by the metal blade.

There is little blood.

"Suction," says David.

Secretions at the back of the throat obscure the view. David suctions them away with a plastic catheter.

"Open," commands David. More gagging. Another pass with the scope. Another thrust with the tube. Violent coughing informs us that the tube is in the right place. It has entered the windpipe. Quickly the balloon is inflated to snug it against the wall of the trachea. A bolus of Pentothal is injected into a vein in the man's arm. It takes fifteen seconds for the drug to travel from his arm to his heart, then on to his brain. I count them. In fifteen seconds, the coughing stops, the man's body relaxes. He is asleep.

"All set?" I ask David.

"Go ahead," he nods.

long incision. You do not know how much room you will need. This part of the operation is swift. Fat . . . muscle . . . fascia . . . the peritoneum is snapped open and a giant shining eggplant presents itself. It is the stomach, black from the blood it contains and that threatens to burst it. We must open that stomach, evacuate its contents, explore.

Silk sutures are placed in the wall of the stomach as guidelines between which the incision will be made. They are like the pitons of a mountaineer. I cut again. No sooner is the cavity of the stomach achieved, then a columnar geyser of blood stands from the small opening I have made. Quickly, I slice open the whole front of the stomach. We scoop out handfuls of clot, great black gelatinous masses that shimmy from the drapes to rest against our own bellies as though, having been evicted from one body, they must find another in which to dwell. Now and then we step back to let them slidder to the floor. They are under our feet. We slip in them. ". . . ," I say. "He is bleeding all over North America." Now my hand is inside the stomach, feeling, pressing. There! A tumor spreads across the back wall of this stomach. A great hard craterous plain, the dreaded linitis plastica (leather bottle) that is not content with seizing one area, but infiltrates between the layers until the entire organ is stiff with cancer. It is that, of course, which is bleeding. I stuff wads of gauze against the tumor. I press my fist against the mass of cloth. The blood slows. I press harder. The bleeding stops.

A quick glance at Roy. His gown and gloves, even his mask, are sprinkled with blood. Now is he dipped; and I, his baptist.

David has opened a second line into the man's veins. He is pumping blood into both tubings.

"Where do we stand?" I ask him.

"Still behind. Three units." He checks the blood pressure.

"Low, but coming up," he says.

"Shall I wait 'til you catch up?"

"No. Go ahead. I'll keep pumping."

I try to remove my fist from the stomach, but as soon as I do, there is a fresh river of blood.

"More light," I say. "I need more light."

Brenda stands on a platform behind me. She adjusts the lamps.

"More light," I say, like a man going blind.

"That's it," she says. "There is no more light."

"We'll go around from the outside," I say. Heriberto nods agreement. "Free up the greater curvature first, then the lesser, lift the stomach up and get some control from behind."

I must work with one hand. The other continues as the compressor. It is the tiredest hand of my life. One hand, then, inside the stomach, while the other creeps behind. Between them . . . a ridge of tumor. The left hand fumbles, gropes toward its mate. They swim together. I lift the stomach forward to find that *nothing* separates my hands from each other. The wall of the stomach has been eaten through by the tumor. One finger enters a large tubular structure. It is the aorta. The incision in the stomach has released the tamponade of blood and brought us to this rocky place.

"Curved aortic clamp."

A blind grab with the clamp high up at the diaphragm. The bleeding slackens, dwindles. I release the pressure warily. A moment later there is a great bang of blood. The clamp has bitten through a cancerous aorta.

"Zero silk on a big Mayo needle."

I throw the heavy sutures, one after the other, into the pool of blood, hoping to snag with my needle some bit of tissue to close over the rent in the aorta, to hold back the blood. There is no tissue. Each time, the needle pulls through the crumble of tumor. I stop. I repack the stomach. Now there is a buttress of packing both outside and inside the stomach. The bleeding is controlled. We wait. Slowly, something is gathering here, organizing. What had been vague and shapeless before is now declaring itself. All at once, I know what it is. There is nothing to do.

For what tool shall I ask? With what device fight off this bleeding? A knife? There is nothing here to cut. Clamps? Where place the jaws of a hemostat? A scissors? Forceps? Nothing. The instrument does not exist that knows such deep red jugglery. Not all my clever picks, my rasp . . . A miner's lamp, I think, to cast a brave glow.

David has been pumping blood steadily.

"He is stable at the moment," he says. "Where do we go from here?"

o place. He's going to die. The minute I take away my pressure, he'll bleed to death."

I try to think of possibilities, alternatives. I cannot; there are none. Minutes pass. We listen to the cardiac monitor, the gassy piston of the anesthesia machine.

"More light!" I say. "Fix the light."

The light seems dim, aquarial, a dilute beam slanting through a green sea. At such a fathom the fingers are clumsy. There is pressure. It is cold.

"Dave," I say, "stop the transfusion." I hear my voice coming as from a great distance. "Stop it," I say again.

David and I look at each other, standing among the drenched rags, the smeared equipment.

"I can't," he says.

"Then I will," I say, and with my free hand I reach across the boundary that separates the sterile field from the outside world, and I close the clamp on the intravenous tubing. It is the act of an outlaw, someone who does not know right from wrong. But I know. I know that this is right to do.

"The oxygen," I say. "Turn it off."

"You want it turned off, you do it," he says.

"Hold this," I say to Heriberto, and I give over the packing to him. I step back from the table, and go to the gas tanks.

"This one?" I have to ask him.

"Yes," David nods.

I turn it off. We stand there, waiting, listening to the beeping of the electrocardiograph. It remains even, regular, relentless. Minutes go by, and the sound continues. The man will not die. At last, the intervals on the screen grow longer, the shape of the curve changes, the rhythm grows wild, furious. The line droops, flattens. The man is dead.

It is silent in the room. Now we are no longer a team, each with his circumscribed duties to perform. It is Evelyn who speaks first.

"It is a blessing," she says. I think of her husband's endless dying.

"No," says Brenda. "Better for the family if they have a few days . . . to get used to the idea of it."

"But, look at all the pain he's been spared."

"Still, for the ones that are left, it's better to have a little time."

I listen to the two women murmuring, debating without rancor, speaking in hushed tones of the newly dead as women have done for thousands of years.

"May I have the name of the operation?" It is Brenda, picking up her duties. She is ready with pen and paper.

"Exploratory laparotomy. Attempt to suture malignant aorto-gastric fistula."

"Is he pronounced?"

"What time is it?"

"Eleven-twenty."

"Shall I put that down?"

"Yes."

"Sew him up," I say to Heriberto. "I'll talk to the family."

To Roy I say, "You come with me."

Roy's face is speckled with blood. He seems to me a child with the measles. What, in God's name, is he doing here?

From the doorway, I hear the voices of the others, resuming.

"Stitch," says Heriberto.

Roy and I go to change our bloody scrub suits. We put on long white coats. In the elevator, we do not speak. For the duration of the ride to the floor where the family is waiting, I am reasonable. I understand that in its cellular wisdom, the body of this man had sought out the murderous function of my scalpel, and stretched itself upon the table to receive the final stabbing. For this little time, I know that it is not a murder committed but a mercy bestowed. Tonight's knife is no assassin, but the kind scythe of time.

We enter the solarium. The family rises in unison. There are so many! How ruthless the eyes of the next of kin.

"I am terribly sorry . . . ," I begin. Their faces tighten, take guard. "There was nothing we could do."

I tell them of the lesion, tell of how it began somewhere at the back of the stomach; how, long ago, no one knows why, a cell lost the rhythm of the body, fell out of step, sprang, furious, into rebellion. I tell of how the cell divided and begat two of its kind, which begat four more and so on, until there was a whole race of lunatic cells, which is called cancer.

I tell of how the cancer spread until it had replaced the whole back of the stomach, invading, chewing until it had broken into the main artery of the body. Then it was, I tell them, that the great artery poured its blood into the stomach. I tell of how I could not stop the bleeding, how my clamps bit through the crumbling tissue, how my stitches would not hold, how there was nothing to be done. All of this I tell.

A woman speaks. She has not heard my words, only caught the tone of my voice.

 o you mean he is dead?"

Should I say "passed away" instead of "died"? No. I cannot. "Yes." I tell her, "he is dead."

Her question and my answer unleashes their anguish. Roy and I stand among the welter of bodies that tangle, grapple, rock, split apart to form new couplings. Their keening is exuberant, wild. It is more than I can stand. All at once, a young man slams his fist into the wall with great force.

"Son of a . . . !" he cries.

"Stop that!" I tell him sharply. Then, more softly, "Please try to control yourself."

The other men crowd about him, patting, puffing, grunting. They are all fat, with huge underslung bellies. Like their father's. A young woman in a nun's habit hugs each of the women in turn.

"Damn!" says one of the men.

The nun hears, turns away her face. Later, I see the man apologizing to her.

The women, too, are fat. One of them has a great pile of yellowish hair that has been sprayed and rendered motionless. All at once, she begins to whine. A single note, coming louder and louder. I ask a nurse to bring tranquilizer pills. She does, and I hand them out, one to each, as though they were the wafers of communion. They urge the pills upon each other.

"Go on, Theresa, take it. Make her take one."

Roy and I are busy with cups of water. Gradually it grows quiet. One of the men speaks.

"What's the next step?"

"Do you have an undertaker in mind?"

They look at each other, shrug. Someone mentions a name. The rest nod.

"Give the undertaker a call. Let him know. He'll take care of everything."
I turn to leave.

"Just a minute," one of the men calls. "Thanks, Doc. You did what you could."

"Yes," I say.

Once again in the operating room. Blood is everywhere. There is a wild smell, as though a fox had come and gone. The others, clotted about the table, work on. They are silent, ravaged.

"How did the family take it?"

"They were good, good."

Heriberto has finished reefing up the abdomen. The drapes are peeled back. The man on the table seems more than just dead. He seems to have gone beyond that, into a state where expression is possible—reproach and scorn. I study him. His baldness had advanced beyond the halfway mark. The remaining strands of hair had been gallantly dyed. They are, even now, neatly combed and crenellated. A stripe of black moustache rides his upper lip. Once, he had been spruce!

We all help lift the man from the table to the stretcher.

"On three," says David. "One . . . two . . . three."

And we heft him over, using the sheet as a sling. My hand brushes his shoulder. It is cool. I shudder as though he were infested with lice. He has become something that I do not want to touch.

More questions from the women.

"Is a priest coming?"

"Does the family want to view him?"

"Yes. No. Don't bother me with these things."

"Come on," I say to Roy. We go to the locker room and sit together on a bench. We light cigarettes.

"Well?" I ask him.

"When you were scooping out the clots, I thought I was going to swoon."

I pause over the word. It is too quaint, too genteel for this time. I feel, at that moment, a great affection for him.

"But you fought it."

"Yes. I forced it back down. But, almost . . ."

"Good," I say. Who knows what I mean by it? I want him to know that I count it for something.

"And you?" he asks me. The students are not shy these days.

t was terrible, his refusal to die."

I want him to say that it was right to call it quits, that I did the best I could. But he says nothing. We take off our scrub suits and go to the shower. There are two stalls opposite each other. They are curtained. But we do not draw the curtains. We need to see each other's healthy bodies. I watch Roy turn his face directly upward into the blinding fall of water. His mouth is open to receive it. As though it were milk flowing from the breasts of God. For me, too, the water is like a well in a wilderness.

In the locker room, we dress in silence.

"Well, goodnight."

Awkwardly our words come out in unison.

"In the morning . . ."

"Yes, yes, later."

"Goodnight."

I watch him leave through the elevator door.

For the third time I go to that operating room. The others have long since finished and left. It is empty, dark. I turn on the great lamps above the table that stands in the center of the room. The pediments of the table and the floor have been scrubbed clean. There is no sign of the struggle. I close my eyes and see again the great pale body of the man, like a white bullock, bled. The line of stitches on his abdomen is a hieroglyph. Already, the events of this night are hidden from me by these strange untranslatable markings.

Author's Profile
RICHARD SELZER

Richard Selzer is a retired physician, surgeon, medical school surgery instructor, and writing teacher, the last two professions at Yale University.

The son of a medical doctor, Selzer was born in Troy, New York, in 1928. He was educated at Union College, Albany Medical College, and Yale University. He was in the practice of general surgery and was on the faculty of the Yale School of Medicine, both from the early 1960s.

Selzer's books of short stories and essays on life, literature, and surgery, which quite often are indistinguishable to him, include *Rituals of Surgery* (1974), *Mortal Lessons: Notes on the Art of Surgery* (1974), *Confessions of a Knife* (1979), *Letters to a Young Doctor* (1982), *Taking the World in for Repairs* (1986), and *Down from Troy: A Doctor Comes of Age* (1992). In a 1987 speech to the National Council of Teachers of English, Selzer described the relationship between surgery and writing:

> Surgery is not such a different thing from writing
>
> . . . Where I used to suture the tissue of the body together, now I suture words together. (Stories and essays) are rather like surgical operations . . . You make the incision, you rummage around a little bit, and then you stitch it up.

Retired from medicine and teaching, Selzer continues to write full time at his home in New Haven, Connecticut.

Nancy Miles: The Political Conscience of the Class

BY STUDS TERKEL

ANTICIPATING: Write about your future in terms of the work you will choose. Will you always choose to go for the most money, or will you choose jobs that you consider "meaningful"?

he's twenty-three. She's an engineer working for a nonprofit group: Center for Neighborhood Technology. ▦ She graduated from Cornell in 1985. "For a long time I wanted to be an engineer. I always wanted to work with trains, right?" (Laughs.) ▦ "The attrition rate is enormous, people leaving engineering, especially women. There's a lot against us. There are engineering fraternities, all your professors are men. There was only one woman teacher and she was on leave while I was there." ▦ She is diffident in manner and speaks softly. ▦

We work with people in the neighborhoods to figure out how their economy works, to develop jobs in their own community rather than chains like McDonald's: in controlling their economic future.

When I graduated, all sorts of offers came, because companies were looking for women engineers. I was on the dean's list most of the time, top ten percent or something. I got offers from AT&T, Pacific Gas and Electric—to start at $27,000. A lot of money. Much more than I get paid now (laughs). I didn't think I'd be happy. I think it's real hard to spend eight hours a day working on something you don't believe in. If I went into management, I probably would have wound up making six figures. But it wouldn't have been any challenge.

Many of the jobs, especially large engineering firms, have contracts with the Defense Department to build rockets or communications systems, a real waste of money, so . . .

My dad is really afraid of political activity. His father had to appear before a grand jury during the McCarthy era. Lost his job, lost all their money, lost everything. He's very afraid.

When I got politically active, he said, "Nancy, I know you're doing what you believe in, but you're on somebody's list. You're gonna find out later in life that you've been on somebody's list and you're gonna lose your job or something's gonna happen to you." He thinks it's fine for me to have my beliefs, but he's real concerned about my acting on 'em.

My mother's much more willing to encourage me. She encourages us to do whatever we want. She was a graduate student at Northwestern when all the Vietnam protests were going on. She's not politically active now. She's spending all her time on her career.

In engineering school, we get this constant barrage of companies coming to hire us and telling us how much money is spent on defense in this country. Many of them are real clear about the politics they use to get that kind of money from the Pentagon. It's an old boys' network. Seeing how it worked disgusted me.

I became the political conscience of the class. There were three women in our class. I was the one who would get upset when they made sexist jokes. I developed a reputation.

The men were all in fraternities. Some would agree with me at times, but then they'd say, I have to worry about myself. I have to get a good job, I have to pay back enormous debts that I've accrued. I thought, well, sure, I have to worry about myself, but what am I gonna get out of working for AT&T or McDonnell Douglas? Besides money, which I'm not gonna have time to spend, I didn't think I'd get very much. So it was a conscious decision not to work in any of these places.

During the interviews, the company would ask if you could get security clearance. Wow, I'm gonna be working at a place where the government has to know about me, know what I do, know my politics. How much of myself am I willing to give up to work in Silicon Valley?

At the time of these interviews, the South African protest had become big. In '85, there had hardly been any political activity. We helped protest against the companies when they would come and recruit. We had a small discussion group and most of my activity was outside the engineering school. We were trying to get the school to divest.

In the spring of my senior year, everything exploded. Campuses all over the country were doing it. We held daily protests of two thousand people. People were getting arrested. A lot of them were real concerned: What is this going to mean to my security clearance? They decided to do it anyway, which made me hopeful. I said, How are you gonna feel working for these companies with big investments in South Africa, now that you've registered your complaint? Most of 'em were thinking of this protest as a one-time shot.

Political involvement is real scary for some people. The first time you do it, you realize maybe it's not so scary and you wonder what holds people back. But it's uncomfortable. How are other people gonna react to them after they do it?

ummer of '86, I went to Nicaragua to work with Técnica: it's a technical assistance program for their schools, hospitals, water projects. I worked with the Central Bank, helping to set up a system to track loans to small farmers. There were seven of us from Chicago.

When I got back, I needed a job. I had heard about this center. I had been looking for a place like this and hadn't found it, 'cause they don't come to campuses to recruit. I got hired in twenty minutes (laughs).

Our program is targeted at lower-income neighborhoods. Daycare centers, shelters, schools. In some of the projects, I oversee the work: assess building conditions, write specifications, recommend. I like the work because it's challenging. When I'm working at something until eight o'clock at night, it's for a reason. Right now, I'm working with Latino Youth Services in Pilsen. They're rehabbing a building and I'm designing the heating system. Teenagers, along with contractors, are doing some of the work and they're really good, learning fast.

If I were working at Grumman Aerospace until eight o'clock at night, I'd get a headache. I'd wonder what I was doing. To design a rocket?

My parents want me to go to graduate school. I think my dad gets a kick out of it, but he figures I'll get tired of it. They're worried about what's going to happen ten years from now. What kind of security do I have? And they're right. In the meantime, I support myself and actually save money (laughs).

Just last week, the FBI visited twelve people who had been with Téc-nica in Nicaragua. It was a coordinated effort at their workplaces. It was some-what threatening. For the other six from Chicago, it could jeopardize their jobs.

When I got back to the office, our executive director told me about it. Half an hour later, I got a call from one of the agents. In Chicago, they used fourteen agents to talk to seven of us all at the same time. With me they used a man-woman team. She did the talking (laughs).

She told me it was an issue of national security and she couldn't dis-cuss it on the phone. It was urgent that she speak to me. I told her I wasn't inter-ested. She asked if she could come tomorrow. I said no. I had a lawyer call up and say if she had any questions, she could go through him.

I was certainly shocked. I was a little bit scared and then real angry. I'm lucky I chose to work at the center, because they don't care. It's nice to know I don't have to hide my politics. Some of the others are real concerned about their jobs. I'm not. I'm planning to go back to Nicaragua in a few weeks. I haven't told my father yet (laughs). I'm worried about what will happen when he sees the story about the press conference. It'll be in the *Trib* next week. It'll scare him. I need to prepare him for it.

My brother disagrees with me. My sister has become very support-ive. She wants me to get active again. She played a role in getting me inter-ested in these things when I was younger. Now I've influenced her (laughs). I don't see people my age changing their views a lot. With the Iran-Contragate scandal, maybe they don't trust the federal government as much as they used to, but aside from that, no.

Nick Salerno

BY STUDS TERKEL

ANTICIPATING: Describe yourself as a worker. How do you feel about the work you do, either on the job, around your home, at school, or on a team. Discuss what you believe in when it comes to work. Do you believe in working hard, no matter what the reward, just for personal satisfaction? Do you believe in just getting by, doing enough but not more? What satisfaction do you get in a job well-done?

_H_e has been driving a city garbage truck for eighteen years. He is forty-one, married, has three daughters. He works a forty-hour, five-day week, with occasional overtime. He has a crew of three laborers. "I usually get up at five-fifteen. I get to the city parking lot, you check the oil, your water level, then proceed for the ward yard. I meet the men, we pick up our work sheet." 📖 You get just like the milkman's horse, you get used to it. If you remember the milkman's horse, all he had to do was whistle and whooshhh! That's it. He knew just where to stop, didn't he? You pull up until you finish the alley. Usually thirty homes on each side. You have thirty stops in an alley. I have nineteen alleys a week. They're called units. Sometimes I can't finish 'em, that's how heavy they are, this bein' an old neighborhood. 📖 I'll sit there until they pick up this one stop. You got different thoughts. Maybe you got a problem at home. Maybe one of the children aren't feeling too good. Like my second one, she's a problem with homework. Am I doin' the right thing with her? Pressing her a little bit with math. Or you'll read the paper. You always daydream. 📖

Some stops, there's one can, they'll throw that on, then we proceed to the next can. They signal with a buzzer or a whistle or they'll yell. The pusher blade pushes the garbage in. A good solid truckload will hold anywhere from eight thousand to twelve thousand pounds. If it's wet, it weighs more. Years ago, you had people burning, a lot of people had garbage burners. You would pick up a lot of ashes. Today most of 'em have converted to gas. In place of ashes, you've got cardboard boxes, you've got wood that people aren't burning any more. It's not like years ago, where people used everything. They're not too economy-wise today. They'll throw anything away. You'll see whole packages of meat just thrown into the garbage can without being opened. I don't know if it's spoiled from the store or not. When I first started here, I had nearly thirty alleys in this ward. Today I'm down to nineteen. And we got better trucks today. Just the way things are packaged today. Plastic. You see a lot of plastic bottles, cardboard boxes.

We try to give 'em twice-a-week service, but we can't complete the ward twice a week. Maybe I can go four alleys over. If I had an alley Monday. I might go in that alley Friday. What happens over the weekend? It just lays there.

After you dump your garbage in the hopper, the sweeper blade goes around to sweep it up, and the push blade pushes it in. This is where you get your sound. Does that sound bother you in the morning? (Laughs.) Sometimes it's irritating to me. If someone comes up to you to talk, and the men are working in the back, and they press the lever, you can't hear them. It's aggravating but you get used to it. We come around seven-twenty. Not too many complaints. Usually you're in the same alley the same day, once a week. The people know that you're coming and it doesn't bother them that much.

Some people will throw, will literally throw garbage out of the window—right in the alley. We have finished an alley in the morning and that same afternoon it will look like it wasn't even done. They might have a cardboard carton in the can and garbage all over the alley. People are just not takin' care of it. You get some people that takes care of their property, they'll come out and sweep around their cans. Other people just don't care or maybe they don't know any better.

Some days it's real nice. Other days, when you get off that truck you're tired, that's it! You say all you do is drive all day, but driving can be pretty tiresome—especially when the kids are out of school. They'll run through a gangway into the alley. This is what you have to watch for. Sitting in that cab, you have a lot of blind spots around the truck. This is what gets you. You watch out that you don't hit any of them.

At times you get aggravated, like your truck breaks down and you get a junk as a replacement. This, believe me, you could take home with you. Otherwise, working here, if there's something on your mind, you don't hold anything in. You discuss anything with these guys. Golf, whatever. One of my laborers just bought a new home and I helped him move some of his small stuff. He's helped me around my house, plumbing and painting.

We've got spotters now. It's new. (Laughs.) They're riding around in unmarked cars. They'll turn you in for stopping for coffee. I can't see that. If you have a coffee break in the alley, it's just using a little psychology. You'll get more out of them. But if you're watched continually, you're gonna lay down. There's definitely more watching today, because there was a lot of layin' down on the job. Truthfully, I'd just as soon put in my eight hours a day as easy as possible. It's hard enough comin' to work. I got a good crew, we get along together, but we have our days.

f you're driving all day, you get tired. By the time you get home, fighting the traffic, you'd just like to relax a little bit. But there's always something around the house. You can get home one night and you'll find your kid threw something in the toilet and you gotta shut your mind and take the toilet apart. (Laughs.) My wife drives, so she does most of the shopping. That was my biggest complaint. So now this job is off my hands. I look forward to my weekends. I get in a little golf.

People ask me what I do, I say, "I drive a garbage truck for the city." They call you G-man, or, "How's business, picking up?" Just the standard . . . Or sanitary engineer. I have nothing to be ashamed of. I put in my eight hours. We make a pretty good salary. I feel I earn my money. I can go any place I want. I conduct myself as a gentleman any place I go. My wife is happy, this is the big thing. She doesn't look down at me. I think that's more important than the white-collar guy looking down at me.

They made a crack to my children at school. My kids would just love to see me do something else. I tell 'em, "Honey, this is a good job. There's nothing to be ashamed of. We're not stealin' the money. You have everything you need."

I don't like to have my salary compared to anybody else's. I don't like to hear that we're makin' more than a schoolteacher. I earn my money just as well as they do. A teacher should get more money, but don't take it away from me.

Author's Profile
STUDS TERKEL

Studs Terkel has made a valuable contribution to Americans' self-image by following people around with a tape recorder and getting them to talk about their hopes, dreams, and memories. His interviews, as he puts it, are with real people: "I celebrate the non-celebrated."

Born Louis Terkel in New York City on May 16, 1912, he attended the University of Chicago, where he obtained his undergraduate degree in 1932 and his law degree in 1934. He worked briefly as an actor, then as a movie theater manager, and later as a host of a series of radio and television interview and variety shows.

By the late 1960s, Terkel was interviewing everyday people with his tape recorder. In 1970, he published *Hard Times: An Oral History of the Great Depression.* He followed this with *Working: People Talk about What They Do All Day and How They Feel about What They Do* in 1974. He turned his microphone on himself in his 1977 book *Talking to Myself: A Memoir of My Times.* His next book, *American Dreams: Lost and Found* (1980), explored a wide range of people on their views of "What is the American Dream?" He returned to earlier times with *The Good War: An Oral History of World War II* in 1984, and he focused on ethnic issues in *Race: How Blacks and Whites Think and Feel About the American Obsession,* published in 1993.

In reviewing *Working: People Talk about What They Do All Day and How They Feel about What They Do, Newsweek* critic Peter S. Prescott describes Terkel's approach to interviewing, which underscores the success of all of his books:

> Terkel understands that what people need—more than sex,
> almost as much as food—and what they perhaps will never
> find, is a sympathetic ear. I'm sure Terkel takes pains never to
> ask an embarrassing question. Gently he draws his subjects
> out, encourages them to make—perhaps for the first time—
> some kind of pattern of their lives; then he edits and condenses
> his material.

Essay

Pablo Picasso: Living in His Own Shadow

BY ELLEN GOODMAN

ANTICIPATING: Think of a woman or a man you admire: an athlete, a singer, an actor, a politician, an artist, a business leader, a community leader.

Write everything you know about this person off the top of your head; just get the information down on paper. Discuss what this person has done, why you admire her or him, and how s/he ended up in their career, if this last part is applicable.

e were one hour into the Picasso exhibit when we stopped in front of a cubist painting called "The Accordionist."  Behind us were five huge rooms full of gorgeous Impressionist children and massive seated women, of perfectly reproduced realism, of shattered forms of revolutionary cubism. At the bottom of this one picture, we checked the date: 1911. He had done all this before his thirtieth birthday. The age impressed me more than it did the twelve-year-old next to me. We live on opposite sides of that dividing line. Yet, we were both struck by the volume and versatility of Picasso's life work in this exhibit.

Surrounded, even overwhelmed, as we moved among the 900 Picassos that have taken over the Museum of Modern Art for the summer in a massive retrospective, it was obvious why this man still dominates art the way Shakespeare dominates literature or Mozart dominates music.

It is said that when Picasso was a teenager, his artist-father gave the boy his own palette, brushes and colors, and never painted again. It is known that when he died at the age of ninety-one, Picasso was arranging for a show of his latest work. In between he was astonishingly productive.

Here was a man who produced some 13,000 to 14,000 canvases, 100,000 prints or engravings, and 34,000 book illustrations. He worked in virtually every medium from stage sets to ceramics, ranging back and forth from one to the other with as much energy as genius.

et as we wandered through the last thirty years of his life, you could see it all slip. The exhibit kindly excludes the commercial peace doves and greeting-card poster art of the last years. But still, it is easy to see the versatility turning frenetic, the search turning downhill. There is even a sense that perhaps he began to imitate himself—not just to create, but to create "Picassos."

There is nothing bad on these walls. The worst of this artist is very, very good. But winding down through his age and out again onto 54th Street, it was hard not to wonder what it was like to be Picasso at seventy, or eighty, or ninety, competing with Picasso at forty.

What is it like to keep working in the present while your past has already been written into history books? What is it like to compete with your own best?

It is something that I've thought of before. I've thought of it whenever Tennessee Williams turns up in the news, alive but rarely well, writing poorly in comparison to his own brilliant retrospectives. I've thought of it when Frank Sinatra goes on stage, all blue eyes and strained vocal cords. They are pale versions of themselves.

Living in your own shadow is a problem of aging athletes and beautiful women and artists and actors and, to an extent, all of us.

The American ideal is that people should quit with the gold medals around their necks and the stars on their doors.

We want them to stay on top or move on. We want to laurelize them like Jesse Owens or ignore them like Mark Spitz. We hope that, like Beverly Sills, they will "move on" at the right moment, off of one stage and onto the next . . . before their voices crack in public.

There are very few ways for our stars to retreat gracefully back into the chorus line. We live in such an achievement-oriented world that anyone who is not doing his or her best, breaking records, going onward and upward, is somehow or other failing.

We feel saddened that Joe DiMaggio sells coffee-makers and uncomfortable that Willie Mays "stayed too long." Few of us know quite how to deal with the man or woman who "used to be" somebody.

Picasso was hardly a failure in his later life. He refused to be canonized. He refused to rest on his laurels. He chose productivity. He got up in the morning, nearly paralyzed by pessimism about his own ability, and went to work.

There is something, not sad but remarkable, in this refusal to "act his age," or to retire gracefully. Surrounded by his own collection of his favorite cubist work, he must have known his limits. But out of compulsion or conviction, he kept working.

"Creation," Picasso said, "is the only thing that interests me." So for ninety-one years, he did something remarkable. He stayed interested.

July 1980

Author's Profile
ELLEN GOODMAN

*B*oston Globe columnist Ellen Goodman is syndicated in more than 300 newspapers across the United States. In addition, she is a frequent guest commentator on network radio and television programs.

Born in Boston in 1941, Goodman has been a columnist with the *Boston Globe* since 1971. She won the Pulitzer Prize for commentary in 1980. She summed up her perspective towards news commentary in a 1986 interview with Gannett News Service Reporter Andrea Stone:

> *If you're telling people what you think, you've got to be really sure. Not just of your facts, but you have to be sure of your point of view.*

Avoiding such usual "tags" as "liberal" or "conservative," Goodman says her political bent is for "sanity." As one of a small group of nationally syndicated columnists, she says she has resisted the temptation to become "a spokeswoman for women":

> *You speak for yourself. There are some ways in which my column has been a place where things that are important to women are discussed, not settled. There's nothing definitive. It's a personal voice.*

Her collections of her commentary columns include *Turning Home, Close to Home, At Large* (1981), and *Keeping in Touch* (1986). Goodman offers us this perspective on her work:

> *Often in my column I connect something very small and personal . . . to something very large. And I think that's both the way my mind works and that's the way things work.*

Insert Flap "A" and Throw Away

BY S. J. PERELMAN

ANTICIPATING: Describe a time when you had to put something together or operate something using the manufacturer's directions. Describe what you were trying to build or achieve and how it turned out.

An alternative to this is to interview a parent or grandparent about an experience with a home project or perhaps a Christmas toy.

One stifling summer afternoon last August, in the attic of a tiny stone house in Pennsylvania, I made a most interesting discovery: the shortest, cheapest method of inducing a nervous breakdown ever perfected. In this technique, the subject is placed in a sharply sloping attic heated to 340°F and given a mothproof closet known as the Jiffy-Cloz to assemble. The Jiffy-Cloz, procurable at any department store or neighborhood insane asylum, consists of half a dozen gigantic sheets of red cardboard, two plywood doors, a clothes rack, and a packet of staples. With these is included a set of instructions mimeographed in pale-violet ink, fruity with phrases like "Pass Section F through Slot AA, taking care not to fold tabs behind washers (see Fig. 9)." The cardboard is so processed that as the subject struggles convulsively to force the staple through, it suddenly buckles, plunging the staple deep into his thumb. He thereupon springs up with a dolorous cry and smites his knob (Section K) on the rafters (RR). As a final demonic touch, the Jiffy-Cloz people cunningly omit four of the staples necessary to finish the job, so that after indescribable purgatory, the best the subject can possibly achieve is a sleazy, capricious structure which would reduce any self-respecting moth to helpless laughter. The cumulative frustration, the tropical heat, and the soft, ghostly chuckling of the moths are calculated to unseat the strongest mentality. In a period of rapid technological change, however, it was inevitable that a method as cumbersome as the Jiffy-Cloz would be superseded. It would be superseded at exactly nine-thirty Christmas morning by a device called the Self-Running 10-Inch Scale-Model Delivery-Truck Kit Powered by Magic Motor, costing twenty-nine cents. About nine on that particular morning, I was spread-eagled on my bed, indulging in my favorite sport of mouth-breathing, when a cork fired from a child's air gun mysteriously lodged in my throat. The pellet proved awkward for a while, but I finally ejected it by flailing the little marksman (and his sister, for good measure) until their welkins rang, and sauntered in to breakfast. Before I could choke down a healing fruit juice, my consort, a tall, regal creature indistinguishable from Cornelia, the Mother of the Gracchi, except that her foot was entangled in a roller skate, swept in. She extended a large, unmistakable box covered with diagrams. "Now don't start making excuses," she whined. "It's just a simple cardboard toy. The directions are on the back—"

"Look, dear," I interrupted, rising hurriedly and pulling on my overcoat, "it clean slipped my mind. I'm supposed to take a lesson in crosshatching at Zim's School of Cartooning today." "On Christmas?" she asked suspiciously.

"Yes, it's the only time they could fit me in," I countered glibly. "This is the big week for crosshatching, you know, between Christmas and New Year's."

"Do you think you ought to go in your pajamas?" she asked.

"Oh, that's O.K.," I smiled. "We often work in our pajamas up at Zim's. Well, goodbye now. If I'm not home by Thursday, you'll find a cold snack in the safe-deposit box." My subterfuge, unluckily, went for naught, and in a trice I was sprawled on the nursery floor, surrounded by two lambkins and ninety-eight segments of the Self-Running 10-Inch Scale-Model Delivery-Truck Construction Kit.

The theory of the kit was simplicity itself, easily intelligible to Kettering of General Motors, Professor Millikan, or any first-rate physicist. Taking as my starting point the only sentence I could comprehend, "Fold down on all lines marked 'fold down'; fold up on all lines marked 'fold up,'" I set the children to work. In a few moments, my skin was suffused with a delightful tingling sensation and I was ready for the second phase, lightly referred to in the directions as "Preparing the Spring Motor Unit." As nearly as I could determine after twenty minutes of mumbling, the Magic Motor ("No Electricity—No Batteries—Nothing to Wind—Motor Never Wears Out") was an accordion-pleated affair operating by torsion, attached to the axles. "It is necessary," said the text, "to cut a slight notch in each of the axles with a knife (see Fig. C.). To find the exact place to cut this notch, lay one of the axles over diagram at bottom of page."

"Well, *now* we're getting some place!" I boomed, with a false gusto that deceived nobody. "Here, Buster, run in and get Daddy a knife."

"I dowanna," quavered the boy, backing away. "You always cut yourself at this stage." I gave the wee fellow an indulgent pat on the head that flattened it slightly, to teach him civility, and commandeered a long, serrated bread knife from the kitchen. "Now watch me closely, children," I ordered. "We place the axle on the diagram as in Fig. C, applying a strong downward pressure on the knife handle at all times." The axle must have been a factory second, because an instant later I was in the bathroom grinding my teeth in agony and attempting to stanch the flow of blood. Ultimately, I succeeded in contriving a rough bandage and slipped back into the nursery without awaking the children's suspicions. An agreeable surprise awaited me. Displaying a mechanical aptitude clearly inherited from their sire, the rascals had put together the chassis of the delivery truck.

"Very good indeed," I complimented (naturally, one has to exaggerate praise to develop a child's self-confidence). "Let's see—what's the next step? Ah, yes, 'Lock into box shape by inserting tabs C, D, E, F, G, H, J, K, and L into slots C, D, E, F, G, H, J, K, and L. Ends of front axle should be pushed through holes A and B.'" While marshalling the indicated parts in their proper order, I emphasized to my rapt listeners the necessity of patience and perseverance. "Haste makes waste, you know," I reminded them. "Rome wasn't built in a day. Remember, your daddy isn't always going to be here to show you."

"Where *are* you going to be?" they demanded.

"In the movies, if I can arrange it," I snarled. Poising tabs C, D, E, F, G, H, J, K, and L in one hand and the corresponding slots in the other, I essayed a union of the two, but in vain. The moment I made one set fast and tackled another, tab and slot would part company, thumbing their noses at me. Although the children were too immature to understand, I saw in a flash where the trouble lay. Some idiotic employee at the factory had punched out the wrong design, probably out of sheer spite. So that was the game, eh? I set my lips in a grim line and, throwing one hundred and fifty-seven pounds of fighting fat into the effort, pounded the component parts into a homogeneous mass.

"There," I said with a gasp, "that's close enough. Now then, who wants candy? One, two, three—everybody off to the candy store!"

e wanna finish the delivery truck!" they wailed. "Mummy, he won't let us finish the delivery truck!" Threats, cajolery, bribes were of no avail. In their jungle code, a twenty-nine-cent gew-gaw bulked larger than a parent's love. Realizing that I was dealing with a pair of monomaniacs, I determined to show them who was master and wildly began lock-ing the cardboard units helter-skelter, without any regard for the directions. When sections refused to fit, I gouged them with my nails and forced them together, cack-ling shrilly. The side panels collapsed; with a bestial oath, I drove a safety pin through them and lashed them to the roof. I used paper clips, bobby pins, any-thing I could lay my hands on. My fingers fairly flew and my breath whistled in my throat. "You want a delivery truck, do you?" I panted. "All right, I'll show you!" As merciful blackness closed in, I was on my hands and knees, bunting the infernal thing along with my nose and whinnying, "Roll, confound you, roll!"

"Absolute quiet," a carefully modulated voice was saying, "and fif-teen of the white tablets every four hours." I opened my eyes carefully in the darkened room. Dimly I picked out a knifelike character actor in a Vandyke beard and pencil-striped pants folding a stethoscope into his bag. "Yes," he added thoughtfully, "if we play our cards right, this ought to be a long, expen-sive recovery." From far away, I could hear my wife's voice bravely trying to control her anxiety.

"What if he becomes restless, Doctor?"

"Get him a detective story," returned the leech. "Or better still, a nice, soothing picture puzzle—something he can do with his hands."

Author's Profile
S. J. PERELMAN

As both a screenwriter and regular contributor to *New Yorker* magazine, Sidney Joseph Perelman was considered one of the funniest writers alive during his 50-year career, which lasted from the late 1920s until the late 1970s. He loved to poke fun at various aspects of American life and he loved to play with words.

Perelman was born in Brooklyn, New York, on February 1, 1904. After his graduation from Brown University in 1925, he went to work as a cartoonist and writer, first for *Judge* magazine (1925-1929) and later for *College Humor* magazine (1929-1930). He became a columnist for *New Yorker* magazine in 1931, continuing to write short stories and pieces for this publication for most of his career.

In 1930, Perelman began his Hollywood screenwriting career and worked with the Marx Brothers on two of their most important films, *Monkey Business* (1931) and *Horse Feathers* (1932). His screenplay for the 1956 movie *Around the World in Eighty Days* won him both a New York Film Critics Award and an Academy Award.

Essayist E. B. White once paid this tribute to Perelman, his fellow *New Yorker* magazine colleague:

> I'm sure Sid's stuff influenced me in the early days. His pieces usually had a lead sentence, or lead paragraph, that was as hair-raising as the first big dip on a roller coaster: it got you in the stomach, and when it was over you were relieved to feel deceleration setting in.

Among the many collections of Perelman's comic pieces are *Look Who's Talking* (1937), *Crazy Like a Fox* (1944), *The Swiss Family Perelman* (1950), and *The Open Form: Essays for Our Time* (1961).

His many plays include *The Third Little Show* (1932), *One Touch of Venus* (1943), and *The Beauty Part* (1961).

Perelman died in 1979.

Shorthand Grad Is Shortchanged

BY MIKE ROYKO

ANTICIPATING: Write a description of a time in your life when you feel you were cheated or not given what was promised you. Be sure to include the "who-what-where-when-why-how" of this situation.

his story would be kind of funny if it wasn't so sad. 📖 A downtown lawyer, David Schultz, recently had a job opening for a part-time secretary in his office. 📖 He was looking for someone at the starting level: basic secretarial skills, right out of school, no experience necessary, who could be trained by the firm. 📖 So he opened the Yellow Pages to "Schools" and saw a big ad for a secretarial college. The ad boasted of the success its students had after completing the 10 month secretarial course. 📖

Schultz called the school and told someone about the job opening.

"I said we wanted someone bright with good language skills. They said they would send me two young women who were graduating in June and were ready for the job market.

"When they came in, I looked at their resumés and I was surprised. They were filled with typos and spelling errors."

Based on the resumés, he wasn't inclined toward hiring either of them. But he decided to give one of them a test.

The test consisted of his slowly dictating a series of sentences to the woman. She was then asked to type the sentences.

This is what he dictated:

"To be effective, secretaries must possess an efficient mind and a congenial personality. Errors and omissions must be kept to a minimum.

"On Wednesday, February 23rd, the library will probably have its lease cancelled.

"The Joneses are plaintiffs in this case, but their lien was thoroughly dissolved, nevertheless.

"It's indefinite whether yours, or ours, will be adequate to achieve our purposes.

"The ambulance arrived and brought the Smiths' dog to the canine hospital.

"The Bookkeeping Department will announce its recommendations through the Liaison Committee regarding all of the officers' accommodations for the Hawaiian cruise."

The young woman took her notebook, sat down at a typewriter, and this is what Schultz got back:

"To be a affective secteraries must an effective mind and a ginle persoanity. Errors and omission must be keep to a mindmen.

"One Wednesday, February 23 the libiary will probily can its lease cancel.

"The Jones' are platiff in this case but there lean was throughly desovlued nevertheless.

"Its whether yours or ours will be adquied to achive our purposes.

"The abolus, arrived and brought the Smith's dog to the cannie hospital.

"The bookeeping department, will announce its recommondations throw the Leasize commiittee, regrading all the officers accomondation for the Hawii."

No, I'm not kidding, nor is Attorney Schultz. He showed me a copy of the woman's effort.

After he gently told her that she needed more training, he wrote a letter to the secretarial school in which he said:

"I am appalled [a] at the thought that such students have 'successfully' completed a program of secretarial training; [b] that you send these women out as representatives of your program; [c] that you, apparently, do not take the time or interest to even proofread their resumés; and [d] that you send these poor, unsuspecting souls out into the business world to embarrass themselves and, of more interest to you, your entire program.

"You can be sure that I feel sorry for the young ladies who, apparently, have paid a considerable sum of money for an education and are then, unwittingly, cast out your door guaranteed to fail."

Yes, it is appalling. We called the school and asked how much the tuition is for the 10 month course, which the girl allegedly took. Including a registration fee, it is $5,510.

If the school actually took $5,510 from that woman, they should give her a complete refund, with interest, and an apology.

e asked the owner of the school for her response to Schultz's allegations and letter. She said she wasn't aware of the letter but would check and get back to us. She hasn't.

But the incident is appalling for other reasons. Schultz said that the young woman was black and, according to her resumé, was a product of the Chicago public school system.

Does that surprise anyone?

Does it surprise the school superintendent, who would have us believe he's done a splendid job?

Take a look at that test, Mr. Superintendent. It was done by a person who was passed on from one grade to another, handed a diploma, and she is borderline illiterate.

Does it surprise the head of the teachers union, who opposed school reform legislation and whose reaction to a state income tax was something like: "Good, it will mean there will be more money for the teachers."

More money for the teachers? If they can't teach someone who is applying for a secretarial job how to spell "secretary," maybe they ought to take a pay cut, instead.

The mayor says improving the schools is his top priority. I hope so and wish him luck, since it obviously wasn't the priority of the incompetents who got that kid ready for the real world.

Author's Profile

MIKE ROYKO

One of America's best-known newspaper columnists, Mike Royko is syndicated in more than 600 newspapers in four countries around the world. He is sometimes referred to as "the Mark Twain of the Chicago River."

Born in Chicago in 1933, Royko spent his teenage years tending bar in several of his father's establishments. He dropped out of junior college at age nineteen, joined the Air Force, and was sent to Korea. Claiming that he had worked for the *Chicago Daily News*, Royko was appointed editor of his base's newspaper, and his journalism career was born. After the Korean War, he worked as a reporter for several newspapers.

In 1963, his big break came when he landed a job with the *Chicago Daily News*, and soon Chicago readers were howling over his exposes of graft and corruption in Cook County politics and acts of injustice against everyday citizens. Reporter John Culhane says that the question, "Juhread Royko?" has become a substitute in Chicago for "Good morning." Culhane also describes his colleague's work schedule:

> *Though he has been writing his column for over three decades, he can still get excited over his 900-word pieces, five days a week, 47 weeks a year. Monday through Friday, he puts in nearly ten hours a day on his column.*

Winner of the Pulitzer Prize and countless other journalism awards, Royko has published a number of collections of his newspaper columns, including *Like I was Sayin'...* (1984). He has also written the political biography *Boss: Richard J. Daley of Chicago* (1971).

In 1978, Royko moved to the *Chicago Sun Times* when that paper bought out the *Chicago Daily News*. When the *Sun Times* was purchased by Rupert Murdoch in 1983, Royko made another move, this time to the *Chicago Tribune*, where he continues to write his column.

POETRY

THEME *Coping*

*ANTICIPATING: **What do you daydream about most? When do you daydream? Write a
journal entry on daydreams and how they make the boring tasks easier to perform.
Use examples from your job, from school, from home, etc.***

Woman Work

*'ve got the children to tend
The clothes to mend
The floor to mop
The food to shop
Then the chicken to fry
The baby to dry
I got company to feed
The garden to weed
I've got the shirts to press
The tots to dress
The cane to be cut
I gotta clean up this hut
Then see about the sick
And the cotton to pick.*

*Shine on me sunshine
Rain on me, rain
Fall softly, dewdrops
And cool my brow again.*

Storm, blow me from here
With your fiercest wind
Let me float across the sky
'Til I can rest again.

Fall gently, snowflakes
Cover me with white
Cold icy kisses and
Let me rest tonight.

Sun, rain, curving sky
Mountain, oceans, leaf and stone
Star shine, moon glow
You're all that I can call my own.

Maya Angelou

Factory Jungle

ight after the seven o'clock break
the ropes start shining down,
thin light through the factory windows,
the sun on its way to the time clock.
My veins fill with welding flux —
I get that itchy feeling that I don't belong here.

I stand behind the biggest press in the plant
waiting for the parts to drop down into the rack,
Thinking about what that mad elephant
could do to a hand.

I'd like to climb one of those ropes of light
swing around the plant
between presses, welders, assembly lines
past the man working the overhead crane
everyone looking up, swearing off booze, pills,
whatever they think made them see me.
I'd shed my boots, coveralls, safety glasses, ear plugs,
and fly out the plant gate
past the guard post
and into the last hour of twilight.

The parts are backing up
but I don't care
I rip open my coveralls and pound my chest
trying to raise my voice
above the roar of the machines
yelling louder than Tarzan ever had to.

Jim Daniels

The Song of the Factory Worker

ed brick building
With many windows,
You're like a vampire,
For wherever I go
You know I'm coming back to you.
You have held many under your spell,
Many who have sewed their life away
Within your walls.
You say to me,
"Oh, you may leave
But you'll come back.
You'll miss
The whir, whir of the machinery,
The click of the tacker,
The happy laughter of the girls,
Telling jokes.
You'll miss the songs
They sing,
And the tired-eyed ones,
Watching the clock.
The pieceworkers,
Sewing fast,
So fast till it makes you dizzy
to watch.
(They haven't time to look up.)
And under the skylight,
The red-haired girl,
When the sun sets her head aflame.
You'll miss the noise and the bustle and the hurry,

And you'll come back,
You'll see."
All this and more
You say to me,
Red brick building
With many windows.

Ruth Collins

Pee Wee

ee Wee has that automatic smile
for anyone he sees,
that smile, no teeth, just gums, lips,
pillows of flesh.

Pee Wee fits in coveralls
like a kid in a clown costume,
the material blossoming out loose
over his tiny bones.

Pee Wee's been here 29 years.
He smiles that smile.
He looks through glassy eyes.
He pops pills every day.

Pee Wee has an easy job,
painting lock-tite on axle-housing welds
as they ride by on hooks.
He cranes his long neck around the housings
looking for the foreman
then, after letting a few pass by
he grabs one he likes,
light and graceful,
his neck resting on the warm steel,
and dances the stiff housing
toward the paint house at the end of the line,
that black spraying he calls death.

Jim Daniels

Old Man Pike

ld man Pike was a sawyer at the mill
over in Craftsbury.
He lived just down the road from here.
Every morning he walked six miles through the woods
over Dunn Hill saddle while the sun rose.
He took dinner and supper in the village
then walked home across the mountain in the dark.
Sally Tatro who used to live on my place
would hear him coming through the night, singing.
Sometimes he'd stop to gossip
but mostly she only saw him stride by the window
and disappear.

The old man could have stayed at home,
milked cows, like everybody else,
but he needed an excuse to go and come
through the mountains, every day,
all his life, alone.

Old man Pike didn't believe in the local religion of work,
but out of deference, to his neighbors maybe,
he bowed to it,
placed its dullness at the center of his life,
but he was always sure, because of his excuse,
to wrap it at the edges of his days
in the dark and solitary amblings of his pleasure.

David Budbill

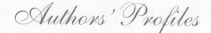

Authors' Profiles

MAYA ANGELOU

See notes under poetry on Family.

JIM DANIELS

See notes under poetry on Survivors.

RUTH COLLINS

Ruth Collins was a young woman who studied at the Vineyard Shore Worker's School in New York in the 1920s.

DAVID BUDBILL

David Budbill (1940-) has made a career as a writer, but he has experienced the world of work from many viewpoints. He has been a street gang worker, groundskeeper, short-order cook, forester, and carpenter's apprentice. He attended Columbia University and earned a master's degree in divinity from Union Theological Seminary in New York City. He has four poetry collections: Pulp Cutter's Nativity, From Down to the Village, The Chain Saw Dance, *and* Why I Came to Judevine.

THEME *Downtrodden*

ANTICIPATING: Who do you believe are the downtrodden in our society today? Write in your journal about these people and the problems you believe they face. What do you believe should be done to help them?

An Old Charcoal Seller

 n old charcoal seller
Cuts firewood, burns coal by the southern mountain.
His face, all covered with dust and ash, the color of smoke,
The hair at his temples is gray, his ten fingers black.
The money he makes selling coal, what is it for?
To put clothes on his back and food in his mouth.
The rags on his poor body are thin and threadbare;
Distressed at the low price of coal, he hopes for colder weather.
Night comes, an inch of snow has fallen on the city,
In the morning, he rides his cart along the icy ruts,
His ox weary, he hungry, and the sun already high.
In the mud by the south gate, outside the market, he stops to rest.
All of a sudden, two dashing riders appear;
An imperial envoy, garbed in yellow (his attendant in white),
Holding an official dispatch, he reads a proclamation.
Then turns the cart around, curses the ox, and leads it north.
One cartload of coal—a thousand or more catties!
No use appealing to the official spiriting the cart away:
Half a length of red lace, a slip of damask
Dropped on the ox—is payment in full!

Po Chü-Yi
Translated from the Chinese by Eugene Eoyang

Share-Croppers

ust a herd of Negroes
Driven to the field,
Plowing, planting, hoeing,
To make the cotton yield.

When the cotton's picked
And the work is done
Boss man takes the money
And we get none,

Leaves us hungry, ragged
As we were before.
Year by year goes by
And we are nothing more

Than a herd of Negroes
Driven to the field—
Plowing life away
To make the cotton yield.

Langston Hughes

Weaving at the Window

Sighing high and
        again a sigh!
In the garden are dates
        which the passers-by crave;
A girl of poor family
        for a rich one must weave,
Her parents beyond the wall
        can give her no help;
Cold water, rough hands,
        and fine thread so easily breaks!
Stitch in, stitch out,
        it tears at her heart!
Insects swarm in the grass,
        to cry beneath her loom,
In two days she must do
        one roll and a half;
When each tax is paid
        only odd pieces are left!
Her mother-in-law has no new dress,
        how could she wear one?
From her window she can even envy
        those green-bower girls,
Their ten fingers idle
        while clothes fill the hamper.

Wang Chien
Translated from the Chinese
by William H. Nienhauser

"Butch" Weldy

After I got religion and steadied down
They gave me a job in the canning works,
And every morning I had to fill
The tank in the yard with gasoline,
That fed the blow-fires in the sheds
To head the soldering irons.
And I mounted a rickety ladder to do it,
Carrying buckets full of the stuff.
One morning, as I stood there pouring,
The air grew still and seemed to heave,
And I shot up as the tank exploded,
And down I came with both legs broken,
And my eyes burned crisp as a couple of eggs.
For someone left a blow-fire going.
And something sucked the flame in the tank.
The Circuit Judge said whoever did it
Was a fellow-servant of mine, and so
Old Rhodes' son didn't have to pay me.
And I sat on the witness stand as blind
As Jack the Fiddler, saying over and over,
"I didn't know him at all."

Edgar Lee Masters

Song of the Weaving Woman

usy is the life of the weaving woman!
Silkworms are about to grow old after their third sleep,
And soon the silkworm goddess will start to make silk;
Early too comes this year's levy of the silk tax.
This early tax is not the evil doing of the officials—
The government has been waging wars since last year:
Soldiers in bitter fighting bandage their sword wounds;
The great general, his merits high, changes his gauze curtain.

She'd continue her effort to reel threads and weave silk,
But the tangled skeins on the loom give her trouble.

In the house to the east, a white-haired man has two daughters;
He won't marry them off because they're skilled in embroidery.
Amid the floating gossamers on the eaves,
A spider nimbly plies back and forth.
Admirable are the insects that understand Heaven's way:
They know how to spin a gossamer web in the void.

Yüan Chen
Translated from the Chinese by Wu-chi Liu

Authors' Profiles

PO CHÜ-YI

*P*o Chü-yi (772-846) is one of China's earliest popular poets. He is unique because he was successful as well as semiprofessional, achieving fame in his lifetime. He was acclaimed not only by literary men, but also by common people. His fame also reached into Korea and Japan, with foreigners paying large sums of money for his poems. He wrote more than 2,800 poems, acting as his own editor. Po Chü-yi writes social criticism of the taxing of the people. "An Old Charcoal Seller" is an example of his criticism of the abuses of the T'ang dynasty.

LANGSTON HUGHES

*J*ames Mercer Langston Hughes (1902-1967) wrote prose and poetry about life for African-American people in America. His poetry collections, The Weary Blues *(1926) and* Fine Clothes to the Jew *(1927), explored African-American consciousness, while his* Lament for Dark People and Other Poems *(1944) stressed the commonality of suffering and cultures. Hughes' prose works include his 1925 essay "The Negro Artist and the Racial Movement," his 1940 autobiography* The Big Sea, *and his 1956 travel journals* I Wonder as I Wander.

WANG CHIEN

*W*ang Chien (768-833) was a native of Honan, China, whose career included being a government official, a soldier, a courtier, and a recluse. He is known for his 100 "Palace Poems" which recount happenings in the court of Emperor Te-tsung. His themes are realistic and reflect his social concern. "Weaving at the Window" focuses on the solitude, sadness, and despair of young women who were unmarried and unmatched. He refers to the unfair taxes on silk.

EDGAR LEE MASTERS

See notes under poetry on Endings.

YÜAN CHEN

Yüan Chen (779-831) enjoyed success as the most colorful poet of the mid-T'ang period in China. He was intelligent and well-educated. His political life was unsettled and he was repeatedly banished. During his exile, he was brought closer to the commoners and became sympathetic with their sufferings. "Song of the Weaving Woman" is an example of his feelings for the downtrodden. He was a close friend of poet Po Chü-Yi and shared his philosophy that literature should reflect the social conditions and concerns.

THEME *Endings*

*ANTICIPATING: Day I: Write descriptions and stories of older people you know. What
is your relationship with these people and how do you feel about them?*

*Day II: Do you ever think about where you'll be when you've grown old?
Write in your journals what your life will be like after age 65. Will you still be working? Why or why not? How will you spend your time when not working?*

*Day III: How would you like to be remembered by family, friends, and
neighbors when you die? Discuss this point and how you intend to live your life so
you are remembered in this way.*

Enough!

*nd now they are no longer
man and father,
woman and mother,
but 2
workers in old age:
heroic and used up
as smoldering rags.*

*Her, she's
a tiny cell of light
—40 watts, say,
against 3 backyards
and one small, dirty sidestreet—
in an immense night.*

*She dreams no more
than the dog, Toro,
chained to the back porch.*

Six days she goes
out in the marbled mist
of streetlamps, dawn, dripping trees,
the sky
with its wisp of moon.

Sundays she sleeps.

Across the city, by the harbor,
the cable coiling
machines she tends
are not what they are,
but the oily roar
of her horizon.
An end.

And him?
Back from the hospital
he sits in the kitchen.
His brain scatters
wishes
and insights, like fireflies
through the terrible spring night

only to say
how dark it is,

how 38 years
boxing chemicals and beakers,
grinding glass,
add up
to $57.60 each month
for life: enough
for dog food, cheap
stupefying wine,
rest beyond belief.

It is more
than enough.

James Scully

Cooney Potter

inherited forty acres from my Father
And, by working my wife, my two sons and two daughters
From dawn to dusk, I acquired
A thousand acres. But not content.
Wishing to own two thousand acres,
I bustled through the years with axe and plow,
Toiling, denying myself, my wife, my sons, my daughters.
Squire Higbee wrongs me to say
That I died from smoking Red Eagle cigars.
Eating hot pie and gulping coffee
During the scorching hours of harvest time
Brought me here ere I had reached my sixtieth year.

Edgar Lee Masters

Their Bodies

to the students of anatomy at Indiana University

That gaunt old man came first, his hair as white
As your scoured tables. Maybe you'll recollect him
By the scars of steel-mill burns on the backs of his hands,
On the nape of his neck, on his arms and sinewy legs,
And her by the enduring innocence
Of her face, as open to all of you in death
As it would have been in life: she would memorize
Your names and ages and pastimes and hometowns
If she could, but she can't now, so remember her.

They believed in doctors, listened to their advice,
And followed it faithfully. You should treat them
One last time as they would have treated you.
They had been kind to others all their lives
And believed in being useful. Remember somewhere
Their son is trying hard to believe you'll learn
As much as possible from them, as he did,
And will do your best to learn politely and truly.

They gave away the gift of those useful bodies
Against his wish. (They had their own ways
Of doing everything, always.) If you're not certain
Which ones are theirs, be gentle to everybody.

David Wagoner

Authors' Profiles

JAMES SCULLY

James Scully (1937-) is a university professor who has published in several collections, among them Modern Poets on Modern Poetry *(Collins, 1966) and* Avenue of the Americas *(University of Massachusetts, 1971). He is a distinguished translator and editor. He won the Ingram Merrill Foundation Fellowship in 1962 and the Guggenheim Fellowship in 1973.*

EDGAR LEE MASTERS

Edgar Lee Masters (1869-1950) was a leader in the Chicago Renaissance. His most successful work was the 1915 book of poems Spoon River Anthology, *a collection of monologues from the citizens in the Spoon River cemetery. The author of a number of novels and biographies, his* Lincoln the Man *(1931) was the most successful.*

DAVID WAGONER

David Wagoner (1926-) has published 14 books of poems and ten novels. He is a professor of English at the University of Washington and editor of Poetry Northwest. *He is one of 12 chancellors of the Academy of American Poets. Wagoner is also an accomplished novelist. He is known as a master craftsman of language in both genres. Among his poetry collections are* Staying Alive *(1966),* Sleeping in the Woods *(1974), and* In Broken Country *(1979).*

THEME *Family*

ANTICIPATING: Think about your plans for the future. Do they include marriage and a family? What kind of job will you seek? What training will you need? What salary range will you require? Will you be happy? Write about these plans in your journal.

Me And My Work

 got a piece of a job on the waterfront.
Three days ain't hardly a grind.
It buys some beans and collard greens
and pays the rent on time.
       Course the wife works, too.

Got three big children to keep in school,
need clothes and shoes on their feet,
give them enough of the things they want
and keep them out of the street.
       They've always been good.

My story ain't news and it ain't all sad.
There's plenty worse off than me.
Yet the only thing I really don't need
is strangers' sympathy.
That's someone else's word for
    caring.

Maya Angelou

That Day

ust once
my father stopped on the way
into the house from work
and joined in the softball game
we were having in the street,
and attempted to play in our
game that his country had never
known.

Just once
and the day stands out forever
in my memory
as a father's living gesture
to his son,
that in playing even the fool
or clown, he would reveal
that the lines of their lives
were sewn from a tougher fabric
than the son had previously known.

David Kherdian

The Rope

heir voices still wake me
as I woke for years to that rise and fall,
the rope pulled taut between them,

both afraid to break or let go.
Years spilled on the kitchen table,
picked over like beans or old bills.

What he owed to the mill, what she wanted
for him. Tears swallowed and hidden
under layers of paint, under linoleum rugs,

new piled on old, each year the pattern
brighter, costlier. The kids
he would say, if it weren't for

She'd hush him and promise
to smile, saying This is what
I want, this is all I ever wanted.

Patricia Dobler

Mag

I wish to God I never saw you, Mag.
I wish you never quit your job and came along with me.
I wish we never bought a license and a white dress
For you to get married in the day we ran off to a minister
And told him we would love each other and take care of each other
Always and always long as the sun and the rain lasts anywhere.
Yes, I'm wishing now you lived somewhere away from here
And I was a bum on the bumpers a thousand miles away dead broke.

    I wish the kids had never come
    And rent and coal and clothes to pay for
    And a grocery man calling for cash,
    Every day cash for beans and prunes.
    I wish to God I never saw you, Mag.
    I wish to God the kids had never come.

Carl Sandburg

Authors' Profiles

MAYA ANGELOU

*M*aya Angelou *(1928-) is a renowned poet, autobiographer, playwright, actress, director, singer, composer, and teacher. Her autobiography* I Know Why the Caged Bird Sings *(1971) was made into a television film. In addition, she has produced other volumes of memoirs:* Gather Together in My Name *(1974),* Singin' and Swingin' and Gettin' Merry Like Christmas *(1976),* The Heart of a Woman *(1981), and* All God's Children Need Traveling Shoes *(1986). Her volumes of poetry include* Just Give Me a Cool Drink of Water 'fore I Die *(1971),* Oh Pray My Wings Are Gonna Fit Me Well *(1975),* And Still I Rise *(1978), and* Shaker, Why Don't You Sing? *(1983). In 1993, she wrote her personal insights in* Wouldn't Take Nothin' for My Journey Now *(Random House).*

DAVID KHERDIAN

*D*avid Kherdian *(1931-) has distinguished himself as a poet as well as a fiction and nonfiction writer of books totaling 40 in all. His collections of poetry include* I Remember Root River *(1978),* Threads of Light *(1985), and* The Dividing River *(1990). He wrote a two-volume tribute to his mother's life,* The Road from Home *and* Finding Home *(Greenwillow, 1979 and 1981), which addresses the struggles of her life in Armenia and her immigration to America. He has received the Boston Globe-Horn Award (1979), the Newbery Honor Book Award (1980), and the Friends of American Writers Award (1982).*

PATRICIA DOBLER

*P*atricia Dobler *(1939-) was raised in a small steel town, Middletown, Ohio. The themes of her first book of poetry,* Talking to Strangers *(University of Wisconsin Press, 1986), focus on family members involved in industrial steel work. For this work she won the 1986 Brittingham Prize in Poetry. In 1991, Mill Hunk Books published her second major book,* UXB: Poems and Translations. *These poems explore her German heritage and World War II. She includes translations of works by German poet Ilse Aichinger. Dobler is director of the Women's*

Creative Writing Center at Carlow College in Pittsburgh, and she teaches a poetry and fiction workshop entitled "Mad Women in the Attic."

CARL SANDBURG

*C*arl Sandburg *(1878-1967) wrote poetry about urban and rural life, always celebrating the working class.* Chicago Poems *(1916) was his first collection, and* The Complete Poems *(1970) is a collection of all the poems published during his lifetime. He was also a noted biographer of Abraham Lincoln:* The Prairie Years *(1925) and* The War Years *(1939). His other works include* The Chicago Race Riots *(journalism, 1919),* The American Songbook *(1927),* Remembrance Rock *(historical novel, 1948), and* Always the Young Strangers *(autobiography, 1952).*

THEME *Pride*

ANTICIPATING: Make a list of all the tasks you perform on the job or in some other area of your life (on a team, around your home). Next to each task, write down how you feel about that aspect of the work.

Old Men Working Concrete

*on't be rushed; will take
their own sweet time.
Now and then, will stop
for snuff (reaching in
the pocket where the circle
of can has worn a circle
in the cloth); and then
get back to work, mix mud
and fill and walk that barrow
back and back and back.
Soon enough the slab end
takes shape. The one man
on his knees with a float
checks it with his eye
stopping time and again
to run his striker saw-wise
and level across the top.
Soon enough it gets long;
smooth with broad swings
of trowel it gets long.
Finally they stop the mixer.*

One trowels out the last space,
one works the edger.
Done, they stand back.
They look one more time.
It's good. Yes sir, it's good.
They talk. They dip snuff.
They are happy.

Phil Hey

Old Florist

hat hump of a man bunching chrysanthemums
Or pinching back asters, or planting azaleas,
Tamping and stamping dirt into pots, —
How he could flick and pick
Rotten leaves or yellowy petals,
Or scoop out a weed close to flourishing roots,
Or make the dust buzz with a light spray,
Or drown a bug in one spit of tobacco juice,
Or fan life into wilted sweet-peas with his hat,
Or stand all night watering roses, his feet blue in rubber boots.

Theodore Roethke

Factory Work

ll day I stand here, like this,
over the hot-glue machine,
not too close to the wheel
that brings up the glue,
and I take those metal shanks,
slide the backs of them in glue
and make them lie down
on the shoe-bottoms, before the sole
goes on. It's simple, but the lasts
weigh, give you big arms.
If I hit my boyfriend now,
in the supermarket parking lot,
he knows I hit him.

Phyllis, who stands next to me,
had long hair before the glue machine
got it. My machine ate up my shirt once.
I tried to get it out, the wheel
spinning on me, until someone with a brain
turned it off. It's not bad
here, people leave you alone,
don't ask you what you're thinking.

It's a good thing, too, because all this morning
I was remembering last night,
when I really thought my grandpa's soul
had moved into the apartment,
the way the eggs fell, and the lamp
broke, like someone was trying

to communicate to me, and he
just dead this week. I wouldn't
blame him. That man in the next aisle
reminds me of him, a little.

It's late October now, and Eastland
needs to lay some people off.
Last week they ran a contest
to see which shankers shanked fastest.
I'm not embarrassed to say
I beat them all. It's all
in economy of motion, all the moves
on automatic.
I almost
don't need to look at what
I'm doing. I'm thinking of the way
the leaves turn red when the cold
gets near them. They fall until
you're wading in red leaves up to your knees,
and the air snaps
in the tree-knuckles, and you begin
to see your breath rise
out of you like your own ghost
each morning you come here.

Deborah Boe

The Closing of the Rodeo

he lariat snaps; the cowboy rolls
    His pack, and mounts and rides away.
Back to the land the cowboy goes.

Plumes of smoke from the factory sway
    In the setting sun. The curtain falls,
A train in the darkness pulls away.

    Good-by, says the rain on the iron roofs.
        Good-by, say the barber poles.
    Dark drum the vanishing horses' hooves.

William Jay Smith

Authors' Profiles

PHIL HEY

*P*hil Hey (1942-) is the author of four collections of poetry: In Plain Sight, Reorganizing the Stars, Plain Label Poems, *and* A Change of Clothes. *In addition to teaching creative writing and presenting at scholarly and professional organizations, he is a teacher of business writing. Hey has coedited the Iowa Poets series and is the senior writer on the roster of the Iowa Arts Council's Writers in the Schools program. He has been writing and teaching at Briar Cliff College since 1969.*

THEODORE ROETHKE

*T*heodore Roethke (1908-1963) was an important teacher and poet, who translated the psychology of the subconscious into vivid images. Such collections as Open House *(1941) and* Lost Son and Other Poems *(1948) made him a leader among younger American poets. He won the 1954 Pulitzer Prize for poetry for* The Waking *and both the National Book Award and the Bollingen Prize for* Words for the Wind *(1957). The posthumously published* The Far Field *further solidified his reputation. His notebooks* Straw for the Fire, *published in 1972, show an artist constantly refining his insights about life and nature.*

DEBORAH BOE

*D*eborah Boe attended Bowdoin College and Columbia University and began freelance writing in New England. Her first major collection of poems is Mojave, *printed by Hanging Loose Press in 1987. Her poems have been published in* Poetry, Poetry Northwest, *and other magazines. She is a recipient of grants from the National Endowment for the Arts and the New Jersey State Council on the Arts. Boe is presently pursuing her career in Santa Barbara, California.*

WILLIAM JAY SMITH

*W*illiam Jay Smith (1918-) is the author of ten volumes of poetry, the most recent of which is Collected Poems 1939-1989 *(Scribner's, 1990). Consultant in Poetry to the library of Congress (1968-70), he has translated poetry from several languages, written more than a dozen books of poetry, and edited several* *anthologies for children. He was elected a member of the American Academy of Arts and Letters in 1975 and was its Vice President for Literature (1986-89). Smith was also Poet-in-Residence at the Cathedral of St. John the Divine in New York, in charge of the Poets' Corner (1985-88).*

THEME Society

ANTICIPATING: What do you admire most in workers? What are the characteristics of those who work hard? What is the importance of working hard?

To Be of Use

he people I love the best
jump into work head first
without dallying in the shallows
and swim off with sure strokes almost out of sight.
They seem to become natives of that element,
the black sleek heads of seals
bouncing like half-submerged balls.

I love people who harness themselves, an ox to a heavy cart,
who pull like water buffalo, with massive patience,
who strain in the mud and the muck to move things forward,
who do what has to be done, again and again.

I want to be with people who submerge
in the task, who go into the fields to harvest
and work in a row and pass the bags along,
who stand in the line and haul in their places,
who are not parlor generals and field deserters
but move in a common rhythm
when the food must come in or the fire be put out.

The work of the world is common as mud.
Botched, it smears the hands, crumbles to dust.
But the thing worth doing well done
has a shape that satisfies, clean and evident.
Greek amphoras for wine or oil,
Hopi vases that held corn, are put in museums
but you know they were made to be used.
The pitcher cries for water to carry
and a person for work that is real.

Marge Piercy

The Country of Everyday: Literary Criticism

"*h*e was in a hurry," Wood said, "the young foreman
only 26, down on his knees at the base of
the heavy lamppost, impatient to push it back on the block.
He was yelling at the rest of us to give him a hand
and didn't see the top of the pole, as it
swayed over and touched the powerline.

"I was looking right at him. There was a flash
and he just folded over onto his side and
turned black: his ears melted.
There were two holes burned in the pavement
where his knees were. Somebody started giving him
mouth-to-mouth and I said Forget it. I mean, he's dead."

And there are poets who can enter in
to the heart of a door, and discover the rat inside us
that must be kept caged in the head because it is perfectly sane.

There are poets who claim to know what it's like
to have a crucifix wedged in the throat
unable to swallow, and how the knot of the stomach
turns into a bowl of fire.

But around and ahead of them
is the housewife endlessly washing
linoleum, sheets, fruit dishes, her hands
and the face of a child. And there is the girl who stands
in the cannery line twelve hours in season
to cut out the tips of the fish.

For the paper they tear out to write on
is pulled from the weeks of working graveyard
and all the weariness of millwork, the fatigue
of keeping it going, the urge to reclaim the body
for the hours not working or sleeping
when the body ends too tired for much but a beer and a laugh.

Beside every dazzling image, each line
desperate to search the unconscious
are the thousand hours someone is spending
watching ordinary television.
For every poet who considers the rhythm
of the word "dark" and the word "darkness"
a crew is balancing high on the grid
of a new warehouse roof, gingerly taking the first load of lumber
hauled thirty feet up to them.

For every hour someone reads critical articles
Swede is drunk in a bar again
describing how he caught his sleeve once in the winch of an oil rig
whirling him round till his ribs broke.
And for every rejection of a manuscript
a young apprentice is riding up on the crane
to work his first day on high steel.
"Left my fingerprints in the metal
when I had to grab a beam to get off," he says.
And Ed Shaw stands looking down into the hold
where a cable sprang loose lifting a pallet
and lashed across the dock, just touching one of the crew
whose body they are starting to bring up from the water.

When the poet goes out for a walk in the dusk
listening to his feet on the concrete, pondering
all of the adjectives for rain, he is walking on work
of another kind, and on lives that wear down like cement.
Somewhere a man is saying, "Worked twenty years for the City
but I'm retired now."
Sitting alone in a room, in the poorhouse of a pension
he has never read a modern poem.

Tom Wayman

Authors' Profiles

MARGE PIERCY

Marge Piercy (1936-) is a native of Detroit, renowned as the most widely anthologized feminist poet of her generation. She is also a novelist. Her first volume of poetry, Breaking Camp *(Wesleyan University Press), was published in 1968. Other anthologies of poetry are* To Be of Use *(Doubleday, 1973),* Circles on the Water *(Knopf, 1982),* Available Light *(Knopf, 1988), and* Mars and Her Children *(Knopf, 1992). She has written 11 novels which have been highly praised. Among them are* Small Changes *(Doubleday, 1973),* Braided Lives *(Summit, 1982), and the recent* He, She and It *(Knopf, 1991).*

TOM WAYMAN

Tom Wayman (1945-) is a distinguished Western-Canadian poet whose themes often focus on the worker. He has published numerous collections for which he has won several awards. Among the collections are Free Time: Industrial Poems *(Macmillan, 1975) and* Living on the Ground: Tom Wayman Country *(McClelland & Stewart, 1980). According to Wayman, "It is my intention to set at the heart of my writing what is the center of my daily existence. Hence my interest in writing about the jobs I have had." He won the first prize in the U.S. National Bicentennial Poetry Awards for his poem "Garrison" (1976) and has been a writer-in-residence and instructor at several universities.*

THEME *Survivors*

ANTICIPATING: Write about a situation where you considered yourself a survivor. Did you have a narrow escape? Did you work through a problem? Did you fight the odds? Describe how you felt and what you told yourself to keep going.

Saturday's Child

 ome are teethed with a silver spoon,
   With the stars strung for a rattle;
 I cut my teeth as the black raccoon—
   For implements of battle.

 Some are swaddled in silk and down,
  And heralded by a star;
They swathed my limbs in a sackcloth gown
 On a night that was black as tar.

  For some, godfather and goddame
   The opulent fairies be;
  Dame Poverty gave me my name,
   And Pain godfathered me.

 For I was born on Saturday—
  "Bad time for planting a seed,"
Was all my father had to say,
  And, "One mouth more to feed."

Death cut the strings that gave me life,
And handed me to Sorrow,
The only kind of middle wife
My folks could beg or borrow.

Countee Cullen

Dynamiter

*I sat with a dynamiter at summer in a German saloon eating steak and
  onions.*

*And he laughed and told stories of his wife and children and the cause of
  labor and the working class.*

*It was laughter of an unshakable man knowing life to be a rich and red-
  blooded thing.*

*Yes, his laugh rang like the call of gray birds filled with a glory of joy
  ramming their winged flight through a rain storm.*

*His name was in many newspapers as an enemy of the nation and few
  keepers of churches or schools would open their doors to him.*

*Over the steak and onions not a word was said of his deep days and
  nights as a dynamiter.*

*Only I always remember him as a lover of life, a lover of children, a lover
  of all free, reckless laughter everywhere—lover of red hearts and red
  blood the world over.*

Carl Sandburg

5000 Apply for 100 Jobs

 stood in line, drunk with the cold
shuffling toward the factory door.
Hundreds danced slowly in front of me
hundreds behind. Some of us I knew were poor
with pink skin sticking out
of what we wore.
When the man said go home, that's it
some kicked the ground and swore.
Others moved on quickly
having been here before.
At least I have another job—minimum wage—
washing windows, sweeping floors,
so I felt a bit of joy inside that big sadness,
like Happy Hour at the Goodwill Store.

Jim Daniels

Authors' Profiles

COUNTEE CULLEN

Countee Cullen (1903-1946) was a leader in the Harlem Renaissance of the 1920s. He studied at New York University and graduated from Harvard in 1926, winning a coveted Guggenheim Foundation Fellowship. Later he studied at the Sorbonne and lectured in Europe. His writings became a favorite of Parisians. Returning to America, he ignored offers from universities and opted to teach at Frederick Douglass Jr. High School in Harlem. Cullen celebrated the lives of African-Americans in such verse collections as Color (1925), Copper Sun (1927), and The Ballad of a Brown Girl (1927).

CARL SANDBURG

See notes under poems on Family.

JIM DANIELS

Jim Daniels (1956-) grew up in a blue-collar suburb in Michigan, received a master's degree in fine arts from Bowling Green State University in Ohio, and now teaches in the creative writing program at Carnegie Mellon University in Pittsburgh. His books include Places/Everyone (University of Wisconsin Press, 1985); Punching Out (Wayne State University Press, 1990); and M-80 (University of Pittsburgh Press, 1993). Two recently published fiction works are The Bridge and The Long Story.

DRAMA

The Oyster and the Pearl

WILLIAM SAROYAN

ANTICIPATING: **What do you collect? In your journal, discuss the special items you have saved over the years. Why do you continue to keep them? What do they represent to you? How have they continued to hold their value in your eyes?**

HARRY VAN DUSEN, a barber

CLAY LARRABEE, a boy with Saturday off from school

VIVIAN McCUTCHEON, a new schoolteacher

CLARK LARRABEE, Clay's father

MAN, a writer

ROXANNA LARRABEE, Clay's sister

GREELEY, Clay's pal

JUDGE APPLEGARTH, a beachcomber

WOZZECK, a watch repairer

A GARAGE ATTENDANT

CENE: Harry Van Dusen's barber shop in O.K.-by-the-Sea, California, population 909. The sign on the window says: HARRY VAN DUSEN, BARBER. It's an old-fashioned shop, crowded with stuff not usually found in barber shops. . . . Harry himself, for instance. He has never been known to put on a barber's white jacket or to work without a hat of some sort on his head: a stovepipe, a derby, a western, a homburg, a skull-cap, a beret, or a straw, as if putting on these various hats somewhat expressed the quality of his soul, or suggested the range of it. ✷ On the walls, on shelves, are many odds and ends, some apparently washed up by the sea, which is a block down the street: abalone and other shells, rocks, pieces of driftwood, a life jacket, rope, sea plants. There is one old-fashioned chair. ✷ When the

play begins, HARRY *is seated in the chair. A boy of nine or ten named* CLAY LARRABEE *is giving him a haircut.* HARRY *is reading a book, one of many in the shop.* 🙙

CLAY. Well, I did what you told me, Mr. Van Dusen. I hope it's all right. I'm not a barber, though. *(He begins to comb the hair)*

HARRY. You just gave me a haircut, didn't you?

CLAY. I don't know *what* you'd call it. You want to look at it in the mirror? *(He holds out a small mirror)*

HARRY. No thanks. I remember the last one.

CLAY. I guess I'll never be a barber.

HARRY. Maybe not. On the other hand, you may turn out to be the one man hidden away in the junk of the world who will bring merriment to the tired old human heart.

CLAY. Who? Me?

HARRY. Why not?

CLAY. Merriment to the tired old human heart? How do you do that?

HARRY. Compose a symphony, paint a picture, write a book, invent a philosophy.

CLAY. Not me! Did you ever do stuff like that?

HARRY. I did.

CLAY. What did you do?

HARRY. Invented a philosophy.

CLAY. What's that?

HARRY. A way to live.

CLAY. What way did you invent?

HARRY. The Take-it-easy way.

CLAY. Sounds pretty good.

HARRY. All philosophies sound good. The trouble with mine was, I kept forgetting to take it easy. Until one day. The day I came off the highway into this barber shop. The barber told me the shop was for sale. I told him all I had to my name was eighty dollars. He sold me the shop for seventy-five, and threw in the haircut. I've been here ever since. That was twenty-four years ago.

CLAY. Before I was born.

HARRY. Fifteen or sixteen years before you were born.

CLAY. How old were you then?

HARRY. Old enough to know a good thing when I saw it.

CLAY. What did you see?

HARRY. O.K.-by-the-Sea, and this shop—the proper place for me to stop. That's a couplet. Shakespeare had them at the end of a scene, so I guess that's the end of this haircut. *(He gets out of the chair, goes to the hat tree, and puts on a derby)*

CLAY. I guess I'd never get a haircut if you weren't in town, Mr. Van Dusen.

HARRY. Nobody would, since I'm the only barber.

CLAY. I mean, free of charge.

HARRY. I give you a haircut free of charge, you give me a haircut free of charge. That's fair and square.

CLAY. Yes, but you're a barber. You get a dollar a haircut.

HARRY. Now and then I do. Now and then I don't.

CLAY. Well, anyhow, thanks a lot. I guess I'll go down to the beach now and look for stuff.

HARRY. I'd go with you, but I'm expecting a little Saturday business.

CLAY. This time I'm going to find something *real* good, I think.

HARRY. The sea washes up some pretty good things at that, doesn't it?

CLAY. It sure does, except money.

HARRY. What do you want with money?

CLAY. Things I need.

HARRY. What do you need?

CLAY. I want to get my father to come home again. I want to buy Mother a present—

HARRY. Now, wait a minute, Clay, let me get this straight. Where *is* your father?

CLAY. I don't know. He went off the day after I got my last haircut, about a month ago.

HARRY. What do you mean, he went off?

CLAY. He just picked up and went off.

HARRY. Did he say when he was coming back?

CLAY. No. All he said was, Enough's enough. He wrote it on the kitchen wall.

HARRY. Enough's enough?

CLAY. Yeah. We all thought he'd be back in a day or two, but now we know we've got to *find* him and *bring* him back.

HARRY. How do you expect to do that?

CLAY. Well, we put an ad in *The O.K.-by the Sea Gull* . . . that comes out every Saturday.

HARRY. *(Opening the paper)* This paper? But your father's not in town. How will he see an ad in this paper?

CLAY. He *might* see it. Anyhow, we don't know what else to do. We're living off the money we saved from the summer we worked, but there ain't much left.

HARRY. The summer you worked?

CLAY. Yeah. Summer before last, just before we moved here, we picked cotton in Kern County. My father, my mother, and me.

HARRY. *(Indicating the paper)* What do you say in your ad?

CLAY. *(Looking at it)* Well, I say . . . Clark Larrabee. Come home. Your fishing tackle's in the closet safe and sound. The fishing's good, plenty of cabazon, perch, and bass. Let bygones be bygones. We miss you. Mama, Clay, Roxanna, Rufus, Clara.

HARRY. That's a good ad.

CLAY. Do you think if my father reads it, he'll come home?

HARRY. I don't know, Clay. I hope so.

CLAY. Yeah. Thanks a lot for the haircut, Mr. Van Dusen.

CLAY *goes out.* HARRY *takes off the derby, lathers his face, and begins to shave with a straight-edged razor.* A PRETTY GIRL *in a swimming suit comes into the shop, closing a colourful parasol. She has long blonde hair.*

HARRY. Miss America, I presume.

THE GIRL. Miss McCutcheon.

HARRY. Harry Van Dusen.

THE GIRL. How do you do.

HARRY. *(Bowing)* Miss McCutcheon.

THE GIRL. I'm new here.

HARRY. You'd be new anywhere—brand new, I might say. Surely you don't live here.

THE GIRL. As a matter of fact, I do. At any rate, I've been here since last Sunday. You see, I'm the new teacher at the school.

HARRY. You are?

THE GIRL. Yes, I am.

HARRY. How do you like it?

THE GIRL. One week at this school has knocked me for a loop. As a matter of fact, I want to quit and go home to San Francisco. At the same time I have a feeling I ought to stay. What do you think?

HARRY. Are you serious? I mean, in asking me?

THE GIRL. Of course I'm serious. You've been here a long time. You know everybody in town. Shall I go, or shall I stay?

HARRY. Depends on what you're looking for. I stopped here twenty-four years ago because I decided I wasn't looking for anything any more. Well, I was mistaken. I *was* looking, and I've found exactly what I was looking for.

THE GIRL. What's that?

HARRY. A chance to take my time. That's why I'm still here. What are *you* looking for, Miss McCutcheon?

THE GIRL. Well. . . .

HARRY. I mean, besides a husband. . . .

THE GIRL. I'm not looking for a husband. I expect a husband to look for me.

HARRY. That's fair.

THE GIRL. I'm looking for a chance to teach.

HARRY. That's fair too.

THE GIRL. But this town! . . . The children just don't seem to care about anything— whether they get good grades or bad, whether they pass or fail, or anything else. On top of that, almost all of them are unruly. The only thing they seem to be interested in is games, and the sea. That's why I'm on my way to the beach now. I thought if I could watch them on a Saturday I might understand them better.

HARRY. Yes, that's a thought.

THE GIRL. Nobody seems to have any sensible ambition. It's all fun and play. How can I teach children like that? What can I teach them?

HARRY. English.

THE GIRL. Of course.

HARRY. *(Drying his face)* Singing, dancing, cooking. . . .

THE GIRL. Cooking? . . . I must say I expected to see a much older man.

HARRY. Well! Thank you!

THE GIRL. Not at all.

HARRY. The question is, Shall you stay, or shall you go back to San Francisco?

THE GIRL. Yes.

HARRY. The answer is, Go back while the going's good.

THE GIRL. Why? I mean, a moment ago, I believed you were going to point out why I ought to stay, and then suddenly you say I ought to go back. Why?

HARRY. *(After a pause)* You're too good for a town like this.

THE GIRL. I am not!

HARRY. Too young and too intelligent. Youth and intelligence need excitement.

THE GIRL. There are *kinds* of excitement.

HARRY. Yes, there are. You need the big-city kind. There isn't an eligible bachelor in town.

THE GIRL. You seem to think all I want is to find a husband.

HARRY. But only to teach. You want to teach him to become a father, so you can have a lot of children of your own—to teach.

THE GIRL. *(She sits down angrily in the chair and speaks very softly)* I'd like a poodle haircut if you don't mind, Mr. Van Dusen.

HARRY. You'll have to get that in San Francisco, I'm afraid.

THE GIRL. Why? Aren't you a barber?

HARRY. I am.

THE GIRL. Well, this is your shop. It's open for business. I'm a customer. I've got money. I want a poodle haircut.

HARRY. I don't know how to give a poodle haircut, but even if I knew how, I wouldn't do it.

THE GIRL. Why not?

HARRY. I don't give women haircuts. The only women who visit this shop bring their small children for haircuts.

THE GIRL. I want a poodle haircut, Mr. Van Dusen.

HARRY. I'm sorry, Miss McCutcheon. In my sleep, in a nightmare, I would *not* cut your hair. *(The sound of a truck stopping is heard from across the street)*

THE GIRL. *(Softly, patiently, but firmly)* Mr. Van Dusen, I've decided to stay, and the first thing I've got to do is change my appearance. I don't fit into the scenery around here.

HARRY. Oh, I don't know—if I were a small boy going to school, I'd say you look just right.

THE GIRL. You're just like the children. They don't take me seriously, either. They think I'm nothing more than a pretty girl who is going to give up in despair and go home. If you give me a poodle haircut I'll look more—well, plain and simple. I plan to dress differently, too. I'm determined to teach here. You've got to help me. Now, Mr. Van Dusen, the shears, please.

HARRY. I'm sorry, Miss McCutcheon. There's no need to change your *appearance* at all.

CLARK LARRABEE *comes into the shop.*

HARRY. You're next, Clark. (HARRY *helps* MISS MCCUTCHEON *out of the chair. She gives him an angry glance)*

THE GIRL. *(Whispering)* I won't forget this rudeness, Mr. Van Dusen.

HARRY. *(Also whispering)* Never whisper in O.K.-by-the-Sea. People misunderstand. *(Loudly)* Good day, Miss.

MISS MCCUTCHEON *opens her parasol with anger and leaves the shop.* CLARK LARRABEE *has scarcely noticed her. He stands looking at Harry's junk on the shelves.*

HARRY. Well, Clark, I haven't seen you in a long time.

CLARK. I'm just passing through, Harry. Thought I might run into Clay here.

HARRY. He was here a little while ago.

CLARK. How is he?

HARRY. He's fine, Clark.

CLARK. I been working in Salinas. Got a ride down in a truck. It's across the street now at the gasoline station.

HARRY. You've been home, of course?

CLARK. No, I haven't.

HARRY. Oh?

CLARK. *(After a slight pause)* I've left Fay, Harry.

HARRY. You got time for a haircut, Clark?

CLARK. No thanks, Harry. I've got to go back to Salinas on that truck across the street.

HARRY. Clay's somewhere on the beach.

CLARK. *(Handing Harry three ten-dollar bills)* Give him this, will you? Thirty dollars. Don't tell him I gave it to you.

HARRY. Why not?

CLARK. I'd rather he didn't know I was around. Is he all right?

HARRY. Sure, Clark. They're *all* O.K. I mean. . . .

CLARK. Tell him to take the money home to his mother.

He picks up the newspaper, The Gull.

HARRY. Sure, Clark. It came out this morning. Take it along.

CLARK. Thanks. *(He puts the paper in his pocket)* How've things been going with *you,* Harry?

HARRY. Oh, I can't kick. Two or three haircuts a day. A lot of time to read. A few laughs. A few surprises. The sea. The fishing. It's a good life.

CLARK. Keep an eye on Clay, will you? I mean—well, I *had* to do it.

HARRY. Sure.

CLARK. Yeah, well. . . . That's the first money I've been able to save. When I make some more, I'd like to send it here, so you can hand it to Clay, to take home.

HARRY. Anything you say, Clark. *(There is the sound of the truck's horn blowing)*

CLARK. Well. . . . *(He goes to the door)* Thanks, Harry, thanks a lot.

HARRY. Good seeing you, Clark.

CLARK LARRABEE *goes out.* HARRY *watches him. A truck shifting gears is heard, and then the sound of the truck driving off.* HARRY *picks up a book, changes hats, sits down in the chair and begins to read.* A MAN *of forty or so, well-dressed, rather swift, comes in.*

MAN. Where's the barber?

HARRY. I'm the barber.

MAN. Can I get a haircut, real quick?

HARRY. *(Getting out of the chair)* Depends on what you mean by real quick.

MAN. *(Sitting down)* Well, just a haircut, then.

HARRY. *(Putting an apron around the man)* O.K. I don't believe I've seen you before.

MAN. No. They're changing the oil in my car across the street. Thought I'd step in here and get a haircut. Get it out of the way before I get to Hollywood. How many miles is it?

HARRY. About two hundred straight down the highway. You can't miss it.

MAN. What town is *this*?

HARRY. O.K.-by-the-Sea.

MAN. What do the people do here?

HARRY. Well, I cut hair. Friend of mine named Wozzeck repairs watches, radios, alarm clocks, and sells jewellery.

MAN. Who does he sell it to?

HARRY. The people here. It's imitation stuff mainly.

MAN. Factory here? Farms? Fishing?

HARRY. No. Just the few stores on the highway, the houses further back in the hills, the church, and the school. You a salesman?

MAN. No, I'm a writer.

HARRY. What do you write?

MAN. A little bit of everything. How about the haircut?

HARRY. You got to be in Hollywood tonight?

MAN. I don't have to be anywhere tonight, but that was the idea. Why?

HARRY. Well, I've always said a writer could step into a place like this, watch things a little while, and get a whole book out of it, or a play.

MAN. Or if he was a poet, a sonnet.

HARRY. Do you like Shakespeare's?

MAN. They're just about the best in English.

HARRY. It's not often I get a writer in here. As a matter of fact you're the only writer I've had in here in twenty years, not counting Fenton.

MAN. Who's he?

HARRY. Fenton Lockhart.

MAN. What's he write?

HARRY. He gets out the weekly paper. Writes the whole thing himself.

MAN. Yeah. Well. . . . How about the haircut?

HARRY. O.K.

HARRY *puts a hot towel around the man's head.* MISS McCUTCHEON, *carrying a cane chair without one leg and without a seat, comes in. With her is* CLAY *with something in his hand, a smaller boy name* GREELEY *with a bottle of sea water, and* ROXANNA *with an assortment of shells.*

CLAY. I got an oyster here, Mr. Van Dusen.

GREEL. Miss McCutcheon claims there *ain't* a big pearl in it.

HARRY. *(Looking at Miss McCutcheon)* Is she willing to admit there's a *little* one in it?

GREEL. I don't know. I know I got sea water in this bottle.

MISS M. Mr. Van Dusen, Clay Larrabee seems to believe there's a pearl in this oyster he happens to have found on the beach.

CLAY. I didn't *happen* to find it. I went looking for it. You know Black Rock, Mr. Van Dusen? Well, the tide hardly ever gets low enough for a fellow to get around to the ocean side of Black Rock, but a little while ago it did, so I went around there to that side. I got to poking around and I found this oyster.

HARRY. I've been here twenty-four years, Clay, and this is the first time I've ever heard of anybody finding an oyster on our beach—at Black Rock, or anywhere else.

CLAY. Well, *I did*, Mr. Van Dusen. It's shut tight, it's alive, and there's a pearl in it, worth at least three hundred dollars.

GREEL. A *big* pearl.

MISS M. Now, you children listen to me. It's never too soon for any of us to face the truth, which is supposed to set us free, not imprison us. The truth is, Clay, you want money because you need money. The truth is also that you have found an oyster. The truth is also that there is no pearl in the oyster.

GREEL. How do you know? Did you look?

MISS M. No, but neither did Clay, and inasmuch as only one oyster in a million has a pearl in it, truth favours the probability that this is not the millionth oyster . . . the oyster with the pearl in it.

CLAY. There's a *big* pearl in the oyster.

MISS M. Mr. Van Dusen, shall we open the oyster and show Clay and his sister Roxanna and their friend Greeley that there is no pearl in it?

HARRY. In a moment, Miss McCutcheon. And what's that *you* have?

Miss M. A chair, as you see.

Harry. How many legs does it have?

Miss M. Three of course. I can count to three, I hope.

Harry. What do you want with a chair with only three legs?

Miss M. I'm going to bring things from the sea the same as everybody else in town.

Harry. But everybody else in town *doesn't* bring things from the sea—just the children, Judge Applegarth, Fenton Lockhart, and myself.

Miss M. In any case, the same as the children, Judge Applegarth, Fenton Lockhart, and you. Judge Applegarth? Who's he?

Harry. He judged swine at a county fair one time, so we call him Judge.

Miss M. Pigs?

Harry. Swine's a little old-fashioned but I prefer it to pigs, and since both mean the same thing—Well, I wouldn't care to call a man like Arthur Applegarth a pig judge.

Miss M. Did he actually judge swine, as you prefer to put it, at a county fair—one time? Did he even do *that*?

Harry. Nobody checked up. He *said* he did.

Miss M. So that entitled him to be called Judge Applegarth?

Harry. It certainly did.

Miss M. On that basis, Clay's oyster has a big pearl in it because he *says* so, is that it?

Harry. I didn't say that.

Miss M. Are we living in the Middle Ages, Mr. Van Dusen?

Greel. No, this is 1953, Miss McCutcheon.

Miss M. Yes, Greeley, and to illustrate what I mean, that's water you have in that bottle. Nothing else.

Greel. *Sea* water.

Miss M. Yes, but there's nothing else in the bottle.

Greel. No, but there's little things in *the water*. You can't see them now, but they'll show up later. The water of the sea is full of things.

Miss M. Salt, perhaps.

Greel. No. *Living* things. If I look hard I can see some of them now.

Miss M. You can *imagine* seeing them. Mr. Van Dusen, are you going to help me or not?

Harry. What do you want me to do?

Miss M. Open the oyster, of course, so Clay will see for himself that there's no pearl in it. So he'll begin to face reality, as he should, as each of us should.

HARRY. Clay, do you mind if I look at the oyster a minute?

CLAY. *(Handing the oyster to Harry)* There's a big pearl in it, Mr. Van Dusen.

HARRY. *(Examining the oyster)* Clay . . . Roxanna . . . Greeley . . . I wonder if you'd go down the street to Wozzeck's. Tell him to come here, the first chance he gets. I'd rather *he* opened this oyster. I might damage the pearl.

CLAY, GREEL., AND ROXANNA. O.K., Mr. Van Dusen. *(They go out)*

MISS M. What pearl? What in the world do you think you're trying to do to the minds of these children? How am I ever going to teach them the principles of truth with an influence like yours to fight against?

HARRY. Miss McCutcheon. The people of O.K.-by-the-Sea are all poor. Most of them can't afford to pay for the haircuts I give them. There's no excuse for this town at all, but the sea is here, and so are the hills. A few people find jobs a couple of months every year North or South, come back half dead of homesickness, and live on next to nothing the rest of the year. A few get pensions. Every family has a garden and a few chickens, and they make a few dollars selling vegetables and eggs. In a town of almost a thousand people there isn't one rich man. Not even one who is well off. And yet these people are the richest I have ever known. Clay doesn't really want money, as you seem to think. He wants his father to come home, and he thinks money will help get his father home. As a matter of fact his father is the man who stepped in here just as you were leaving. He left thirty dollars for me to give to Clay, to take home. His father and his mother haven't been getting along. Clark Larrabee's a fine man. He's not the town drunk, or anything like that, but having four kids to provide for he gets to feeling ashamed of the showing he's making, and he starts drinking. He wants his kids to live in a good house of their own, wear good clothes, and all the other things fathers have always wanted for their kids. His wife wants these things for the kids, too. They don't have these things, so they fight. They had one too many fights about a month ago, so Clark went off—he's working in Salinas. He's either going to keep moving away from his family, or he's going to come back. It all depends on—well, I don't know what. This oyster maybe. Clay maybe. *(Softly)* You and me maybe. *(There is a pause. He looks at the oyster.* MISS MCCUTCHEON *looks at it, too)* Clay believes there's a pearl in this oyster for the same reason you and I believe whatever *we* believe to keep *us* going.

MISS M. Are you suggesting we play a trick on Clay, in order to carry out your mumbo-jumbo ideas?

HARRY. Well, maybe it *is* a trick. I know Wozzeck's got a few pretty good-sized cultivated pearls.

MISS M. You plan to have Wozzeck pretend he has found a pearl in the oyster when he opens it, is that it?

HARRY. I plan to get three hundred dollars to Clay.

MISS M. Do you *have* three hundred dollars?

HARRY. Not quite.

MISS M. What about the other children who need money? Do you plan to put pearls in oysters for them, too? Not just here in O.K.-by-the-sea. Everywhere. This isn't the only town in the world where people are poor, where fathers and mothers fight, where families break up.

HARRY. No, it isn't, but it's the only town where I live.

MISS M. *I* give up. What do you want me to do?

HARRY. Well, could you find it in your heart to be just a little less sure about things when you talk to the kids—I mean, the troubled ones? You can get Clay around to the truth easy enough just as soon as he gets his father home.

ARTHUR APPLEGARTH *comes in.*

HARRY. Judge Applegarth, may I present Miss McCutcheon?

JUDGE. *(Removing his hat and bowing low)* An honour, Miss.

MISS M. How do you do, Judge.

HARRY. Miss McCutcheon's the new teacher at the school.

JUDGE. We are honoured to have you. The children, the parents, and—the rest of us.

MISS M. Thank you, Judge. *(To Harry, whispering)* I'll be back as soon as I change my clothes.

HARRY. *(Whispering)* I told you not to whisper.

MISS M. *(Whispering)* I shall expect you to give me a poodle haircut.

HARRY. *(Whispering)* Are you out of your mind?

MISS M. *(Aloud)* Good day, Judge.

JUDGE. *(Bowing)* Good day, Miss. *(While he is bent over he takes a good look at her knees, calves, ankles, and bow-tied sandals.* MISS McCUCTHEON *goes out.* JUDGE APPLE-GARTH *looks from the door to Harry)*

JUDGE. She won't last a month.

HARRY. Why not?

JUDGE. Too pretty. Our school needs an old battle-axe, like the teachers we had when we went to school, not a bathing beauty. Well, Harry, what's new?

HARRY. Just the teacher, I guess.

JUDGE. You know, Harry, the beach isn't what it used to be—not at all. I don't mind the competition we're getting from the kids. It's just that the quality of the stuff the sea's washing up isn't good any more. *(He goes to the door)*

HARRY. I don't know. Clay Larrabee found an oyster this morning.

JUDGE. He did? Well, one oyster don't make a stew, Harry. On my way home I'll drop in and let you see what I find.

HARRY. O.K., Judge. *(*THE JUDGE *goes out.* HARRY *comes to life suddenly and becomes businesslike)* Now, for the haircut! *(He removes the towel he had wrapped around the writer's head)*

WRITER. Take your time.

HARRY. *(He examines the shears, clippers, and combs)* Let's see now. *(*THE WRITER *turns and watches.* A GARAGE ATTENDANT *comes to the door)*

ATTEND. *(To The Writer)* Just wanted to say your car's ready now.

WRITER. Thanks. *(*THE ATTENDANT *goes out)* Look. I'll tell you what. How much is a haircut?

HARRY. Well, the regular price is a dollar. It's too much for a haircut, though, so I generally take a half or a quarter.

WRITER. *(Getting out of the chair)* I've changed my mind. I don't want a haircut after all, but here's a dollar just the same. *(He hands Harry a dollar, and he himself removes the apron)*

HARRY. It won't take a minute.

WRITER. I know.

HARRY. You don't have to pay me a dollar for a hot towel. My compliments.

WRITER. That's O.K. *(He goes to the door)*

HARRY. Well, take it easy now.

WRITER. Thanks. *(He stands for a moment, thinking, then turns)* Do you mind if I have a look at that oyster?

HARRY. Not at all.

THE WRITER *goes to the shelf where Harry has placed the oyster, picks it up, looks at it thoughtfully, puts it back without comment, but instead of leaving the shop he looks around at the stuff in it. He then sits down on a wicker chair in the corner, and lights a cigarette.*

WRITER. You know, they've got a gadget in New York now like a safety razor that anybody can give anybody else a haircut with.

HARRY. They have?

WRITER. Yeah, there was a full-page ad about it in last Sunday's *Times*.

HARRY. Is that where you were last Sunday?

WRITER. Yeah.

HARRY. You been doing a lot of driving.

WRITER. I like to drive. I don't know, though—those gadgets don't always work. They're asking two-ninety-five for it. You take a big family. The father could save a lot of money giving his kids a haircut.

HARRY. Sounds like a great idea.

WRITER. Question of effectiveness. If the father gives the boy a haircut the boy's ashamed of, well, that's not so good.

HARRY. No, a boy likes to get a professional-looking haircut all right.

WRITER. I thought I'd buy one, but I don't know.

HARRY. You got a big family?

WRITER. I mean for myself. But I don't know—there's something to be said for going to a barber shop once in a while. No use putting the barbers out of business.

HARRY. Sounds like a pretty good article, though.

WRITER. *(Getting up lazily)* Well, it's been nice talking to you. *(*WOZZECK, *carrying a satchel, comes in followed by* CLAY, ROXANNA, *and* GREELEY*)*

WOZZ. What's this all about, Harry?

HARRY. I've got an oyster I want you to open.

ROX. *He* doesn't believe there's a pearl in the oyster, either.

WOZZ. Of course not! What foolishness!

CLAY. There's a *big* pearl in it.

WOZZ. O.K., give me the oyster. I'll open it. Expert watch repairer, to open an oyster!

HARRY. How much is a big pearl worth, Louie?

WOZZ. Oh, a hundred. Two hundred, maybe.

HARRY. A very *big* one?

WOZZ. Three, maybe.

WRITER. I've looked at that oyster, and I'd like to buy it. *(To Clay)* How much do you want for it?

CLAY. I don't know.

WRITER. How about three hundred?

GREEL. Three hundred dollars?

CLAY. Is it all right, Mr. Van Dusen?

HARRY. *(He looks at* THE WRITER, *who nods)* Sure it's all right.

THE WRITER *hands Clay the money.*

CLAY. *(Looking at the money and then at The Writer)* But suppose there ain't a pearl in it?

WRITER. There *is*, though.

WOZZ. Don't you want to open it first?

WRITER. No, I want the whole thing. I don't think the pearl's stopped growing.

CLAY. He says there *is* a pearl in the oyster, Mr. Van Dusen.

HARRY. I think there is, too, Clay; so why don't you just go on home and give the money to your mother.

CLAY. Well. . . . I *knew* I was going to find something good today!

The children go out. WOZZECK *is bewildered.*

WOZZ. Three hundred dollars! How do you know there's a pearl in it?

WRITER. As far as I'm concerned, the whole thing's a pearl.

WOZZ. *(A little confused)* Well, I got to get back to the shop, Harry.

HARRY. Thanks for coming by.

WOZZECK *goes out.* THE WRITER *holds the oyster in front of him as if it were an egg, and looks at it carefully, turning it in his fingers. As he is doing so,* CLARK LARRABEE *comes into the shop. He is holding the copy of the newspaper that Harry gave him.*

CLARK. We were ten miles up the highway when I happened to see this classified ad in the paper. *(He hands the paper to Harry and sits down in the chair)* I'm going out to the house, after all. Just for the weekend of course, then back to work in Salinas again. Two or three months, I think I'll have enough to come back for a long time. Clay come by?

HARRY. No, I've got the money here.

CLARK. O.K., I'll take it out myself, but first let me have the works—shave, haircut, shampoo, massage.

HARRY. *(Putting an apron on Clark)* Sure thing, Clark.

He bends the chair back, and begins to lather Clark's face. MISS MCCUTCHEON, *dressed neatly, looking like another person almost, comes in.*

MISS M. Well?

HARRY. You look fine, Miss McCutcheon.

MISS M. I don't mean that. I mean the oyster.

HARRY. Oh, that! There *was* a pearl in it.

MISS M. I don't believe it.

HARRY. A *big* pearl.

MISS M. You might have done me the courtesy of waiting until I had come back before opening it.

HARRY. Couldn't wait.

MISS M. Well, I don't believe you, but I've come for my haircut. I'll sit down and wait my turn.

HARRY. Mr. Larrabee wants the works. You'll have to wait a long time.

MISS M. Mr. Larrabee? Clay's father? Roxanna's father?

(CLARK sits up)

HARRY. Clark, I'd like you to meet our new teacher, Miss McCutcheon.

CLARK. How do you do.

MISS M. How do you do, Mr. Larrabee. *(She looks bewildered)* Well, perhaps some other time, then, Mr. Van Dusen. *(She goes out. CLARK sits back. JUDGE APPLEGARTH stops at the doorway of the shop)*

JUDGE. Not one thing on the beach, Harry. Not a blessed thing worth picking up and taking home. *(JUDGE APPLEGARTH goes on. THE WRITER looks at Harry).*

HARRY. See what I mean?

WRITER. Yeah. Well . . . so long. *(He puts the oyster in his coat pocket)*

HARRY. Drop in again any time you're driving to Hollywood.

WRITER. Or away. *(He goes out)*

CLARK. *(After a moment)* You know, Harry, that boy of mine, Clay . . . well, a fellow like that, you can't just go off and leave him.

HARRY. Of course you can't, Clark.

CLARK. I'm taking him fishing tomorrow morning. How about going along, Harry?

HARRY. Sure, Clark. Be like old times again. *(There is a pause)*

CLARK. What's all this about an oyster and a pearl?

HARRY. Oh, just having a little fun with the new teacher. You know, she came in here and asked me to give her a poodle haircut? A poodle haircut! I don't believe I remember what a poodle *dog* looks like, even.

CURTAIN

🎭 🎭 🎭

Author's Profile
WILLIAM SAROYAN

*W*illiam Saroyan is one of America's most prolific writers, often writing a short story a day, and producing more than 500 stories between 1934 and 1940. Born in Fresno, California, in 1908, he started writing at the age of thirteen but left high school at the age of fifteen, working odd jobs as grocery clerk, vineyard worker, postal employee, and messenger. His first collection of short stories was published in 1934, when he was twenty-six, and was followed by a book nearly every year throughout the remainder of the thirties.

In 1940, he published the play *The Time of Your Life,* which was awarded the Drama Critics Circle Award and the Pulitzer Prize. Like Sinclair Lewis, Saroyan turned down the Pulitzer, saying it was patronizing of art by the wealthy. However, this play remains the only one to win both prestigious awards. Other significant works include the play *My Heart is in the Highlands* (1937), which was produced on film by United Artists in 1948; the novel *The Human Comedy* (1943), filmed in 1943 by M-G-M; "The Unstoppable Gray Fox" produced by CBS-TV (1962); and *My Name is Aram,* a book of short stories (1940).

Although Saroyan produced novels, plays, musical numbers, a ballet-play, and children's stories, it is for his short stories that he became immediately famous and remains so. Critics consider him the most significant talent to appear in San Francisco since Frank Norris and Jack London.

Saroyan's themes include man's goodness, the difficulties of immigrants holding on to the old world values, and the changing of dreams with the passing of time. He is both optimistic and nostalgic, and uses rural and small-town environments to frame his characters.

Sometimes criticized for his lack of background on them, Saroyan lets his characters reveal themselves by talking. Their language is down-home, everyday speech, making them seem vital and genuine.

Saroyan claims, "Everything I write, everything I have ever written, is allegorical." (An allegory is a story told to teach a lesson about life.) This accounts for the criticism that his stories are "soft," meaning unrealistic or sentimental. As allegories, they need not portray life's harsh reality; the author can choose the elements that represent his central themes. *The Oyster and the Pearl* is one of these, a tale of wisdom and magic in a small town by the sea.

Saroyan died of cancer on May 18, 1981.

(continued from copyright page)

"The Boy and the Bank Officer". Reprinted by permission of Roberta Pryor Inc. Copyright ©1979 by Philip Ross.

"Butch Weldy" from SPOON RIVER ANTHOLOGY by Edgar Lee Masters. Originally published by the Macmillan Company. Permission by Ellen C. Masters.

"The Catbird Seat". Reprinted by permission of Rosemary A. Thurber.

"The Closing of the Rodeo" from COLLECTED POEMS 1939-1989 by William Jay Smith, published in 1990 by Charles Scribner's Sons, copyright ©1947, 1980, 1990 by William Jay Smith. Reprinted by permission of William Jay Smith.

"Cooney Potter" from SPOON RIVER ANTHOLOGY by Edgar Lee Masters. Originally published by the Macmillan Company. Permission by Ellen C. Masters.

"Cotton-Picking Time" from I KNOW WHY THE CAGED BIRD SINGS by Maya Angelou. Copyright © 1969 by Maya Angelou. Reprinted by permission of Random House, Inc.

"The Country of Everyday: Literary Criticism". Reprinted by permission of Harbour Publishing Co. Ltd.

"Darkness at Noon," by Harold Krents. Copyright © 1976 by The New York Times Company. Reprinted by permission.

"A Doctor's Visit". Reprinted with the permission of Macmillan Publishing Company from THE LADY WITH THE DOG AND OTHER STORIES by Anton Chekhov, translated from the Russian by Constance Garnett. Copyright 1917 by Macmillan Publishing Company, renewed 1945 by Constance Garnett.

"Dynamiter" by Carl Sandburg. Reprinted by permission of Harcourt Brace & Company.

"Enough!" is reprinted from RAGING BEAUTY, Azul Editions, 1994. Permission to reprint granted by James Scully.

"Factory Jungle" reprinted from PLACES/EVERYONE by Daniels. Reprinted by permission of The University of Wisconsin Press.

"Factory Work" by Deborah Boe first appeared in POETRY, was copyrighted in the appropriate year by The Modern Poetry Association, and is reprinted by permission of the Editor of POETRY.

"5000 Apply for 100 Jobs" reprinted from PLACES/EVERYONE by Daniels. Reprinted by permission of The University of Wisconsin Press.

"Forty-Five A Month", from MALGUDI DAYS by R. K. Narayan. Copyright ©1972, 1975, 1978, 1980, 1981, 1982 by R. K. Narayan. Used by permission of Viking Penguin, a division of Penguin Books USA Inc.

"From Man to Boy". Reprinted from BLUE COLLAR JOURNAL, ©1974 by John R. Coleman, by permission of Collier Associates, P.O. Box 688, Boca Raton, FL 33429, USA.

"Perfection Is an Insult to the Gods" from HOUSE by Tracy Kidder. Copyright ©1985 by John Tracy Kidder. Reprinted by permission of Houghton Mifflin Company. All rights reserved.

"The Rope" from TALKING TO STRANGERS by Patricia Dobler. Reprinted by permission of The University of Wisconsin Press.

"Saracophagus". Copyright© 1979 by Richard Selzer. Reprinted by permission of John Hawkins & Associates, Inc.

"Saturday's Child". Reprinted by permission of GRM Associates, Inc., Agents for the Estate of Ida M. Cullen. From the book COLOR by Countee Cullen. Copyright © 1925 by Harper & Brothers; copyright renewed 1953 by Ida M. Cullen.

"Share-Croppers". From SELECTED POEMS by Langston Hughes. Copyright 1942 by Alfred A. Knopf Inc. and renewed 1970 by Arna Bontemps and George Houston Bass. Reprinted by permission of the publisher.

"Shooting an Elephant" from SHOOTING AN ELEPHANT AND OTHER ESSAYS by George Orwell, copyright 1950 by Sonia Brownell Orwell and renewed 1978 by Sonia Pitt-Rivers, reprinted by permission of Harcourt Brace & Company.

"Song of the Weaving Woman" by Yüan Chen as found in SUNFLOWER SPLENDOR. Permission to reprint granted by Dr. Irving Yucheng Lo.

"Spring 17. Smoke, Wind, and Soap Bubbles" by Italo Calvino. Reprinted by permission of Harcourt Brace & Company.

"That Day" from I REMEMBER ROOT RIVER by David Kherdian. Copyright © 1978 David Kherdian. Published by The Overlook Press, Woodstock, NY 12498.

"The Richer, the Poorer" from THE RICHER, THE POORER by Dorothy West. Copyright © 1995 by Dorothy West. Used by permission of Doubleday, a division of Bantam Doubleday Dell Publishing Group, Inc.

"Their Bodies" from THROUGH THE FOREST. Used by permission of Grove/Atlantic, Inc. Copyright ©1987 by David Wagoner.

"To Be Of Use" from CIRCLES ON THE WATER by Marge Piercy. Copyright © 1982 by Marge Piercy. Reprinted by permission of Alfred A. Knopf Inc.

"To Bid the World Farewell". THE AMERICAN WAY OF DEATH. Reprinted by permission of Jessica Mitford. All rights reserved. Copyright © 1963, 1978 by Jessica Mitford.

"True Stories and Other Dreams" from TRUST YOUR HEART by Judy Collins. Copyright ©1987 by Judy Collins. Reprinted by permission of Houghton Mifflin Company. All rights reserved.

"Weaving at the Window" translated by William H. Nienhauser, Jr. Permission to reprint granted by William H. Nienhauser, Jr.

"Woman Work" from AND STILL I RISE by Maya Angelou. Copyright © 1978 by Maya Angelou. Reprinted by permission of Random House, Inc.

Note: The authors and editors have made every effort to trace the ownership of all copyright selections found in this book and to make full acknowledgment for their use.